Brandscendence

Brandscendence

THREE ESSENTIAL ELEMENTS
OF ENDURING BRANDS

Kevin A. Clark

Dearborn™
Trade Publishing
A **Kaplan Professional** Company

Vice President and Publisher: Cynthia A. Zigmund
Acquisitions Editor: Michael Cunningham
Senior Project Editor: Trey Thoelcke
Interior Design: Lucy Jenkins
Cover Design: Design Solutions
Typesetting: Elizabeth Pitts

Published by Dearborn Trade Publishing
A Kaplan Professional Company

Printed in the United States of America

04 05 06 10 9 8 7 6 5 4 3 2 1

Library of Congress Cataloging-in-Publication Data

Clark, Kevin A.
      Brandscendence : three essential elements of enduring brands / Kevin A. Clark.
        p.   cm.
      Includes index.
      ISBN 0-7931-8303-0
   1. Brand name products. 2. Brand name products—Management. 3. Brand name products—Valuation—Management.   I. Title.
      HD69.B7C53 2004
      658.8′27—dc22

                                                                                    2004006707

ADVANCED PRAISE FOR *BRANDSCENDENCE*

Brandscendence *blends all the schools of branding to articulate the last word in branding for generations to come. Kevin Clark's book is balanced and inspiring, and it brings together all the major branding concepts in a book that should be a reference document for CEOs, marketing executives, and marketing schools. If you want to find your brand "holon," this is your book.*

MARC GOBÉ
President and CEO, Desgrippes Gobé Group
Author of *Emotional Branding*

Kevin Clark has created a powerful new way to explain both the power and the long-term implications of branding. Well worth the time.

JOEL A. BARKER
The "Paradigm Man" and Co-author of *Five Regions of the Future,*
To Be Released January 2005

Executives seeking the power of branding without knowing exactly how to get it will welcome Kevin Clark's thoughtful guide and devour every useful detail.

ROSABETH MOSS KANTOR
Harvard Business School, and Author of *Confidence:*
How Winning Streaks and Losing Streaks Begin and End

I have known Kevin Clark for some time and had the pleasure to work with him on several Archetype Discoveries at IBM. Kevin is not only brilliant, but he has a great sense of humor and ample culture on brand. This is his "Brand Essence." Because branding is becoming more crucial then ever, this book is must reading for anyone involved in brand strategy.

Dr. G. CLOTAIRE RAPAILLE
Chairman and CEO, Archetype Discoveries Worldwide

The ideas in Brandscendence *will vault companies to transcend the current limits of their brands by adapting to a changing world while remaining true to what each brand stands for.*

B. JOSEPH PINE II and JAMES H. GILMORE
Co-founders, Strategic Horizons LLP
Co-authors, *The Experience Economy*

Not only has Kevin Clark read all the books on branding in the process of writing Brandscendence, *he's synthesized their best points in a deceptively simple original framework. It's both philosophical and pragmatic. Philomatic? Pragsophical? Worth reading, in any case!*

ROBERT F. LAUTERBORN
James L. Knight Professor of Advertising
University of North Carolina

This has got to be one of the finest tutorials–primers–that exists to fundamentally guide one through the process of developing, building and maintaining a brand. You can find it all in one place from a world-class expert in the business of brand husbandry. If you or your company's future depends upon establishing a positive, powerful image for your customers, this is the book for you.

JOHN L. PETERSEN
President and Founder, The Arlington Institute

I got to see Kevin in action the other day and I thought to myself, as I always do, "This guy gets marketing right down to the DNA." Brandscendence *is a book to take you through the mysteries of branding.*

GRANT MCCRACKEN
Adjunct Professor, Department of Art History and
Communications Studies, McGill University

Brands do one thing: they simplify choice! Kevin Clarke with Brandscendence *offers the most relevant, practical, and enlightening treatise on the increasingly critical topic of branding. It will become the text of choice for executives and educators alike.*

CHRIS D. BEAUMONT
President and CEO, Grey Global Group Japan

Kevin Clark ably guides us on a thoughtful journey through the life stages and complex ecology of successful, enduring brands, articulating the qualities that enable brands to achieve lasting meaning and strength. Brandscendence *draws on a rich variety of sources and experience to forge a unique perspective on understanding and managing brands in context and over time.*

NAPIER COLLYNS
Co-founder of Global Business Network

Brandscendence *is an intriguing guide for practitioners and a must-read for anyone who has always been interested in the transcendence side of branding.*
ERICH JOACHIMSTHALER, Ph.D.
Vivaldi Partners

In my global work of "Designing the Future for Success" for 30 years with companies, boards, investors and individuals, one of the key ingredients in the framework remains a consideration of the brand. Kevin's book, Brandscendence, *offers an exceptional and fact-based expose on the merits and successful application of branding, as well as the enduring value it enables. Reading this book will provide an important and easy-to-acquire foundation for everyone, given how central branding remains in our collective futures.*
WILLIAM C. WEISS
Chairman and CEO, The Promar Group, LLC

C o n t e n t s

PART FOUR

THE NEXT STAGE

How do brands become so important that they can transcend cultures, geography, and time? As any marketer or strategist can tell you, the holy grail of all marketing is to establish a positioning in the marketplace that becomes so entrenched in the customer's mind that it is only yours to lose. This is what we're in business fighting for every day. This is where profits are generated, where shareholder value is created, and where marketing is fun and exciting. Creating brands of value may be a once in a lifetime experience or, for some, may never happen.

In this book, the author brings together the forces that create brands, hold on to them, and build them over time.

This book is a rare look at what makes a successful brand and what keeps it alive and relevant in an ever-changing world and marketing environment.

How important is this pursuit? Think about a brand and its the potential points of contact as one travels around the country and even around the world. To create and maintain brand relevance is no accident. It happens through building purpose, character, and a following. When a brand is in full stride, its image is like a beacon of light that shines in unfamiliar surroundings. In times of economic and political uncertainty, these images can provide a sense of comfort. The shared values of consumers that use those brands provide a sense of unity and, sometimes, of community.

Because of this, Kevin's book becomes an important read for anyone involved in brand strategy. He digs deeply into the fundamental nature of brands to uncover how they succeed and how to keep them relevant in a fast-paced economy and an ever-changing marketplace. This book will give you mileposts and guidelines in your search and will lead you in new directions of thought, raising your awareness of the importance of strong brand management.

I have known the author for almost two decades. Over that time, he has studied and refined his thinking on brand strategy and communication. For the last 20 years, the author has studied how companies treat their brands and the communication strategies they chose. The student has now become the teacher with this book. By studying different industries and brands in different stages of their maturity, he has compiled a very interesting approach to looking at brand strategy and communication. A good book makes you think, and in this book, the author has done just that. He considers what makes a truly effective brand both for the business entity and the consumer.

If you are looking for a step-by-step guide to creating powerful brands, you will not find it here. Instead, the author has provided a guide to thinking about the essence that connects long-lasting brands that have a place in the consumer psyche—brands that have meaning and consequently, purpose in the mind of consumers, thus creating a defensible position and the opportunity for long-term success and economic value.

Brandscendence pulls it all together and provides a fresh view of branding—one I am sure you will enjoy.

Jon G. Rubin, Vice President
General Manager Trade Marketing
News America Marketing
New York
February 2004

Brandscendence™ is about understanding brands that go beyond ordinary limits to be considered supreme over long periods of time. Some brands are already well along on the journey to Brandscendence, and others show every indication of being on the right path. This book is about helping you understand and cultivate the transcendent elements of enduring brands.

Brandscendence is a journey, not a destination.

Over ten years ago, I started to form an idea about marketing called Return on Relationships.™ The idea was delivered in a lot of speeches over the years but didn't appear in print until the publication of *Wireless Rules* in 2000. Authors Frederick Newell and Katherine Newell Lemon graciously asked me to contribute a chapter to the book: "The Future of Marketing in a Wireless World."

Since then, I've redoubled my interest in the Return on Relationships concept, and it has evolved into Brandscendence.

I've also delivered a speech over the years called "Products are Solids, Customers are Liquids.™" You have to freeze the specifications of any product well before it comes to market—and while you're busy making it, the tastes and temperaments of your customers are changing. The same is true for this book.

I've frozen my thoughts for you about brand strategy over the year 2003. The ideas on these pages will continue to evolve beyond what you read here before the first printing is out the door and on the shelves.

What you're about to receive is my heightened perception of branding as a practicing brand strategist. These are my thoughts, my impressions, grounded in the first world of global brands and in the local world of the brands we live with every day.

Brand strategy can be applied to many aspects of our personal and professional lives.

That's a key premise of this book—branding is not just for large businesses. The same techniques work equally well for local businesses, nonprofits, governments, nongovernmental organizations—and individual citizens.

As I write this introduction in the spring of 2003, the marketing world is grappling with changes wrought by the war in Iraq. What does it mean to be an American company or an American brand? Or to be of any other country that weighed in on this conflict?

Some brands are paid the highest complement and may pay the economic price for being strong "brand ambassadors." McDonald's is a symbol of the United States around the world, and it paid a price by being burned to the ground in Paris by protestors. Simultaneously, France's brand ambassador—wine—was being emptied by the bottle into the streets and rivers of U.S. cities to protest France's not joining in "the coalition of the willing." Spring 2003 sales of French wine are down significantly in the United States.

But even as McDonald's burned, I skied peacefully with friends in France just south of Geneva, Switzerland. It confirmed my belief about ski resorts as a brand—they are apolitical, sanctuaries for people of all nationalities and beliefs to come together as kindred spirits of the slopes.

In emerging economies such as China, India, and Eastern Europe, brand strategy is a sought-after topic. In first world economies, branding is answering questions about how to differentiate offerings when prices are falling, overcapacity and market saturation is occurring, and population birthrates are stable or declining.

If the first world challenge of the 20th century was creating production capacity, the 21st century's challenge is differentiating an increasing overcapacity of physical goods.

On the other hand, a developing country's challenge is to be in the brand game at all—especially in a positive way. India is a country doing a good job of branding itself as an emerging economy—attracting new businesses and educating a new generation of global knowledge workers, who can export skills worldwide without ever leaving the country.

In the third section of this book, you will find stories of brands that are well along the journey to Brandscendence. Tales from the kitchen, vineyard, small screen and big screen, and even the nonprofit world are told in "Brandscendence in Action." The chapter "Becoming the Category" is a cautionary story about being so good at branding that your product becomes synonymous with the product category, such as Q-tips or Kleenex.

At the end of this book, we are in the future, looking at some of the ways brand practices may change in the face of new technologies and new insights into customers and the cultures they live in. The professional futurists I know and work with never talk about "predictions;" they talk "probabilities" and "possibilities." I see the wisdom in this distinction and offer up the ideas in Chapter 16, "BrandNext,™" in the spirit of probabilities and possibilities for the future of branding.

If you're looking for one of the branding books about "cool hunters" and how to detect leading edge trends that can drive brand fads, please close the book now and set it on the bookshelf for a later stage in your professional life.

Are you still with me, or is it several years later?

In any event, as you likely guessed, this book is about seeking the timeless and transcendent values that drive enduring brands over time. That doesn't mean that they stop adapting, but it does mean they hold fast to something fundamental for their customers and constituencies.

These transcendent values provide a foundation for a brand to survive and thrive—to make a lasting difference—to seek and to have Brandscendence.

DEFINING BRANDSCENDENCE

When a key word is introduced in this book, the dictionary definition is provided in the glossary at the end of the chapter. In the case of *Brandscendence,* it's a combination of the words *brand* and *transcendence*—so here are the Webster's definitions that underlie this trademarked word.

> **brand,** *n.* **1.** kind, grade, or make, as indicated by a stamp, trademark, or the like: *the best brand of coffee.* **2.** a mark made by burning or otherwise, to indicate kind, grade, make, ownership, etc. **3.** a mark formerly put upon criminals with a hot iron. **4.** any mark of disgrace; stigma. **5.** See **branding iron. 6.** a kind or variety of something distinguished by some distinctive characteristic: *The movie was filled with slapstick—a brand of humor he did not find funny.* **7.** a partly burned piece of wood. **8.** *Archaic.* a sword.[1]
>
> **transcendence,** *n.* the quality or state of being transcendent.[2]
>
> **transcendent,** *adj.* **1.** going beyond ordinary limits; surpassing; exceeding. **2.** superior or supreme. **3.** *Theol.* (of the Deity) transcending the universe, time, etc. **4.** *Philos.* **a.** *Scholasticism.* above all possible modes of the infinite. **b.** *Kantianism.* transcending experience; not realizable in human experience. **c.** (in

modern realism) referred to, but beyond direct apprehension, outside consciousness. —*n. Math* **5.** a transcendental function.[3]

The definition I intend for *Brandscendence* is as follows:

brandscendence, *n.* a brand that has the quality or state of being transcendent.

Or, more fully defined:

Brandscendence is a kind or make of brand, as indicated by a name, stamp, trademark, or the like that goes beyond ordinary limits; a brand that surpasses; a brand that exceeds; a brand that is superior or supreme over time.

ORGANIZATION OF THIS BOOK

This book is organized so you can move from one chapter to another with an intentional flow. The chapters are organized into four major sections.

1. Discovering Brandscendence
2. Experiencing Brandscendence
3. Brandscendence in Action
4. The Next Stage

Part One, "Discovering Brandscendence," should be read straight through to understand the basic concepts in the next three sections. This is also the section you'll likely reread over the years when you're searching for clarity on a specific brand decision that you're about to make.

I encourage you to read the rest of the book as written to get the full impact of the Brandscendence framework. However, I know myself well enough to think there are some fellow nonlinear readers out there.

If you're interested in specific stories about enduring brands, then after Part One, move on to "Brandscendence in Action." If you're interested in the future of branding, where it's going, and how it can be used in new ways, then skip right to Part Four, "The Next Stage."

Now the journey to discover Brandscendence begins.

Enjoy.

During the past year, I learned that what it really takes to write a book is organization, time management—and something to say that you've personally experienced. The decision to make this book a blend of personal stories with professional insights emerged as I wrote with encouragement from some of my early manuscript reviewers. For organization and time management skills, let me point to my father and a colleague at work.

When I was growing up, my dad, Harley Clark, would be up long before the sun rose or the birds were singing. At the time, he was working for IBM at what was then the Data Processing Division as the director of executive resources (read "internal talent scout"). Twice yearly, he would agonize over large charts spread out on the kitchen table with passport-sized photographs with names that he moved around on layers of organization charts. A thick binder was full of information, that mapped to the pictures, about the candidates that he would recommend to be the next leaders of IBM.

Getting up early and putting the puzzle pieces in place on weekends was a big part of writing this book. To both my parents for being examples of perseverance and discipline—thanks mom, thanks dad.

Mark McNeilly, twice an author and a member of my team at IBM, has also been an inspiration because he is one of the best-organized people I know. If you've ever heard the term *delegate upwards,* then you'll understand what I mean when I say that Mark has the ability to *inspire upwards.*

A note about IBM: Although I work for IBM during the day, this book in no way represents an official position from the company on brand strategy. This book is my thesis paper, without going back to the academy and having my employer pick up the tab.

Which leads me to Leo Suarez, who was my manager at IBM when I started this project with his blessings. Doing this book was written into my career development and executive resources plans. Everything I know about Cuba in this book I learned from Leo.

I penned almost an entire book nine years ago and had a literary agent shop it for me without success. So let's acknowledge an agent who can get a contract for an author:

Ed Knappman of New England Publishing Associates. Thanks Ed for all the advice and counsel that got this into print.

On a related note, thanks to Katherine Newell Lemon and her colleagues for making the introduction to Ed and contributing a valuable appendix for this book on customer equity measurement. Dr. Kazuhiko Yamazaki also contributes in the appendix an article that illuminates the world of design. Thanks to Mark McNeilly for collaborating with me on an article for *Strategy and Leadership* and for Don Beck's recent work on *Spiral Dynamics,* also in the appendix. You'll like the additional gifts they've brought you.

One of the reasons that I'm confident about the content of this book is the support I've received from other authors and experts in brand and business strategy. Many read the book proposal and provided advance praise—and a special few actually read the entire manuscript and provided valuable comments prior to going to press.

For my manuscript review partners, I want first to thank Jon Rubin, who also contributed the foreword. He's been a great friend over the years. Big thanks also go out to Erich Joachimsthaller, Grant McCracken, David Miln, John Petersen, and Shimon Shmueli, who devoted time during the late 2003 holidays to read a ream of paper for you.

For the book proposal reviewers, I want to thank Marc Gobe, Bill Weiss, and Lucy Baney for their early support.

This book was written on an IBM ThinkPad X20 notebook computer.

Most of all, I thank my wife, Heidi Sawyer-Clark, for sacrificing some of our personal time together to make this book possible. She is what every author dreams of—an understanding mate that knows when to leave the writer alone, and when to intervene and tell the writer to ease up and "get a life." Thanks, my love, for keeping me—and our relationship—in balance.

DISCOVERING BRANDSCENDENCE™

(Relevance + Context) × Mutual Benefit

Brandscendence, *n.* a brand that has the quality or state of being transcendent; a kind or make of brand, as indicated by a name, stamp, trademark, or the like that goes beyond ordinary limits; a brand that surpasses; a brand that exceeds; a brand that is superior or supreme over time.

1

THREE KEY ELEMENTS FOR THE JOURNEY TO BRANDSCENDENCE

"It is a luxury to be understood."
RALPH WALDO EMERSON[1]

Executive Summary.   Brandscendence is about understanding and creating brands that endure.

Three elements interact to create Brandscendence: *relevance, context, and mutual benefit*. Relevance is the transcendent core idea, the reason that the brand exists and doesn't change much over time. Context frames where and when the brand exists and helps the brand adapt to new circumstances. Relevance and context work hand in hand to make the brand work for customers and constituents. Mutual benefit is a multiplier effect. When mutual benefit is perceived, trust is built—trust that can overcome problems when they emerge.

THE JOURNEY TO BRANDSCENDENCE

Enduring brands adapt to customer needs, yet stay true to their original purpose.

These are the brands that last. We know them, and they know us. They fill overarching needs that resonate with our minds, fill our hearts, and reach out to our primal instincts.

During the last 20 years, I've been blessed with the opportunity to know and collaborate with some of the most talented branding, marketing, design, public relations and marketing communications professionals around the world. It's been an incredible journey.

What I've come to realize is that in the quest to making branding more sophisticated, we've also complicated matters. Branding models have become richer, deeper—and less accessible to the organizations and clients they are meant to serve.

Brandscendence reduces the branding conversation to three key elements to make brand strategy accessible to anyone—and to any organization.

Brandscendence is a new word—a combination of the word *brand* and the word *transcendence.* Brands that have the quality or state of being transcendent; that is, brands that surpass, exceed, and are superior over time are on the journey to Brandscendence.

Here are the three essential elements of Brandscendence.

1. *Relevance.* A primary idea and character that drives the brand experience.
2. *Context.* Purposeful innovation and adaptive behavior that drives the brand's evolution through time, space, and meaning to specific cultures.
3. *Mutual benefit.* The brand delivers reciprocal advantage for two or more parties and ultimately leads to sustainable, interdependent relationships.

When relevance, context, and mutual benefit combine in the following formula, the Brandscendence model comes alive:

$$B = (R + C) \times Mb$$
Brandscendence equals
Relevance plus Context,
multiplied by Mutual benefit
(over time)

For my friends in the measurement community, I offer my formal disclaimer here that this is not a mathematical formula or a numerical expression of any kind. It's shorthand for the key elements in the Brandscendence model.

Brandscendence is my current assessment and observations about branding. I will use personal stories and examples to illustrate my ideas. Brandscendence is a personal journey documented for your benefit and success in brand strategy and management.

WHERE BRANDS GET TOGETHER

I'm writing these words in a hotel room in Munich, Germany, in late 2002. The hotel is the Kempinski Vier Jahrenzeiten (the Kempinski Four Seasons) on Maximillianstrasse—one of the most brand-rich streets on the planet. Out of my hotel window as the sun sets, I can see two world-class brands: Hermes and Cartier. A short walk to the right are Daks of London, Mont Blanc, Yves St. Laurent, and tucked just behind the Dresdner Bank on a side street, Rolex.

Doubling back on the left-hand side of the street, we find Bvgari, Dior, Polo by Ralph Lauren, Gucci, Escada Sport, Salvatore Ferragamo, Jil Sander, and Giorgio Armani.

How does a street like this become a brand magnet—and a brand itself?

Munich's Maximillianstrasse is well along on the journey to Brandscendence. It is a relevant place for upscale shopping that transcends the individual stores. Its context is tradition and reinvention—and is mutually beneficial to both merchants and customers. It is a place, a symbol, and an attitude.

There are Maximillianstrasses all over the world—for example, Fifth Avenue in New York City, Rodeo Drive in Beverly Hills, and the Ginza shopping district in Tokyo. These shopping locales have been on the journey to Brandscendence for a long time.

When you travel to any international hub airport today or pick up a duty-free catalog en route, there they are again. The luxury brands compress themselves and adapt to the new contexts of airport as shopping district or airline seat as captive audience.

Brandscendence can also be found at Wal-Mart. The relevance of the Wal-Mart brand is centered on acceptable value at a low price. The context of the Wal-Mart shopping experience is self-contained.

Rather than being part of a well-known shopping district, Wal-Mart creates its own context by finding a suitable tract of land, building a superstore on it, and becoming a new destination for the customers it serves. The internal and external layout of a Wal-Mart is essentially the same anywhere in the United States. In fact, there's a full-size prototype store in Bentonville, Arkansas, right next to Wal-Mart headquarters, that serves as layout laboratory to model various ways to display merchandise and direct customer traffic.

Fact: During 2002, Wal-Mart surpassed all other businesses in total revenue.

Observation: Despite its economic status, Wal-Mart as a brand isn't on the following top-ten list, because retailers and distributors aren't considered for inclusion, at least not yet.

THE WORLD'S MOST VALUABLE BRANDS

In the August 4, 2003, issue, *Business Week* reported the "Best Global Brands," with data from Interbrand Corporation.[2]

Rank	Brand Value (billions)	Country of Ownership
1 Coca-Cola	$70.45	U.S.
2 Microsoft	64.09	U.S.
3 IBM	51.77	U.S.
4 GE	42.34	U.S.
5 Intel	31.11	U.S.
6 Nokia	29.44	Finland
7 Disney	28.04	U.S.
8 McDonald's	24.70	U.S.
9 Marlboro	22.18	U.S.
10 Mercedes	21.37	Germany

Source: Interbrand/Business Week 2003.

The list is instructive because each of these very successful commercial brands has large quantities of the three Brandscendence elements: relevance, context, and mutual benefit. They have remained remarkably consistent in their own unique forms of relevance over time, and their managers have understood the changing context of their business environments.

Relevance and context are the fundamental elements in the model and play equally important roles in achieving Brandscendence.

Relevance describes the primary idea behind why a customer would want an offering. Context describes the environment in which a brand is presented and the adaptation needed to keep it fresh. Mutual benefit is a multiplier effect—if relevance plus context are pulling their weight, then perceived mutual benefit brings the customer back again and again over time.

Commercial examples of branding are easy to come by, and we'll start there, but we will also want to build on the basic concepts and move out to other organizations. The three elements of Brandscendence work just as well for the Red Cross as they do for Coke.

DELIVERING MORE THAN VALUE

Take an example well known throughout the world: Harley-Davidson motorcycles. When you buy a Harley, do you buy transportation? Well, this is something you get—but it's not the primary reason for the purchase. Harley owners purchase community and lifestyle. You buy a motorcycle, then join the global HOG (Harley Owners Group) community. This includes a unique vocabulary and member appearance that projects the brand even when the owner isn't riding. Harley-Davidson has achieved Brandscendence. It is the only commercial brand I know of where the members willingly tattoo the company's logo on their bodies.

Harley-Davidson fulfills the three elements of Brandscendence:

1. *A relevant primary idea.* Harley-Davidson is all about riders.
2. *Contextual brand evolution.* Harley innovates on the axis of customer intimacy.
3. *Mutual benefit.* Harley has a brand character that transcends the motorcycle product category and informs member lifestyle.

In the article "Revving Up Auto Branding," in the first quarter 2002 edition of *The McKinsey Quarterly,* the four authors (Chatterjee, Jauchius, Kaas, and Satpathy) provide a compelling example of a strong brand delivering more value and profit.

Workers at the General Motors and Toyota joint venture NUMMI (New United Motor Manufacturing Incorporated) plant in California build the Toyota Corolla and the Chevrolet Prizm side by side. . . .[3]

The article informs readers that Toyota and GM designed both models with only minor changes in trim and components, and that both cars get high marks from *Consumer Reports.* They are even priced the same for similarly equipped models, yet the Prizm,

> requires up to $750 more in buyer incentives to support its sales. Even so, only one-quarter as many Prizms are sold, and their trade-in value depreciates more quickly. Toyota's name on the Corolla attracts customers, while the Prizm is lost among the offerings on a Chevy Dealer's lot.[4]

The McKinsey authors confirm, "the idea that consumers attach significantly greater importance to relationship and emotional benefits than to a car's functional attributes, at least when they meet minimum standards or don't fall short of the competition's. Nevertheless, those intangible benefits are the weakest links in the automakers' performance ratings."

Marc Gobé provides a compelling view of these intangible brand benefits in his book *Emotional Branding.* Gobé asserts that emotions provide the foundation for the power of brands. "Emotional branding provides the means and methodology for connecting products to the consumer in an emotionally profound way. It focuses on the most compelling aspect of the human character; the desire to transcend material satisfaction and experience emotional fulfillment. A brand is uniquely situated to achieve this, because it can tap into the aspirational drives which underlie human motivation."

Another example of branding with which I'm intimately familiar is IBM ThinkPad notebook computers.

As the brand steward for this line of notebook computers from IBM for several years, I have countless customer and marketplace research projects that say that IBM ThinkPad is on the path to Brandscendence. It is a functional classic that displays a serious character to help people succeed in their professional and personal lives.

People recognize IBM ThinkPad at a distance—it has become iconic with its simple, black, rectangular geometry; unique, red-green-blue IBM logo; and red Trackpoint pointing device in the center of the keyboard. Amid the fads in the computer industry, IBM ThinkPad has stayed true to its original idea for over a decade.

More importantly, the research reveals an underlying emotional aspect of notebook computer ownership. A notebook computer, whether you buy one or one is given to you by an employer, is a considered a personal object. It goes where you go—and the brand you use says something about you. People who use IBM ThinkPad notebooks do so to achieve success and are seen by others as successful. It is more than a computer—it is a badge of competence.

It's important to note that IBM is a master brand company—the only brand to be invested in over time is IBM. When I first came to the personal computer world at IBM, we were selling ThinkPads, not *IBM ThinkPads*. This was off our strategy. You need to send brand equity back to the parent organization. This approach is called *brand nesting*—one relevant brand franchise builds into the context of another. IBM and IBM ThinkPad are mutually beneficial to each other for both customers and stakeholders.

As the master brand, IBM promises trust, confidence, and innovation built over a century, while the decade-old IBM ThinkPad notebook subbrand today is one of IBM's most accessible touchstones for customers around the world. Read more about IBM ThinkPad and how we extended its brand equity in Appendix A, where you'll find an article from *Strategy and Leadership* magazine that I cowrote with Mark McNeilly.

Even the lowly french fry can be a fundamental element of a brand strategy. French fries are a signature item and a cornerstone of McDonald's brand equity worldwide along with the "Golden Arches" and "Ronald McDonald." Every person in a first world economy knows this brand asset on the menu and how consistently it is delivered worldwide. It is a familiar taste for both hometown kids and weary global travelers.

Almost a decade ago, I interviewed the founder of McDonald's in Russia. This is a tale of the extraordinary lengths he went to perfect french fries and everything else on the McDonald's menu in that country. It included farming education, cooperative land use, introduction of the Russet potato, and creation of a "McComplex" on the outskirts of Moscow to process potatoes of sufficient length and taste. We'll explore this brand in more depth in Chapter 12, "Fine Wine to Fast Foods."

BRAND SCALE

Now, about those other brands that aren't commercial—they scale from individuals to nations.

Let's start with individual brands. Several books have been published about personal brands and how to build them.

Think about individuals from the past who have achieved high levels of Brandscendence. These names immediately conjure vivid associations: Gandhi, Einstein, Mother Theresa. Now, try to think of some names that have opposite meanings—personal brands that stood for injustice, ignorance, and cruelty. Sometimes, a brand stands for something that we should reject rather than embrace. As you can see, personal brands can have positive or negative associations—either way, they are strong ones.

Let's jump from individuals as brands all the way up to megabrands.

Megabrands include the commercial names in the top ten list at the beginning of the chapter such as Coke, Microsoft, and IBM. But there are other megabrands in our lives such as the United States, the United Nations, the Catholic Church, and the Red Cross.

Notice that referring to these entities as brands just doesn't sound right. The United Nations is a brand?

Sure, the United Nations (UN) is a brand that stands for conflict resolution. You may or may not subscribe to the ability of the UN to achieve its stated mission, or you may even believe the UN is the personification of bureaucracy. In either case, the essential nature of any brand in your mind is a very small but still powerful thought.

We just don't have much room in our minds for brand information. The more concentrated the core idea that is associated with a brand, and the more consistently that idea is portrayed over time, the more likely the brand will achieve Brandscendence.

Look at the jumble of brands below and my assessment of the primary idea association with the brand.

Brand	Category	Primary Association
Michelin	Tires	Safety
Volvo	Cars	Safety
Maytag	Household appliances	Dependability
Middle East	Geographic region	Conflict
McDonald's	Food	Fast
Red Cross	Nonprofit	Help
Nobel Prize	Nonprofit	Innovation
Mercedes	Cars	Luxury
BMW	Cars	Engineering
America	Nation	Freedom
Switzerland	Nation	Finance
French	Culture	Cuisine

Interesting exercise you say, but you can't create the first chart in the book showing the "value" of noncommercial brands. You can't compare the Nobel Prize with McDonald's as brands. Not today, but in the future, it should be possible to compare these brand values as we explore more of the underlying structure of how great brands work and endure.

By the way, I readily accept that some readers will view my examples as provocative at best. Know that I offer them in the spirit of making branding accessible to everyone and to push the boundaries of branding practice forward.

As we explore Brandscendence, we will dive deeper into the elements of relevance, context, and mutual benefit.

Relevance is about having a core brand idea and the values that customers hold about a brand and projecting it through sense and experience.

Context is about purposeful evolution of a brand through time and by culture that is connected to the original brand idea. Brands that adapt to changing wants and needs without losing their core values earn the right to survive.

Mutual benefit is a relationship multiplier, a powerful motivator for having an ongoing relationship.

When put together, Brandscendence describes how brands evolve and how the greater among them endure over time. But the ultimate test for any brand is not when everything's great—it's when things go wrong. This is when the true nature of a brand's character is revealed for all to see. When the crisis hits, the brand will react instinctively and be true to its nature.

CUSTOMER EXPERIENCE

Brands are the sum of the experiences people have when the brand first imprints on them and over time.

We find these experiences rooted in the five senses: seeing, hearing, feeling, tasting, and touching. Of all the ways to communicate Brandscendence, visual design is one of the strongest. The design disciplines have some of the most evolved standards to articulate brand strategy today. A balance of form and function leads to designs that endure over time.

While on a trip to visit my parents for the holidays, I had the chance to drive my wife's mode of transportation for a couple of days. It's a Mercedes ML320 sports utility vehicle, which she's had for a year and was a replacement for a 20-year-old diesel Mercedes 300SD sedan. My impression for the last year was that the vehicles couldn't be more different, until I spent some time in it and truly experienced it for the first time.

The interior design of the SUV was uncannily similar to the sedan made 20 years ago. The color scheme of the instrumentation panel and dashboard, with what I'll call "Mercedes tan" seats and side panels, really spoke to me about the design DNA that had been transferred forward from one generation of car to another. The seats had the same firmness and quality of leather of those in her older car—right down to the pinhole pattern in the center section of the driver and passenger seats. When I got done with the trip, I was more impressed with the sameness of the driving experience than its difference. My experience was a triumph of design consistency over decades.

There are five human senses, and great brands know how to appeal to them. They have distinctive elements that aid us in seeing them, hearing them, touching them, tasting them, and smelling them. Managing brand elements around the five senses provides a useful framework for increasing relevance and context.

Brandscendence is kicked into high gear when all the senses are engaged and a sense of mutual benefit is perceived.

Until now, brand strategy has generally been limited to conversations about commercial success. Brandscendence will explore how branding can be applied to many areas of human activity.

Brands are a shortcut for people. They are known quantities so people don't have to go through an assessment every time they select something. Successful cultures and societies project the same ethos—you know who we are and what you can expect from us. Cultures organize around pivotal principles of core values, just as enduring brands do. Shared values are at the root of why brands work.

As mentioned earlier, some organizations transcend cultures and nations, including the Red Cross, the United Nations, and major religions and sports. These global brands reach across borders and time. What is the secret to these brands' endurance, their ability to hold a place on the global stage for long periods of time? What can every person and organization learn from these enduring brands?

Brands that transcend their original category while staying true to their reason for being endure.

2

STAGES OF BRANDSCENDENCE

"The beginning of wisdom is definition of terms."
SOCRATES[1]

Executive summary. Brandscendence is characterized by the inter-action of three elements: relevance, context, and mutual benefit. Each element manifests itself differently at three major stages of development that map roughly to the development of a person as a child, an adoles-cent/young adult, and a mature adult. The first stage represents general brand dependence, the next independence, and in stage three brand in-terdependence. Understanding each stage of brand behavior provides insight for action to reach the next stage in the successful evolution of a brand.

PURPOSEFUL EVOLUTION

Brandscendence represents the purposeful evolution of enduring brands.

Brandscendence is a journey, not a destination.

When you become familiar with the principles of Brandscendence, you'll be able to see what's going on in the world of brand strategy for yourself. The world of brands will be all around you, but now you'll be able to know them in a new way. You'll be able to assess what customers can perceive and to bridge to the core of what they believe.

Your ability to experience brands will be heightened, so you can continue learning about brand strategy long after you read this book for the first time.

BRAND STRATEGY AND METAPHORS

Much of the current work in branding is based on metaphor. I object to none of them—they all have their place in making sense of branding decisions. In the next few paragraphs, I'll quickly take you through some of the dominant ideas and metaphors used in brand strategy. You'll find all the references to the books and authors I'm referring to in a single endnote for Chapter 2.[2]

Brand equity is a dominant branding idea, which I first met in the writings of David Aaker, especially his books *Managing Brand Equity* and *Building Strong Brands*. The financial equity metaphor has been durable in brand management practice. In Appendix C, you'll find a great contribution to this book from some of the pioneers in the customer equity arena, "Putting the Brand and Branding in Context: Customer Equity Marketing Metrics." Katherine Newell Lemon cowrote the book *Driving Customer Equity* with Roland T. Rust and Valarie A. Zeithaml. Katherine Newell Lemon and her husband, Loren Lemon, spearheaded getting this updated version of their notions about customer equity into Brandscendence. Thanks.

During a lunch with branding luminary David Aaker at Berkeley, several years before David set aside his university duties, he recommended I see Eric Joachimsthaller at the Darden Business School at the University of Virginia. At the time, they were collaborating on a book that would later come to market as the useful and instructive *Brand Leadership*. Here, the brand architecture metaphor comes through loud and clear.

Aaker and Joachimsthaller are in what I call the architectural school of branding. They draw upon management themes that help the business community describe and document brands from the ground up. They prescribe structural models that can guide brand behavior and assist in organizing brand management activities.

Kevin Keller's *Strategic Brand Management* is a good book to have at hand for anyone practicing in the field because it is so comprehensive.

It continues to be the best student text on branding I know of in print today after several editions. Keller is in what I call the descriptive school of branding.

Marc Gobé, author of *Emotional Branding* and the more recent volume, *Citizen Brand,* for me epitomizes the emotional branding school. Also in this school are the authors and practicing professionals who engage in storytelling and myth documentation and development to help strategic marketing efforts. The storyteller model is powerful and has proven its worth many times over in marketing communications and shaping organizational culture. Another title that exhorts readers to leverage storytelling for marketing success is *Legendary Brands,* by Lawrence Vincent. Scott Bedbury, in his book *A New Brand World,* also encourages the use of the brand story to drive successful brand management.

A new brand metaphor drawn from nature is embodied in the book *The Infinite Asset.* Here, the authors create "brand molecules." They follow the progress of brand families over time through brand extensions, creation of brand elasticity to cover new ground, and company mergers and acquisitions that bring new brands into the family through corporate marriage—whether by shotgun or mutual consent. The brand molecule metaphor used in *The Infinite Asset* is truly helpful in describing brand family evolution over time.

I've been most intrigued by research and metaphors from the social sciences and, more recently, cultural anthropology. I've worked with the insightful Dr. Clotaire Rapaille, a medical anthropologist, whose book *Seven Secrets of Marketing* is a good introduction to the "cultural unconscious." Grant McCracken, a cultural anthropologist I first met when he was in residence at Harvard Business School, is now working on a new book, *Flocks and Flows: Anticipating Consumers in a Dynamic Marketplace,* and is a visiting scholar at McGill University in Montreal. Most recently, I have read Gerald Zaltman's ideas in his thoughtful book, *How Customers Think,* which blends marketing practice with the science behind brain function.

I'm going to guide you next toward the human development metaphors from the biological and social sciences to describe brands that endure from one generation to the next.

BRANDSCENDENCE ATTRIBUTES BY STAGE

Brandscendence is a combination of relevance plus context. When working well together, relevance and context can be turbocharged with perceived mutual benefit. Now let's go a bit deeper and explore the attributes associated with relevance, context, and mutual benefit.

Jean Piaget was a Swiss psychologist who created a framework, the stage theory, to understand the development of children on their path to becoming adults.[3] In stage theory, you track the ability of young people to grasp certain concepts. What is not perceivable at one stage can be grasped at the next.

Instead of a smooth continuum of learning and behavior on the journey to adulthood, there are stages, or periods of step function change, where Piaget asserts qualitative differences can be perceived and measured.

In my experience, the concept of stage theory is a good fit to the evolution of enduring brands. As brands mature, they interact with customers and the world at large in very specific and different ways—and they radically change at certain stages.

Some brands are designed to become relevant to you at different stages of life. I can assure you that I wasn't very interested in home health care insurance policies when first entering the workforce, but with fewer years of corporate life ahead than behind, I took out just such a policy several years ago. All financial and health care brands seem to be shifting in relevance as the idea of retirement slowly tries to enter consciousness. I don't think I'll ever fully retire, just stop working for others and wind down over time.

With thanks to Piaget for the stage framework, let me offer a set of adapted brand maturity stages, where stage one generally represents dependence, stage two represents independence, and stage three represents interdependence.

For relevance:

- *Stage 1: Personality development.* The brand behaves as a learning child.
- *Stage 2: Character development.* The brand behaves as a learning adolescent.
- *Stage 3: Defined Purpose.* The brand behaves as a lifelong learning adult.

For context:

- *Stage 1.* The brand *reflects* its surroundings and reacts to the environment.
- *Stage 2.* The brand proactively *adapts* itself to the world to increase its success.
- *Stage 3.* The brand *projects* itself to the world and changes the environment.

For mutual benefit:

- *Stage 1: Conditional.* Mere transactions without ongoing relationships.
- *Stage 2: Reciprocal.* Formation of relationships and memory of the customer.
- *Stage 3: Integrated.* Sustainable relationships that fuel each other's growth.

Each stage is cumulative and builds upon the previous stage.

THE STAGES OF RELEVANCE

In stage one (s1) relevance, the brand functions as would a learning child, perceiving the world locally, forming first impressions, and developing a brand personality.

Brand personality can be uniquely rooted in a larger family of brands, or it can be independent and have a standalone personality. Independent brand personalities can be very successful but can experience arrested development by being unable to become more relevant over time.

Family brands produce brand offspring rooted in the "genetic code" or "DNA" of the parent brand, which provides the basis of their potential. General Electric uses a family brand strategy, as does IBM. Generally, all offerings from both companies start with GE or IBM—there are no standalone branded products or services. What the parent brand stands for informs the rest of the brand family about how to develop and behave, leading to stage two.

In stage two (s2) relevance, the brand forms the features and traits by which it will be known. It is forming a brand character. In the Brandscendence model, s2 cannot be reached if the brand is a fad—constantly changing and never forming a consistent character. As manuscript reviewer David Miln noted to me, "Yes it can—it just is inconsistent by nature." I concede this point. Fads can be an effective brand strategy to take possession of other people's money. However, you're always one fad away from brand extinction. Brandscendence is about a journey of endurance.

A brand with superb character is Johnson & Johnson. Its customers inform the corporate brand character of Johnson & Johnson (J&J). Being primarily a supplier to the medical profession and home health care providers, J&J essentially has done what doctors do—taken the Hippocratic oath: J&J "will do no harm."

The cumulative development of personality and character at this stage holds the potential for graduation to stage three.

Stage three (s3) relevance is defined by purpose—the brand knows what it does for customers. It knows why it was put here on earth and is doing something about it. At stage three, the brand's purpose is known to all and informs everything it does. A brand with purpose is not just conducting commerce; it's driven by a mission. Brands with purpose are focused. Purpose drives employee behavior, customer relationships, shareholder loyalty, and an ability to shape the future. A superb example of brand purpose is the Red Cross. It is such a good example, we'll spend more time with it in a later chapter. For now, let's just remind ourselves that the Red Cross projects itself in such a relevant way that it can overcome race, religion, and geographic and political boundaries anywhere in the world to serve in crisis.

THE STAGES OF CONTEXT

Now that we've explored the three stages of relevance, let's spend some time looking at the ever-changing context and the fitness landscape that drives adaptive behavior.

For context:

- *Stage 1.* The brand *reflects* its surroundings and reacts to the environment
- *Stage 2.* The brand proactively *adapts* itself to the world to increase its success.
- *Stage 3.* The brand *projects* itself to the world and changes the environment.

Fitness landscape is a term, first introduced to me by Ralph Stacey, that complexity theorists use to describe an environment.[4] A particular environment is selected and experiments or modeling is done to show how well organizations adapt when the landscape changes. Substitute brand for organization, and we will explore how well brands adapt when the fitness landscape changes—whether socially, culturally, economically, or technologically.

Stage one (s1) context involves the brand learning to mirror its immediate surroundings. It reflects its environment. Stage one relevance and brand personality development are directly linked to s1 context development, where the brand attempts to reflect its environment. Marketplace entrants at this stage mimic the brand personality and traits of other successful brands. As most business strategists will tell you, being a follower like this will not provide solid market share or revenue returns over time. A more successful strategy is found in stage two.

Stage two (s2) context is where the brand learns to anticipate and adapt to the environment. Adaptive behavior that anticipates is a very successful strategy, especially when it improves the fitness of the brand to survive sudden shifts in market conditions or endure economic downturns. Stage two contextual adaptation is also found when a brand identifies environmental changes and leverages national and global forces affecting it. An example of s2 context brand behavior would be Sony. Here is a brand that not only understands cultural variation but also invests in it in a highly relevant way. All Sony offerings have a mission to entertain. There are design studios in major cities around the world where Sony entertainment product offerings are adapted to meet the tastes of specific countries and cultures. Every business that Sony has acquired, including film, music, and software businesses, focus on the mission to entertain.

Stage three (s3) context holds the power to reshape the environment—the brand has learned to set certain aspects of the social and economic agenda. At this stage, the brand projects itself to the world and changes the fitness landscape for any given category of product or service. An example would be Disney, where a single company has redefined leisure and the meaning of family entertainment and continues to successfully adapt. Disney has taken brand licensing to a new level. The Disney theme park franchises function at an s3 context level in the United States and Japan only, while the Euro Disney park continues to struggle to get the right mix at s2.

An economic example of s3 context changing the rules is Edison's electric light bulb, which took the kerosene lighting business off the map.

THE STAGES OF MUTUAL BENEFIT

Now for the big gun, mutual benefit, and its three stages of development:

- *Stage 1: Conditional.* Mere transactions without ongoing relationships.
- *Stage 2: Reciprocal.* Formation of relationships and memory of the customer.
- *Stage 3: Integrated.* Sustainable relationships that fuel each other's growth.

Stage one (s1) mutual benefit is characterized by conditional transactions where no goodwill is being created that would buffer a bad experience with the brand. You're only one purchase away from the customer switching to another brand. "I'll continue to buy your product as long as . . ." is a typical way a customer frames the conditional form of mutual benefit. You get their patronage only as long as you perform as expected and the competitive landscape doesn't change—a good reason for any brand to consider moving to the next stage.

Stage two (s2) mutual benefit is reciprocal. Both parties perceive an ongoing benefit to being in each other's world. Deposits into the bank of goodwill are being made. Mutual benefit at the reciprocal stage creates relationships that can endure varying degrees of issues and calamities. Brands at this level of maturity are prepared to take a longer view of customer relationships and make necessary investments to move beyond mere conditional transactions. At this stage of mutual benefit, both parties will go the extra mile to make things work. Stage two brands also consider more than customers; they build up goodwill with all stakeholders.

Stage three (s3) mutual benefit is a thing both wondrous and rare. Brands operating at s3 mutual benefit experience integrated benefits with their customers and constituencies. A hallmark of integrated mutual benefit is interdependence. A brand that relies on a web of sustainable, interdependent relationships where everyone benefits can achieve extraordinary results, survive crisis, and endure for long periods.

An example of s3 mutual benefit is eBay. "eBay's mission is to provide a global trading platform where practically anyone can trade practically anything."[5] Forgive me for jumping ahead, but I had a relevant conversation with Scott Elias about sonic branding, which we'll explore more in Chapter 7, "Sensing Relevance: The Power of Perception."

> KC: I think we went through a period where we were trying to send all the characteristics of a three-dimensional environment into a two-dimensional flatland world on the Web. We're now beginning to discover that you can take what the Web can do and introduce it into the store to make it come alive and interactive. That's a much more compelling, experience-based proposition.
>
> For instance, eBay is something of a McLuhan Tetradic reversal[6]—it is retrieving the notion of the large bazaar.
>
> Elias: I agree!
>
> KC: And the fact that you can't physically provide that experience to people on a global scale, being able to do that in a two-dimensional world is just dandy, because it fulfills a need we instinctually want to have.
>
> Elias: And you think about AOL in terms of reducing the world to this whole community where everyone had a different sort of connectivity, not to the whole world, but to everyone you wanted to be connected to.[7]

eBay is an s3 enterprise across each of the Brandscendence elements. It has s3 relevance and purpose that is clearly understood by the customers who use it. "Today, the 1eBay community includes tens of millions of registered members from around the world. People spend more time on eBay than on any other online site, making it the most popular shopping destination on the Internet."[8] eBay redefines the context of shopping online and projects a game that other cyberspace merchants are still trying to match. eBay is also s3 mutually beneficial in an integrated way, by not only providing a shopping experience but by building a community of customers who connect and identify not only with eBay but with each other. In this sense, eBay moves from the role of merchant to the role of matchmaker.

ALL TOGETHER

Let's put the attributes of Brandscendence and the stage development discussion on one chart.

Stages Toward Brandscendence
Brandscendence = (R + C) × Mb

	Relevance	Context	Mutual Benefit
Stage 1 (*dependence*)	personality	reflects	conditional
Stage 2 (*independence*)	character	adapts	reciprocal
Stage 3 (*interdependence*)	purpose	projects	integrated

(Note: each stage is cumulative)

Stage one (s1) development is as if the brand were a child. Relevance, context, and mutual benefit are characterized by a brand personality that reflects its environment and is conditional in its approach to mutual benefit. The time orientation is now.

Stage two (s2) brand development covers adolescence to young adulthood. The brand is forming a character by which it will be known in the world. The brand is learning to adapt to the environment rather than merely reflecting it. The brand is engaging in reciprocally beneficial relationships that are making deposits to the bank of goodwill. The time orientation is now but with a memory of the past.

Stage three (s3) brands demonstrate a high level of maturity. These brands have a sense of purpose that drives relevance—relevance that can be projected to change context and environment—and the fitness landscape for other competitors. Interdependent relationships are being formed to drive brand success. The time orientation is transcendent—standing at once in the past, present, and future.

As you might have guessed, s3 brands are the ones that I believe are on the path to Brandscendence. None actually gets there. At some point, a fatal mistake is made, or, in a moment of cataclysmic, discontinuous change, relevance evaporates in an instant.

To continue with the human development metaphor, the path of Brandscendence is the journey of a long and meaningful life, not immortality.

The next chapters are devoted to an in-depth look at relevance, context, and mutual benefit one at a time—and how to achieve s3 interdependence as an advanced expression of brand maturity.

Our journey to discover Brandscendence continues.

3

I CAN FEEL IT
Relevance and Enduring Brand Values

"The truth is so simple, it is regarded as pretentious banality."
DAG HAMMARSKJOLD[1]

$$\text{Brandscendence} = (Relevance + \text{C}) \times \text{Mb}$$

The attributes of *Relevance* by stage in Brandscendence:

- *Stage 1: Personality.* Brand works to become clear and compelling to the customer. (The brand behaves as a learning child.)
- *Stage 2: Character.* Brand reputation and behaviors are known. (The brand behaves as a young adult: its features, traits, and actions are recognizable; it is sorting out priorities.)
- *Stage 3: Purpose.* The brand's ongoing reason for being is widely perceived and drives brand behavior. (The brand behaves as a mature adult with a mission in life.)

Executive Summary. The first key element in pursuing Brandscendence is to have a brand with enduring relevance for customers and stakeholders. The brand must be known for something, and that reason for being must be understood and believed by customers and key stakeholders. In the stage development of the brand, it should move from transient values to enduring values that are known and trusted. The concept of brand relevance is further explored in this chapter, including ways in which it can manifest itself and be nurtured and a discussion about how to avoid committing "brandicide" (brand suicide).

RELEVANCE

Relevance is the starting point for any brand. Be relevant, or be gone.

Every potential customer waits for your brand to: "Be something to me." Be so compelling that I turn to you for considered purchases and transactions. Be so trustworthy that I seek your counsel in complex or life-changing situations.

Strive to be *relevant* in a particular way over time.

In the Brandscendence model, relevance is the genetic code of the brand, while context is the environmental learning and adapting abilities of the brand. This is not to say brand relevance doesn't evolve over time—it just does it much more slowly, almost glacially. Think of brand relevance as slow adaptation and brand context as fast adaptation.

In this chapter, we want to focus on relevance as a brand's reason for being. What role does a brand play? How does its role help the brand exert influence in its environment so it can survive and thrive for the long run?

Brand development, as we explored in the last chapter, can be compared to that of a person. They first develop a personality, then form a character by which they are known that drives and focuses organizational behavior, and finally have a purpose that can set the agenda for others in the category, industry, or world at large. Tide laundry detergent in the United States sets the agenda for a category, Coke sets the agenda for an entire industry, and the Hollywood, California, brand helps set the cultural and entertainment agenda for the world at large. They are s3, because as brands, their ongoing reason for being is widely perceived by the world at large and drives brand behavior—they have a known purpose.

WHO OWNS THE BRAND?

When I was asked at work to become the "brand steward" for IBM ThinkPad notebook computers, I was uncertain what the company wanted from me. Seven years later, I'm still in the process of working myself out of a job.

Brand stewardship was a concept brought to us in general by our advertising agency, Ogilvy & Mather, and in particular by Charlotte Beers, the leader of O&M at the time. Brand stewardship was the focus of her transformation plan for the agency—but from the client perspective, the message that brand stewardship brought to us was that the customer brings a lot to the table in terms of brand ownership.

The question: Who owns the brand? I can tell you one thing—it's usually not the person designated as the owner. I've come to believe there is a paradoxical answer—one I wanted to explore more.

So in the middle of writing this book, I asked some of my smart, brand-savvy friends, "Who owns the brand?"

The answers fell into three primary camps. The organization owners, the customer/constituent owners, and the "and/both owners." Here are some of the answers.

David Miln, skiing buddy, friend, marketing consultant, and former head of business development for Saatchi and Saatchi:

> It is like asking who owns an idea—the originator and everyone who's heard of it, of course.
>
> Clearly the organization is responsible for the brand and its health; it is parent to the brand as child. The brand changes, grows, and is successful or otherwise depending on what it has to offer the world (cf. the child). What the child, then adult [brand] delivers—hard and soft benefits and its malleability—determines its success and its market value. Ergo, the brand is an idea in the heads of consumers, and each owns it in their own way and so does the organization in its own way. That's my starter!

Jon Rubin, multidecade friend and vice president/general manager of trade marketing for News America Marketing in New York:

> Being the purist that I am, I believe the business owns the brand. I understand the thinking behind the customer owning the brand; i.e., if the customer doesn't agree with the position-

ing or the benefits communicated, they will not buy it. However, it is the organization that sets the mission and objectives for a brand, based on overall product portfolio considerations and the organization's financial demands.

The ownership of a brand for a business must include its purpose in a broader marketing and financial mix for the company. So ultimately the customer owns the brand. However, it is the organization that sets the mission and objectives for a brand, based on overall product portfolio considerations and the organization's financial demands.

Assuming that the role of the company is to maximize ownership value, a brand must be used to that end. So the control of the brand (hence the ownership) remains with the company. There are many products that on their own might be marketed differently; however, because they are part of a larger portfolio, they are used to maximize the overall portfolio. Examples would be Kodak cameras marketed to protect film revenue. They certainly did not set out to manufacture the best-in-class cameras. They simply wanted consumers to continue to take pictures.

Another example is Jeep. When Jeep went upscale to create the Grand Cherokee, it moved to a different class of car. It was a good decision for the company to go upscale. They could have more easily gone downscale based on current consumer attitudes toward Jeep—however, they did not because there was more profit in going upscale.

I understand that if the consumer did not agree to the change, it would have failed. However, I believe brands are first managed by the needs of the organization and the shareholders of that organization, then are marketed for consumer acceptance and nurtured for longevity for the betterment of the organization and the marketplace.

"So in conclusion, the company owns the brand," says Rubin.

Tom Duncan, whose book, *Driving Brand Value,* I reviewed several years ago, is one of the pioneers in Integrated Marketing Communications. Tom directs the IMC graduate program at the Daniels College of Business, part of the University of Denver system. "The brand resides with the customer, but the company is responsible for its nourishment and growth (or death), which the Brandscendence model does a great job of explaining."

Marc Gobé, cofounder of Degrippes/Gobé and author of *Emotional Branding* and *Citizen Brand* says, "On your question, I believe that in a consumer democracy where people vote for brands with their wallet every day, consumers own the brand."

Erich Joachimsthaller, president of Vivaldi Brand Leadership and coauthor of the book *Building Strong Brands* with David Aaker, says,

> Interesting question: "Who owns the brand?"
>
> I like Susan Fornier's thinking about all the actions that a brand does (the stuff that those who manage the brand do on behalf of the brand)—all are indicative of the type of relationship that the company who manages the brand seeks with the customer.
>
> Based on that, a customer decides on the partnership. What a brand does (as managed by the company) expresses its personality. Yahoo!, for example, does things in a fun way, Virgin in an iconoclastic way, and Nike in an irreverent way.
>
> But it is not all the company, because the brand is also something intangible. The perceptions of the actions of the brand count. Thus, the oft-quoted saying: "The brand resides in the minds of customers."
>
> Who owns the brand? The answer is that the company owns the responsibility of managing the brand according to its identity—what it stands for. The customer owns the brand, because the final outcome or whatever is stored in consumers' minds is perceptions.

"So companies have a say in the ownership, an important one, but consumers have the final say." Thanks Erich.

Thanks also to David, Jon, Tom, and Marc for helping to frame this issue.

JOINT VENTURE

Who owns the brand?

Brand relevance and perception is a joint venture between the brand parent organization and the customers and clients who experience the brand.

I'd like to jump off at the deep end and say "Cartesian dualism" might be the way to think about it. I'm only a superficial follower of the philosopher Rene Descartes, but the dictionary definition says dualism

FIGURE 3.1 *Customer/Brand Relationship*

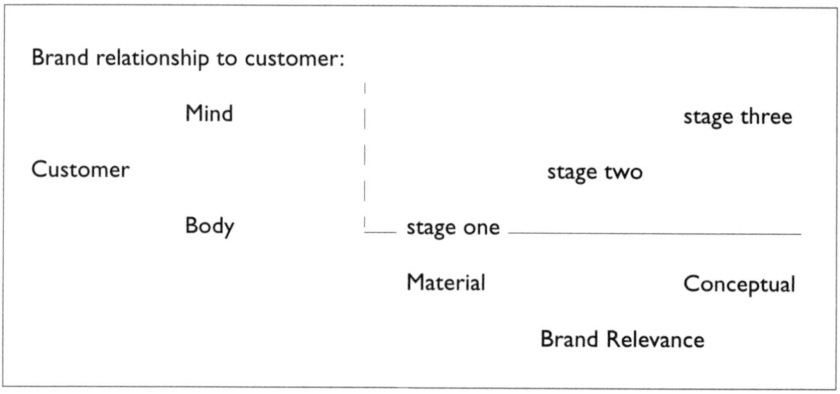

Brand relationship to customer:

Mind		stage three
Customer		stage two
Body	stage one	
	Material	Conceptual
	Brand Relevance	

is "a) the view that there are just two irreducible substances, and, b) the view that substances are either material or mental" is truly fundamental to a discussion of brands. Brands are both material and mental. The customers are both material and mental.

Clearly, the customer indeed has a body and a mind. The brand, likewise, has a body in the sense of a relevance "genetic code"—potential that is essentially unchanging—and a body in the sense of physical delivery of goods and services. The brand has a mind in the sense that it can master how to behave, learn, adapt, and grow in context.

The joint venture between brand and customer grows from one stage to the next as the relationship moves from physical and transactional, to a deeper and more conceptual relevance that touches more of the mind and the heart.

BRAND PERSONALITY

The words *brand* and *image* would probably be some of the first words you would see conjoined as a phrase in a marketing or advertising textbook. *Brand image* is about what customers see and believe about the brand. If the customer view is congruent with the brand's self-image and the brand has relevance, then a healthy brand personality is under development.

For a quick inventory of enduring brand personality at the consumer product level, I will now wander the house using the same technique the legendary Peter Lynch of the Fidelity Magellan Mutual Fund used to pick stocks—through personal experience. Let's see how many brands I can find that have been around "forever," at least in my experience.

Let's start in my kitchen:

- McCormick spices
- LaChoy soy and teriyaki sauce
- Crisco oil and shortening
- Morton salt
- Aunt Jemima syrup
- Campbell's soups
- Hunt's diced tomatoes
- Pillsbury biscuits
- Thomas's English muffins
- Ragu spaghetti sauce
- Green Giant vegetables
- Delmonte vegetables
- Stouffer's TV dinners
- Gorton's frozen fish
- Land O'Lakes butter
- Coke
- Pepsi
- Canada Dry ginger ale
- Schweppes tonic water
- Folgers coffee
- Maxwell House coffee
- Kidde fire extinguisher (seen in public places first)

Master bathroom:

- Crest toothpaste
- Colgate toothpaste
- Johnson's baby powder
- Vaseline petroleum jelly
- Bayer aspirin
- Q-tips cotton swabs
- Phillips's Milk of Magnesia
- Vicks Formula 44 cough syrup
- General Electric clock radio (GE doesn't make these anymore)

Library/Study:

- The Bible
- Webster's dictionary
- Sony television set
- World Book encyclopedia and year books

From these three lists from the kitchen, master bathroom, and library/study, what might you know about my brand perceptions and me?

The brand list for the library in my house is very short. Why? I didn't have a library or study in my house when I was growing up. That's not to say we didn't have books, but they were scattered in various places around the house where they were needed.

BRAND CHARACTER

Brand character is the next stage of brand relevance development.

Brand personality can be associated with a simple product or service, but the next stage of development is needed to move into the realm of brand character. Brand character begins to manifest itself when the brand's reputation and behaviors are known and somewhat uniquely predictable.

At the brand character stage, the brand behaves as a young adult would: features, traits, and actions are becoming recognizable, and a lot of time is being spent sorting out priorities. Who am I? What do I want to be when I grow up? Organizations that manage brands struggle with these questions as surely as an adolescent does.

Young adult brands can be products, services, or the companies themselves as they enter a world where brand families are possible both socially (through brand extensions, cobranding, or ingredient branding) and economically (expense and capital funds are available for customer or geographic expansion).

Some of the most valuable brands on earth are managed as master brands. In a master brand strategy, everything offered falls under one brand umbrella, such as IBM, GE, McDonald's, Microsoft, Intel, and Disney. The master brand strategy aggregates and unifies intangible equity for owners and can increase the effectiveness of integrated marketing activities.

FIGURE 3.2 *Global Brands*

RANK	BRAND VALUE (IN BILLIONS)	COUNTRY OF OWNERSHIP
1. Coca-Cola	$70.45	United States
2. Microsoft	64.09	United States
3. IBM	51.77	United States
4. GE	42.34	United States
5. Intel	31.11	United States
6. Nokia	29.44	Finland
7. Disney	28.04	United States
8. McDonald's	24.70	United States
9. Marlboro	22.18	United States
10. Mercedes	21.37	Germany
11. Toyota	20.78	Japan
12. Hewlett-Packard	19.86	United States
13. Citibank	18.57	United States
14. Ford	17.07	United States
15. American Express	16.83	United States
16. Gillette	15.98	United States
17. Cisco	15.79	United States
18. Honda	15.63	Japan
19. BMW	15.11	Germany
20. Sony	13.15	Japan
21. NesCafé	12.34	Switzerland
22. Budweiser	11.89	United States
23. Pepsi	11.78	United States
24. Oracle	11.26	United States
25. Samsung	10.85	South Korea

Source: Interbrand/Business Week 2003.

Top global brands from the August 4, 2003, Interbrand survey "The Best Global Brands" reported in *Business Week* reinforce the dominance and power of the master brand strategy.[2]

BRAND PURPOSE

Brand purpose gains followers. Brand purpose creates customers who themselves are stewards of brands that reach far beyond commercial intent. I mentioned Harley-Davidson in Chapter 1: this brand delivers more than motorcycles—it informs customers' lifestyles.

The headline from a June 2003 *Business Week* article talks about Helmut Panke, the nuclear physicist turned chief executive of BMW:[3]

> Headline: BMW
> Subhead: Will Panke's high-speed approach hurt the brand?

Why does this *Business Week* article, which talks about a new business strategy to speed up new models to market, point out potential harm to the "brand"—not to the "business"? Is it that business strategy and brand strategy are so closely linked here that they are inseparable? Perhaps it is recognition that brand equity, once built, needs to be protected—especially in the case of a brand that has been consistent and relevant over many years?

I'd say both.

In their writings and speaking engagements, David Aaker and Erich Joachimsthaller preach that brand strategy and business strategy are truly one and the same. In the book *Building the Brand-Driven Business,* authors Scott Davis and Michael Dunn say in the subheadline, "Operationalize your brand to drive profitable growth."[4] That's corporate-speak for linking brand and business strategies together and making them worthy of action. Davis is a managing partner and Dunn is the president and CEO of Prophet, a Chicago-based brand management consulting company that David Aaker helped found years ago. Prophet and Aaker's brand acolytes today still help preach brand purpose as business strategy to help convert the corporate masses to a more effective way of doing business.

In the section about brand personality, I mentioned that there is a library and study in my home. That's where I'm writing this book. On a stand to my right is a venerable companion—*Webster's New Universal Unabridged Dictionary.*

Webster's dictionary is a purely American brand that truly understands its purpose and transcends time in its currency and ongoing usefulness.

Molly Wade McGrath tells the Webster's story:[5]

> *Webster's Dictionary* started life as *The Blue-Backed Speller.* In 1783, *The Blue-Backed Speller* may well have been number one on a very short list of best-selling books. Almost every pioneer family owned a copy; in schoolrooms, it was the ultimate authority in judging many a lively spelling bee.

The primer's official title was *Elementary Spelling Book,* and it was Part 1 of Noah Webster's *An American Dictionary of the English Language,* published in 1828.

Few books have had the impact on their times and on the generations to follow as did this early dictionary, completed when its author was 67, after a quarter of a century of preparation.

David Yerkes, Professor of English at Columbia University, in his introduction to my unabridged version of Webster's Dictionary says, "This fine *Dictionary* continues, in magnificent form, the noble tradition exemplified by Benjamin Franklin of describing and reporting the English language."[6] For people who speak American English, Webster's Dictionary is a very enduring brand.

What was the other book in my library? The *Holy Bible* is the bestselling book in the world. The Bible is an enduring volume that represents a larger religious brand with purpose—Christianity. There are lots of subbrands of Christianity: Catholic, Anglican, Protestant (and lots of sub-subbrands here—Methodist, Baptist, Presbyterian, Lutheran, Pentecostal, etc.). The *Holy Bible* is the text that unites these communities.

Similar roles are played by the *Koran,* the *Talmud, The Teachings of Buddha,* and other sacred texts. I also have some copies of these in my library, they just don't go back to my early childhood as do the other items in my personal brand inventory.

We will spend more time exploring the role of brand strategy in noncommercial settings later on, but I hope these examples give you a sharp taste of enduring relevance.

But what happens when the brand strays from its path? When brand relevance shifts rapidly, customers and constituencies get lost at best and, at worst, feel betrayed. In the branding world, this intentional shift or unintentional loss of relevance is called "committing brandicide."

BRANDICIDE

The fastest path to committing brandicide—a brand suicide—it to stray too far from what people already believe about a brand. New Coke is a classic case study in ignoring core beliefs about relevance.

You know the story: Coke decides it's taking a beating by Pepsi in taste tests, so a ton of money goes into a new formula, which is rigorously tested on the dimension Coca-Cola thinks it is being beaten on—taste.

You know the ending to this story already. The new Coke is introduced, customers rebel and want the old formulation back, and Coke Classic (the only one you can buy today) is back on the shelves and in the fountains within a few short months.

You will learn more about this in Chapter 9, "Creating Context and Integrating Experience," but let's just say for now the people at Coke were worried about taste, when the real issue at hand was tradition versus being contemporary. Taste was not the problem, but because it was the predetermined issue, that's all that blind taste tests studied. Pepsi set the agenda, and Coke tried to manage to it. Big mistake.

Coke as a brand imprints at a very young age, is associated with family and good times, and was a stable part of an ever-changing, fast-paced world. Changing Coke was removing one of the bedrock assumptions of existence for some people—and they drink a lot of Coke.

Brandicide is committed when you have the assumptions wrong on a key branding decision or you ignore the long-held beliefs or needs of your core customers. It's easy to fall into the trap of damaging your brand by churning your executive team too often, failing to listen to key constituencies, or thinking that change is good for its own sake without considering the equity that's already been created in the brand.

BRANDSCENDENCE: CONSISTENCY OVER TIME

Brandscendence argues for a view of building and accumulating brand value over time. That is not to say there aren't "cool hunters" out there that help brands stay on the leading edge of societal trends. The question is whether your brand will be a beacon or a mirror. Will it guide and illuminate a brand proposition over a long period of time and be familiar and known to the customers you choose to serve? Or will your brand reflect a seemingly endless set of changing attitudes. Will it create lasting brand equity?

This question isn't limited to big brands. It includes the local college restaurant everyone goes to years after they've graduated. It includes the college that still draws students for a particular curriculum. It includes the character of the town or city that hosts the college. From transnational to local, Brandscendence is about being consistent over time.

Brand equity is not fostered by being different moment to moment, year to year, decade to decade. Equity is created by making deposits into the bank of goodwill that forms the basis for people wanting to do business with you again.

Do not confuse brand consistency with the ability to adapt to changing circumstances. Consistency is not rigidity. Primary brand relevance can adapt and evolve in context for the mutual benefit of a brand and its constituents.

That's our next chapter—taking enduring relevance forward and helping it adapt to changing contexts over time.

C *h a p t e r* **G** *l o s s a r y*

_____

relevant *adj.* bearing upon or connected with the matter in hand; pertinent: *a relevant remark.*—**relevance, relevancy,** *n.*—**Syn.** Applicable, germane, apposite, appropriate, suitable, fitting. See **apt.**[7]

4

FOREVER YOUNG

Leveraging Context

"We shape our buildings; thereafter, they shape us."
WINSTON CHURCHILL[1]

Brandscendence = (R + *Context*) × Mb

The attributes of *context* in Brandscendence:

- *Stage 1: Reflects.* Mimics the social and economic environment.
- *Stage 2: Adapts.* Actively adapts to changes in the environment.
- *Stage 3: Projects.* Creates new social constructs or economic rules for others to mimic or adapt to.

Executive summary. Brands that reflect live hand to mouth and day to day. Brands that can adapt earn the right to survive over time. Brands that project themselves change the rules, and the fitness landscape, for everyone else. Managing a brand's direction requires connection to and conviction for the original brand idea with innovation that is purposeful to that idea and its current context. Purposeful evolution allows a brand to adapt to changing wants and needs without losing its core relevance in the movement forward.

WINDS OF CHANGE

The winds of change are blowing again. What will you do?

Reflect what's happening after it's happened?

Adapt to the trend as its happening?

Be the force of change?

My advice: Work up the ladder of Brandscendence to be the s3 force that creates and projects context.

Context is the partner of relevance. As relevance is the reason for being, context is the way to interpret that reason for action today. Culture, economic conditions, and customer experience provide the platform for context.

If relevance is the slow and purposeful evolution of the brand's DNA or genetic inheritance over time, then context is the behavioral and situational learning or fast adaptation of the brand.

THE POWER OF CONTEXT

For over a decade, my wife, Heidi, has been an instructor of children's manners. She does this in a class offered by a local parks and recreation department. Heidi is the most senior instructor they have, and her classes are always full.

The same class that is so well received in North Carolina couldn't consistently attract students when we lived in Connecticut. The social context of manners for young people is very different below the Mason-Dixon line versus New England, where the idea of a manners class just didn't attract students or capture the imagination of parents as being relevant.

"Miss Heidi," as she's known around town, has an extended family of children and young adults who have benefited from her work with them over the years. If not for our move south, context would have snuffed out her drive to teach in the north, while context now reinforces her success where we live today. This is an example of cultural context. The class content didn't change; the context did.

Brand relevance is contextual. Relevance without context is a brand without a compass. Context without relevance is meaningless.

STAGE ONE CONTEXT: THE BRAND REFLECTS

You know brands around you that do a serviceable job of meeting customer needs by reflecting their environment. These brands are a mirror of other moderately successful brands. For every McDonald's, there are several other fast food places that have staked a claim in the same neighborhood. Because McDonald's is essentially an expert real estate company and landlord, it's easy for others to follow their lead. Plant your fast food store near a McDonald's; they've done their home-work on traffic and spending habits.

The same is true for car dealerships, furniture stores, and strip malls. You find lots of behavioral imitation but not much leadership or unique adaptation to the environment that can't be quickly copied.

STAGE TWO CONTEXT: THE BRAND ADAPTS

Old Spice was a men's aftershave and cologne when I was growing up. Today, it's my favorite deodorant. The Old Spice brand has adapted to a world where body odor is still an issue, but men's aftershave and cologne are stable, not growing categories.

Brands that actively change in the face of the fitness landscape are s2 contextually adaptive.

Some brands are a lot more adaptive than others.

For instance, Marriott over the past two decades has spawned sev-eral new Marriott brand family hotels to meet the needs of emerging customer pyschographics. In addition to the flagship Marriott Hotels and Resorts, there are J.W. Marriott Hotels that are upscale and located in cities and resorts. The acquisition several years ago of the Ritz-Carl-ton brand complemented the J.W. Marriott initiative.

Marriott acquired Renaissance Hotels to fill the moderate-to-up-scale business part of their portfolio. They developed Courtyard by Mar-riott to meet the needs of the frequent business traveler and Fairfield Inn and Spring Hill Suites to meet the entry-point needs of suburban locations.

I recently stayed at a J.W. Marriott in Seoul, South Korea. The plan-ners had clearly had the Ritz-Carlton and Four Seasons on their mind. The property of the same name in Jakarta, Indonesia, became rubble when a car bomb brought it down. The strength of this American brand gone global also made it a target. It raises the question of high-end lodg-ing in the future—will the most desirable brands be smaller and more discrete?

The airline industry seems to think so. The more nimble private jet and fractional jet ownership/membership companies, not the big carriers, are signing up new customers at a rapid pace. After 9/11, the entire travel infrastructure is likely to get smaller with higher levels of personal service.

MALADAPTIVE LEARNING: ADAPTING BUT STILL MISSING THE MARK

Ralph Stacey, in his book *Complexity and Creativity in Organizations,*[2] puts a spin on adaptive behavior that should be part of every brand manager's intellectual toolbox. It's about something he calls "maladaptive learning."

Stacey says the following about maladaptive learning:

> [Maladaptive learning] occurs when a particularly well-adapted dominant schema enables a system to perform effectively for long periods of time without the need to change the dominant schema. The evaluative schemas then become atrophied, leaving the total system exposed in the event of sudden, unexpected changes. In this case, an organization continues to follow its dominant schema, even though the rivals it is competing with have long since changed the fitness landscape. Maladaptive learning produces stability, because it allows the dominant schema to remain the same and thus permits organizations to follow their preestablished patterns of behavior. They can go on for long periods of time, the length of time depending on how rapidly others are changing the fitness landscape.

In other words, a brand that likes things just the way they are and is not looking, listening, and feeling the environment is likely to find itself out of the game—because the game is changing, sometimes so disruptively that there isn't time to recover.

This would argue for another strategy that Jack Welch, former head of General Electric espoused. Captured so well in the title of the book, *Control Your Destiny or Someone Else Will: How Jack Welch Is Making General Electric the World's Most Competitive Company*[3]—the strategy is to be a brand that projects—a brand that changes the rules for others.

STAGE THREE: THE BRAND PROJECTS

At stage three, context helps the brand create new social constructs or economic rules for others to mimic or adapt to. In military parlance, this stage would be called "projecting power"—and there's no better way to project power than to be "forward deployed." That is, be where you're going to be needed before the need is actually perceived by the enemy, in the case of the military, and by the customer in the case of brand strategy.

No organization is better forward deployed than the U.S. Navy. The Navy is off the coast of almost every hot spot around the world. Is your brand everywhere it should be when a customer need may present itself? Not likely.

The number one brand in any land—Coke—is working on being forward-deployed for its customers. The Coke strategy is to be easily within reach to quench any thirst. They are targeting customer density with greater access to Coke and Coca-Cola products per square block than any other competitor. Remember Jon Rubin in the last chapter? When he read this as a draft, he added, "I'll never forget seeing Coke being sold at the last bar before reaching the Everest base camp. This was at 17,000 feet and had to be carried in about 30 miles."

Douglas Holt at Harvard Business School has done research that indicates, "Customers value some of the most powerful brands in the world primarily for their 'cultural value.' They provide imaginative resources that people use to build their identity."

Holt says, "The most powerful brands are those that are able to traverse disruptive cultural shifts. Many brands falter when disruptions hit. The most impressive brands are those that are able to use disruptions as a platform to enhance the delivery of cultural value." Holt cites Mountain Dew and Nike as such brands.[4]

Brands that project power set the rules for competitors, or they set the agenda for a cause, as do the Red Cross, Doctors without Borders, the European Union, NATO, and the United Nations. Organizations and the brands that project power are the Great Adapters.

EXAMPLES OF GREAT ADAPTERS

The General Electric brand focuses on relevance, because it has so many contexts to express it to customers around the world.

General Electric (GE) creates infrastructure, delivers tools that can be used by that infrastructure, and then provides services. This relevance + context strategy expresses itself not just on a business level but at nation-building level.

GE will help you electrify a country by building power generation stations and an electrical grid (infrastructure). GE will then help you raise your level of medical care with diagnostic devices such as MRI and X-ray machines (tools). GE will sell you "reliable thrust" instead of just an aircraft engine as part of a sale that includes ongoing preventative maintenance (service). GE will also help you finance the project or purchase and get it all to where you need it.

Notice that in each case, GE's brand and business strategy are interlocked, becoming more and more relevant to customers in the context of particular societies with their emerging, unique economic needs. You need electrical infrastructure before you can power the medical tools, and you need to take care of the basic medical needs of the people on the ground before you take to the air with a state airline.

The company I work for, IBM, has changed several times during its 100-year journey toward Brandscendence. IBM has always been in the "reinvention of business" trade—first with simple tabulators and punch card machines, then through a relatively swift transition to electronic computers, and today by embracing a networked world. IBM dubbed this world an "e-business," and it has outlasted the Web bubble and the hysteria that surrounded it. The next big business driver IBM sees is called the "on demand" era, and the company is working to be forward deployed for customers to meet their needs as it emerges.

IBM's defines an on-demand business as "enterprise whose business processes—integrated end-to-end across the company and with key partners, suppliers, and customers—can respond with speed to any customer demand, market opportunity, or external threat." Now that's forward deployed.

STAYING THE COURSE

Three resources are needed to build a brand—time, talent, and money. Time and brand context can overcome large brand-building expenditures. All you need is patience and a willingness to stay the course. Nothing overcomes a lack of talent, but the great brands usually attract great people—another benefit of pursuing the path of Brandscendence.

The college town I live in has a restaurant called the Rathskeller or, as it is affectionately known, "The Rat." It's been an institution in Chapel Hill for decades. If you went to school at the University of North Carolina, you know The Rat. If you're in a U.S. college town, you probably have a similar restaurant, and if you're in Germany, a rathskeller (as a type of pub and dining establishment) is likely one of the oldest in town.

Similarly, my parents grew up in Perry, Oklahoma—population 5,049. In Perry, you can go to the Kumback Lunch on the town square for breakfast, lunch, and dinner. It claims to be Oklahoma's oldest café, open since 1926. If you live or grew up in Perry, you know the Kumback.

Being a megabrand doesn't have to be the objective. These restaurants are not big brands—but they are well known to the customers they serve.

Paying too much attention to brand context and change can move from being productive to being distracting and leading down the path to ruin. Remember, context without relevance is meaningless. Focusing on change without holding fast to core relevance is a disaster in the making.

Bill Weiss, chairman and CEO of the Promar Group, LLC, exhorts his clients, when they ask him to help envision the future of their businesses, to resist jumping into the "what's going to change" dialog first. Bill knows that only a fraction of what's really about to happen to that business will result from change. He worries more about neglecting what's not going to change—or changing something that's working just fine.

Using a technique called "sonaring," Weiss and his colleagues first map an estimate of the future based on what will *not* change, to provide a foundation. Then, the discussion can turn to an exploration of what could change—and what these changes could mean to an enterprise. The wisdom of first understanding what's not changing in a fast-paced world cannot be underestimated.

NO BRAND ZONES

Adrian Slywotsky and David Morrison argue for a "no-profit zone" in their book *The Profit Zone*.[5] I would agree and say that pockets of branding are also emerging that are either "no brand zones" or "radical brand shift zones."

No brand zones are segments of the economy that just don't respond to or need brand management practices to work. If you see a no brand zone emerging in the way you're doing business today, then you'd better hurry up and get out while you can or adapt and find a way to manifest your core relevance in a fresh context.

Radical brand shift zones occur where perceived brand relevance and category value have shifted from one place in the economy to another. For example, Wal-Mart carries a limited number of brands inside the store, in many cases in unique packaging configurations, making price comparisons versus competitors hard to make. In this case, Wal-Mart becomes the primary brand, displacing the primacy of the brands on the shelves. Customers who shop at Wal-Mart believe that the store knows what they need in each category, has selected a good supplier, and has negotiated a rock-bottom price. The new and disruptive context has radically shifted relevance from the brands in the store to the store itself.

By the way, the Wal-Mart business model is a pretty good one—in early 2003, Wal-Mart of Bentonville, Arkansas, became the number-one revenue business anywhere in the world. As of February 18, 2003, Wal-Mart reported total sales of $244.52 billion, an increase of 12 percent over the prior year.

CONTEXT CREATES VALUE

If I'm renovating my house and searching for replacement windows, I have Anderson, Pella, and at lot of other name brands to choose from in the U.S. market. But if I want Windows for my personal computer, the word *windows* changes meaning entirely and becomes a registered trademark of Microsoft Corporation. In this case, context provides the means to lift a word from the dictionary, which no one can protect as a trademark, to the status of an intellectual property asset that can be defended. We'll talk more about brands and names later on, but for now, remember that context can be understood in terms of the following:

- Use and classification, as in the windows example above
- Culture, as in the Harley-Davidson and Coke examples
- Scalability, from local to global relevance, as in the General Electric example
- Purchase occasion and service touch points, such as retail stores or the Web—as in the Wal-Mart example

Different contexts offer the opportunity for creating value.

Relevance and context are equal partners on the road to Brandscendence.

Relevance is the genetic code of the brand and adapts slowly or discontinuously in relation to the fitness landscape.

Context is the environment where relevance is to be found and exploited and requires constant adaptation to ensure brand survival and success. Context can reflect the environment in stage one, can adjust to the environment in stage two, and project and actively change the fitness landscape in stage three.

Brands that quickly adapt to shifting contexts (s1) earn the right to survive. Purposeful evolution allows a brand to adapt to changing wants and needs (s2) without losing its core relevance along the way. Brands that learn to project themselves (s3) change the rules for everyone else, heightening their ability to succeed.

C h a p t e r   G l o s s a r y

---

context, *n.* **1.** the parts of a written or spoken statement that precede or follow a specific word or passage, usually influencing its meaning or effect: *out of context.* **2.** the set of circumstances or facts that surround a particular event, situation, etc. < L *contextus* a joining together, scheme, structure, equiv. to *contex*(ere) to join by weaving.[6]

adapt, *n.* **1.** to make suitable to requirements or conditions; adjust or modify fittingly: *They adapted themselves to change quickly. He adapted the novel for movies.*—*v.i.* **2.** To adjust oneself to different conditions, environment, etc.: *to adapt easily to all circumstances.* [1605-15]; < L *adaptare* to fit, adjust, perh. via F *adapter.* See ADAPT—**adaptedness,** *n.*—**Syn. 1.** Fit, accommodate, suit, reconcile, conform, modify, rework, convert. See **adjust.**[7]

fitness landscape: "This is a conceptual ram for thinking about the evolutionary journey of a system. Strategies that make the system fitter for survival represent movement up a hill, whereas disadvantageous strategies represent movement down into a valley. Each system's landscape is determined by the strategies of the other systems it interacts with. Evolution is therefore a journey across a heaving landscape. Smooth landscapes represent the ordered zone of operation, and very rugged landscapes represent the disordered zone of operation. Landscapes that are rugged but not too rugged are optimal for evolution and constitute the edge of chaos."[8]

5

WE TRUST EACH OTHER

Mutual Benefit over Time

"Treat people as if they were what they ought to be,
and you help them to become what they are capable of being."
JOHANN W. VON GOETHE[1]

Brandscendence = (R + C) × *Mutual benefit*

The attributes of *mutual benefit* in Brandscendence:

- *Stage 1: Conditional.* Simple transactions without ongoing relationships.
- *Stage 2: Reciprocal.* Formation of relationships and memory of the customer.
- *Stage 3: Integrated.* Sustainable interdependent relationships that fuel each other's growth.

Executive summary. Perceived mutual benefit is a relationship multiplier. With just competent amounts of relevance and context, perceiving an obligation to act in kind or sensing mutual benefit is a powerful motivator for having an ongoing relationship.

When you put it all together: relevance, context, and mutual benefit, what is your brand?

The value created by branding efforts is known as "intangible equity" or "goodwill" on the balance sheet of a company. In business strategy, this value is known as brand equity and can help improve margins, increase customer loyalty, provide opportunities to reach into new markets, multiply communications effectiveness, and create a bank of goodwill that can be drawn upon in times of crisis.

MUTUAL BENEFIT

Mutual benefit amplifies and underscores relevance and context in Brandscendence over time. When a brand is both relevant and adapting well over time, it finds allies. These allies know why working with each other is important. They experience mutual benefits, which can lead to integrated relationships and growth, which can make increasing deposits into the bank of goodwill.

Mutual benefit is perceived when two or more parties believe they will benefit in a relationship over time—and disproportionately benefit versus others in the fitness landscape.

This is the concept behind "most favored nation status." We trade with those who disproportionately make our lives better over time. We engage in mutually beneficial acts with those in whom we trust and believe. The ebb and flow of these relationships change over time, with some relationships changing in character and more often than others.

STAGE ONE MUTUAL BENEFIT: CONDITIONAL TRANSACTIONS

At stage one, the concept of mutual benefit is essentially immature. The focus is on the present and is conditional: the immediate sale or the action to be taken now, with little thought either for the future or for ongoing relationships with customers and constituents. Stage one brands are run by transaction-driven organizations. You are surely thinking of some of your own examples right now without prompting. Incentives and coupons can get you to consider switching products and services when a lot of money isn't on the table.

Let's move on in the Brandscendence continuum to the much more interesting, and much more sustainable, idea of creating goodwill in an environment that nurtures reciprocal mutual benefit.

STAGE TWO MUTUAL BENEFIT: GOODWILL

Consider this transaction: Dave Barry, a Pulitzer Prize-winning syndicated columnist and humorist, agreed to let a U.S. television network, CBS, do a half-hour situation comedy based on his life called *Dave's World*. Sarah Lyall, writing in the *New York Times* in the article "Regular Guy on a Laugh Track," says, "He rejected the chance to write for the show. His only connection is that it is based on his books. 'I thought that sounded like a great idea, in the sense that I would have to do nothing,' Barry said. 'You will mail me a check, and I will do nothing. I thought that had great appeal to me as a business concept.'"[2]

This is pure goodwill in action. Barry had plenty of goodwill to exploit based on his previous work, so he let CBS send him a check for "doing nothing." Barry's "doing nothing" is actually years of accumulated intellectual property.

Profit-driven organizations are a combination of many assets. The asset portfolio is comprised of people, property, and ideas.

Because property is counted most easily, people, ideas, and other intangible aspects of doing business have received less attention, but they exert a profound influence on enterprise performance and contribute mightily to the bottom line.

Annual reports, in the letter to stockholders from the company president or CEO, almost inevitably note the talents of people as being the most important asset of the organization.

Henry Ford once said, "We have about $100,000,000 worth of machinery, $100,000,000 worth of buildings, and something more than $100,000,000 in cash, but I have no doubt that we could capitalize what we have for a billion dollars and sell the stock if we wanted to."[3]

Ford's belief he could float this seemingly inflated stock offering at the turn of the century, long before Ford Motor Company traded on the New York Stock Exchange, was based on an unseen asset—commercial goodwill. Ford had not only physical assets, he had bright and energetic people and know-how in the form of the production line and procurement processes that were advanced for the time.

My friend and design colleague, David Hill, told me about Ford specifying the dimensions of shipping crates for parts. The suppliers couldn't quite make heads or tails of why Ford would be so picky about shipping crates, but they wanted to keep the business, so they complied with the seemingly arcane request from Ford. Unknown to the suppliers until later, when dismantled, the planks of wood made perfect floor and running boards for the Model A car and were already cut to size. That's know-how that reads as goodwill in mergers and acquisitions.

In accounting parlace, *goodwill* on the balance sheet is what someone is willing to pay for a company when it is sold, subtracting all the physical assets of the company. Goodwill is essentially an estimate of earning power. That's the simple version. See the sidebar for the detailed version.

A D e f i n i t i o n o f G o o d w i l l i n a M e r g e r

"Fair values as of the date of the combination are assigned to the individual assets acquired and to the liabilities assumed, the difference between (a) the total consideration given and (b) the fair value of the tangible assets and intangibles representing property rights, such as patents, less liabilities is designated intangible. Ordinarily, the designated intangible is referred to as purchased goodwill."[4]

—George R. Catlett and Norman O. Olson, *Accounting for Goodwill.*

THE CHANGING NATURE OF GOODWILL

On a crisp December morning in 1994, Carl Bass agreed to have breakfast with me to discuss the concept of goodwill and what the future might hold for this concept in a rapidly changing global marketplace.[5] This was before the Internet frenzy of the late '90s and long before the financial meltdowns that spawned accounting reform measures worldwide.

At the time, Bass was a practice fellow with the Financial Accounting Standards Board (FASB). These are the folks who set the rules for accountants in the United States. A lot has happened in the ten years since we had our conversation, but I think you'll agree it is as topical as ever, given current headlines.

Practice fellows who work in Norwalk, Connecticut, at FASB headquarters are on loan from some of the best accounting firms in the nation. They are also generally regarded as the future leaders in the profession. At the time, Bass was on the FASB staff from Arthur Andersen's Houston office for two years.

Goodwill "is certainly not on the front of any manager's mind or CEO's mind." said Bass. "But if you listen to some of the things that CEOs are talking about—improving the value of their company by bringing in top-flight people, by having a better trained workforce, by having a better educated workforce—they're really talking about goodwill. They're just not calling it by name.

"They're talking about things that will bring about intangible results to their company over the long term—excess earnings over the future period, because they have a better trained workforce, a more efficient workforce, a better educated workforce. To me, that's a lot of what goodwill should be."[6]

Bass believed that a lot of managers are focused on what they would put into their financial statements, and these goodwill development costs just didn't show up there. "All those costs are expensed and not reflected in their financials or future periods. But they're going to bring value to the company. If you do all those things right, that company's going to have a competitive advantage."

This is mutual benefit in action—doing something today to build capacity and trust that will pay off in the future.

Stage two mutual benefit allows for two or more parties to join in simple or complex transactions where a bank of goodwill is created—intangible deposits are made and withdrawals are taken as needed to buffer brands and the organizations/capabilities they represent from a rainy day.

STAGE THREE MUTUAL BENEFIT: INTEGRATED RELATIONSHIPS

At stage one, mutual benefit is essentially absent; transactions are conditional and no repository of goodwill is being created.

At stage two, mutual benefit is reciprocal—in other words, two or more parties perceive benefit in both directions. At stage two, independent parties feel good about interacting with each other and voluntarily choose to continue because all parties perceive benefit in the relationship.

At stage three, the potential of integrated relationships and benefits becomes possible. Two or more actors can form relationships that are interdependent, that is to say, relationships where the time and energy put in have disproportionately beneficial outcomes.

BRAND ENDURANCE OVER TIME

To get another expert perspective on brand endurance through time, I sought out the thoughts of my friend Chris Beaumont, president of Grey Advertising, Japan. Here is what he shared with me by e-mail.

The dictionary defines *enduring* to be something that is often related to something painful, but on a lifelong timescale.

From a brand perspective, this naturally leads to consideration of brands that have been successful over time—as well as space, as our world accelerates due to globalization. Enduring brands are actually to some extent category driven, although in recent years, globalization and mergers/acquisitions have resulted in the disappearance of some long-term brands, especially in telecommunications, financial services, and the pharmaceutical industries.

Categories that seem to facilitate enduring brands are FMCG (a UK acronym for Fast Moving Consumer Goods), service, and prestige (exclusive) fashion brands, all of which have been greatly enhanced in the last decade or so by globalization. Think Coca-Cola, Persil, Pampers, Kikkoman, American Express, IBM, London Stock Exchange, Louis Vuitton. That last example seems to endure more successfully than the Gucci/Prada upstarts. A good example of a brand, from the United Kingdom, that has endured by keeping up with the times is Lucozade. Until the 1980s, it was a health drink for sick people, but it was repositioned as a sports energy drink. We should also exclude brands that have become category generics: Hoover, Xerox, Kleenex, etc., names that have endured but without sustaining their own economic value. [See Chapter 14, "Becoming the Category."]

People die, buildings become dilapidated, but brands that are nurtured and refreshed endure—put a true timescale to the question, "What endures?" In this context, one needs to consider such enduring institutions as Harvard, *The Economist,* the BBC, Wimbledon, Augusta, Cordon Blue that have, in reality, become true brands in their own right. The commercial implications of sports marketing has clearly been recognized in regard to some of the above events, as well as the World Cup and the Olympics. These are especially potent, because they pit countries against each other.

With globalization, triad trade agreements have ensued. None can have had greater aspirations than the single market notion of Europe, so strongly propagated in 1992. What ensued, withstanding the eternal political, economic, and monetary debate, for the individuals of Europe has been a reaffirmation of the relevancy and nature of their countries as brands. Perhaps Switzerland, the country, is one of the most enduring of brands, with time invariant values and associated personality traits? Moreover, global manufacturers often leverage the parentage of their brands, because the country of origin can have pertinent enduring values.

Thank you, Chris.

SPITZINGSEE

I have been a keynote speaker five times for a remarkable conference held only six times outside of Munich, Germany, in a small ski village in the Bavarian Alps named Spitzingsee. The name of the gathering is the *Deutsche Mobil Komputing Konferenz* (German Mobile Computing Conference). I started delivering the first address at the request of Ralf Hinnenberg, the sponsor, who also published a German mobile computing magazine and was a member of IBM's European Industry Advisory Council.

The conference is remarkable in several ways that have to do with the concept of mutual benefit. This is more than a conference; for the people who come, it is a tradition, almost a family celebration of people interested in mobile computing technology. The closest thing I've experienced in the United States is Esther Dyson's PC Forum (that's personal communications, not personal computing). People come back, good economy or bad, to hear the presentations and see the demonstrations—but, more than anything else, to be with each other. The learning that takes place away from the formal meetings and the networking is incredible. I don't speak German, but it's clear just from the intimacy and body language that these folks know each other and value being together.

OK, it's the seventh year of the conference, and I'm slated to be the keynote speaker for the sixth time. Aren't the people attending this conference getting tired of hearing from Kevin Clark? What's going on here? Mutual benefit.

I always bring a fresh presentation, nothing canned. The audience and Ralf clearly want to see me back, and I'm glad to be there. It gives me a chance every year to gather my thoughts about the state of the mobile computing industry and where it's going. We've climbed up the ladder of mutual benefit from my accepting a single invitation seven years ago to an s3 level of interdependence. I look forward to seeing and sharing with these professionals, and they look forward to seeing me. They're not bored with the same old speaker. Rather, they're taking it as an honor that he would return time after time.

If fate ever separates us, either because I can't come or the conference can't go forward, you know it won't be for lack of perceived mutual benefit.

HARVARD BUSINESS SCHOOL

I recently attended a company-sponsored class called the Senior Leadership Forum, held at Harvard Business School (HBS). I have a long relationship with the school, not from attending Harvard, but in working with Jim Aisner, who is the head of public affairs for HBS, on a variety of projects over the years.

While doing prework for the class, it occurred to me that Harvard Business School is the perfect example to sum up this and the preceding chapters. The driver behind HBS is their not-so-secret weapon—case studies. Case studies drive the curriculum and are used all over the world in both academic and business education settings. HBS case studies are the platinum standard in business education material.

We can use the three key elements of Brandscendence to describe Harvard Business School and its case studies.

1. *Relevance.* HBS case studies show s3 purpose—the ongoing brand reason for being—is widely perceived and drives brand behavior. A Harvard Business School MBA is not just an education, it is indoctrination into a way of thinking and a way to get plugged into a network of powerful business leaders. The permanent relevance of the institution is further ensured by each graduating class.

2. *Context.* Harvard Business School, through its case studies, shows s3 competence; the brand projects—it creates the rules and thought leadership for other business schools to mimic or adapt to. HBS projects power around the world, both through

its case studies in the form of thought leadership and its graduates in the form of being forward deployed to some of the largest business battles in history.

3. *Mutual benefit.* HBS is clearly operating at an integrated s3, where sustainable, interdependent relationships are formed that fuel each other's growth. This is true for both the students that attend Harvard Business School, the other universities that use HBS case studies, and the business community at large around the world that deploys HBS-trained executives to create economic value and change the fitness landscape for competitors.

Harvard Business School by definition has found a full measure of Brandscendence. By definition, it is a business school, but it is so much more. HBS as a brand transcends its educational mission with enduring and purposeful relevance. It has a culture that drives the creation of case studies that contribute to setting the agenda for many organizations worldwide. Finally, it is mutually beneficial in an integrated way to a variety of constituencies, further ensuring the institution's ability to endure.

Now let's see if Harvard can adapt to all the MBA programs being offered online.

Brands really show their true nature and whether they can endure when they are under stress. Let's look at this more closely in the next chapter where culture is destiny.

Chapter Glossary

benefit, *n., v.,* **-fited, fitting.** —*n* **1.** something that is advantageous or good; an advantage: *He explained the benefits of public ownership of the postal system. . . .* —*v.i.* **7.** to derive benefit or advantage; profit; make improvement: *He has never benefited from all that experience.*[7]

conditional, *adj.* **1.** imposing, containing, subject to, or depending on a condition or conditions, not absolute; made or allowed on certain terms; *conditional acceptance.*[8]

integrated, *adj.* **1.** combining or coordinating separate elements so as to provide a harmonious, interrelated whole: *an integrated plot; an integrated course of study.* **2.** Organized or structured so that constituent units function cooperatively: *an integrated economy.*[9]

mutual, *adj.* **1.** possessed, experienced, performed, etc. by each of two or more with respect to the other; reciprocal: *to have mutual respect.* **2.** having the same relation each toward the other: *to be mutual enemies.* **3.** of or pertaining to each of two or more; held in common; shared: *mutual interests.*[10]

reciprocal, *adj.* **1.** given or felt by each toward the other; mutual: *reciprocal respect.* **2.** given, performed, felt, etc.; in return: *reciprocal aid.* **3.** corresponding, matching, complementary, equivalent: *reciprocal privileges at other health clubs.*[11]

6

IN CRISIS, CULTURE IS DESTINY

"Character is destiny."
HERECLITUS[1]

Executive summary. In the previous chapter, we explored mutual benefit and brand equity, which can help improve valuation and margins, attract talent, increase customer loyalty, increase organizational effectiveness, and create a bank of goodwill that can be drawn upon in times of crisis.

The ultimate test for brands is when things go wrong. This is when the true nature and values of a brand are revealed for all to see. When the crisis hits, the brand will act instinctively based on its culture. What instincts and culture does your brand have?

IN CRISIS, CULTURE IS DESTINY

At the opening of this chapter, I quote Hereclitus saying, "Character is destiny." For brands in crisis, let me adapt this to, "Culture is destiny." That is to say, the culture of a brand, just like the character of a person, predetermines a lot about how a brand will behave under stress.

For several years, I lectured about crisis management at Columbia University in New York City and Pace University in Westchester Country, New York. It seems that word of mouth from previous class participants made my lectures both well attended and lively—the questions got better, seeking answers to deeper issues every year.

If you're waiting now for a list of scandals that have tarnished brands over the years, I'm sure you can supply your own examples. We would spend way too much time talking about what not to do. Instead, let's use our time together to understand how brands on the journey to Brandscendence react under stress.

Here is a classic crisis management tale you may have heard before but with corporate culture detail that was likely missing: Tylenol.

In October of 1982, seven people died from cyanide-laced Tylenol capsules.

The Extra-Strength Tylenol capsule product had been tampered with and replaced on store shelves for unsuspecting customers to buy.

Johnson & Johnson, the maker, responded within days by recalling all Extra-Strength Tylenol capsules. Customers were also offered Tylenol tablets in exchange for capsules.

This immediate responsiveness later forms the basis for trust and confidence that would allow the Tylenol brand to quickly reemerge as one of the leading over-the-counter pain medication brands. In 1982, Tylenol was the leading brand in the United States with a one-third share of an estimated $1 billion pain reliever market.

Was this action the result of a speedy cost-benefit analysis of a committee of professionals at J&J? At the time, the value of the recall and exchange program approached $100 million, or 10 percent of total market revenue and one-third of J&J's revenue for the category.[2]

Was it the conviction of the brand manager in charge at the time? Was it the senior leadership team making a quick decision—or the president sending out a mandate? My observation is that no committee was required and no single person can be commended for the rapid actions taken with Tylenol in crisis.

Johnson & Johnson as an organization reacted at the instinct level. There was no other course of action available to the J&J culture than to pull this medication from sale until it could be made safe.

The values of the medical profession were imprinted on J&J early in the company's formation. Most of what the company makes today is still related to supporting physicians and the health care industry at large. In essence, Johnson & Johnson as a company took the Hippocratic oath as a physician would and, therefore, knew at a gut level it should "do no harm."

The key take-away from my university lectures: "In crisis, culture is destiny."

When the crisis hits, the organization is already prewired to react based on existing cultural values.

If you're a spreadsheet culture, the cost-benefit analysis will begin immediately.

If you're a technical culture, a failure mechanism analysis will be performed immediately.

If you're a marketing culture, one or more customer impact analyses will begin immediately.

If you have a high affinity to the industry or profession you serve, as in the case of J&J, then you're likely to react with some of the values of that world in mind and act accordingly.

J&J has a culture that predisposes it to a *Tylenol response,* because it is a category of behavior tightly coupled with an early organization values imprint from the profession being served, in this case medicine.

BRANDS UNDER STRESS

When brands are under stress, their stage level of Brandscendence is exposed for all to see. Core relevance and the motivations behind it are readily visible. If customer satisfaction is the first concern, you'll see that value in the actions of the brand. If immediate gratification is the first motivation, you'll see that in the actions of the brand. Are you seeing the personality (s1), character (s2), or purpose (s3)?

How a brand allocates resources in the context of a crisis also shows stage maturity. Does it reflect the response of an industry as an s1 brand would? Does it adapt and respond to the specific needs of the particular crisis in a more thoughtful way than customers would have expected as an s2 brand would? Does it view the crisis as an opportunity to demonstrate overwhelmingly its core relevance by projecting itself to the world, showing what the brand can do when the spotlight is on (s3)?

The chart in Figure 6.1 shows the quadrants of action in crisis, constructed with the motivations of immediate gratification (s1) or long-term customer satisfaction (s3), and bisected with the goals of acquiring resources over time or minimizing resource allocation today.

If you're faced with a crisis, listen to the words in your team discussions—they'll tell you what quadrant your brand culture is in. If you hear

FIGURE 6.1 *Resource versus Customer Orientation Quadrants*

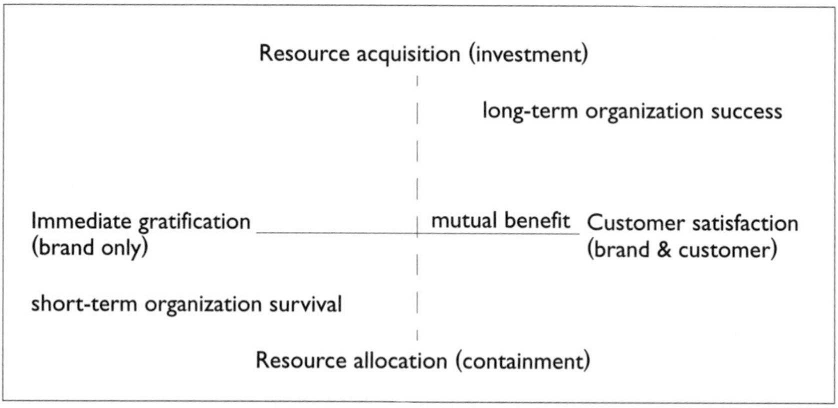

Resource acquisition (investment)

long-term organization success

Immediate gratification _____ | mutual benefit Customer satisfaction
(brand only)   (brand & customer)

short-term organization survival

Resource allocation (containment)

a lot about "containing" the situation this quarter, and "getting out of this at the lowest cost," you're down in the lower left-hand of this quadrant, in survival mode and at a s1 brand behavior level.

If you're faced with a crisis and the words in the team discussion revolve around "best interests of our customers," "investing," "turning this to our advantage," or "showing our customers who we really are"—then you're clearly operating at a s3 brand maturity level in the upper right-hand quadrant.

T *he* **R** *oots* *of* **U** *nderstanding* **E** *conomic* **B** *ehavior*

In *For the Common Good,* John Cobb and Herman Daly talk about the motivations that drive economic behavior. "*Oikonomia*, of course, is the root from which our word *economics* derives. *Chrematisitics* is a word that, these days, is found mainly in unabridged dictionaries. It can be defined as the brand of political economy relating to short-term monetary exchange of value to the owner. *Oikonomia*, by contrast, is the management of the household so as to increase its value to all members of the household over the long run. If we expand the scope of the household to include the larger community of the land, of shared values, resources, biomes, institutions, language, and history, then we have a good definition of *economics for the community*."[3]

There are lots of variations between these two extremes, but notice that *mutual benefit* is also on the chart, mapped distinctly to the right-hand side. It is firmly aligned with customer satisfaction, where both the brand and the customer experience the crisis as a trust-building exercise. "We had a problem, but you took care of me."

During a business trip, I was having a new road put in to our home. One dump truck after another was carrying tons of new gravel. While getting on the commuter jet to come home from New York, I got a call on my cell phone from Heidi, my wife. They had just come past the house with the truck bed all the way up on a final dump of gravel and pulled all the wires down. Two telephone poles were bent in toward each other, and the telephone, electricity, and cable service were gone. Plus, part of the roof was damaged where the electric service pole used to stand upright but was now bent over like a broken toothpick.

Within hours, crews appeared at the request of the owner of the road-building service, and power and telephone service was back that night, cable the next day. He coordinated everything and did it at his own expense. Did I write the check for this road work promptly once completed? You bet. Will I do business with this company again? Unless the road erodes prematurely, there's little doubt. Here's a situation that was a minor crisis for my household but was remedied quickly and created goodwill.

Was this a big, global brand in action? Of course not, this was just a local contractor. But it is also a brand acting at a very mature s2 level in the context of its customers.

EVALUATING DYSFUNCTIONAL BRANDS

Are you comfortable or vaguely uncomfortable right now?

Do you have a sense of how the brands around you will react to stress? If only there was a clearer way to discuss some of the issues you suspect about the behavior of the brands you work with, buy, or manage every day. If only you could put a description with what you're seeing and feeling.

What if you could administer the Minnesota Multiphasic Personality Inventory (MMPI) for your brand?

What is it? The MMPI is a clinical personality test developed in the late 1930s at the University of Minnesota. The legal profession uses the MMPI a lot in parental custody evaluations, because it is considered to be highly reliable and well researched over the last 50 years.

Could you adapt the MMPI for evaluating brand behavior? I think you could.

What is the equivalent of a "custody battle" in the brand world? How about brands in the context of mergers and acquisitions? How much would it be worth to you to know if the company you were about to acquire and the brand(s) it represents had one or more of these "symptoms"?

I've adapted text from an article by Cheryl L. Karp, Ph.D., and Leonard Karp, J.D., on this subject for your consideration.[4]

Scale 1: Hypochondraiasis (Hs). A pattern of vague and nonspecific complaints about the functioning of the brand by customers and employees about an otherwise healthy entity. Companies or brands already in trouble cannot affect this measure greatly. Do you know a brand that people are quietly complaining about?

Scale 2: Depression (D). A brand has a lack of hope for the future, and there is a general dissatisfaction with the brand's current situation. Do you know a brand without a solid business plan?

Scale 3: Hysteria (H). Overreaction to stress; maintaining a façade of superior adjustment, such as avoiding responsibility as a means to resolve conflict. Do you know a brand that "fell down and couldn't get up" after a crisis?

Scale 4: Psychopathic Deviate (Pd). Absence of strongly pleasant experiences; asocial or amoral behavior. Do you know a brand that is sullen and just doesn't seem to care about itself or others?

Scale 5: Masculinity-Femininity (Mf). I choose not to use the MMPI Mf scale for the purpose of a branding discussion based on homosexual versus heterosexual MMPI diagnostics. However, gender clearly can play a significant role in brand relevance and differentiation.

Scale 6: Paranoia (Pa). Brand displays feelings of persecution, grandiose self-concepts, suspiciousness, excessive sensitivity, and rigid opinions and attitudes. Do you know of brands matching this description that just lost a lot of market value?

Scale 7: Psychasthenia (Pt). Not commonly used today, psychasthenia most closely maps to obsessive-compulsive disorder and long-term anxiety. Features measured by scale seven include excessive doubts, compulsions, obsessions, unreasonable fears, self-criticism, difficulties in concentration, and guilt feelings. Do you know a brand that operates on gut feelings without solid customer research?

Scale 8: Schizophrenia (Sc). A brand driven by bizarre thought processes, peculiar conceptions, social alienation, difficulties in concentration and impulse control, and misinterpretations of reality—with a corresponding ambivalence or constriction in emotional responsiveness. Do you know a brand that is a loner—going its own way without consideration for customers or the marketplace?

Scale 9: Hypomania (Ma). A brand characterized by elevated mood, accelerated speech and motor activity, irritability, flight of ideas, and brief periods of depression. Do you know a brand that succeeds in spurts and then goes into hibernation?

Scale 0: Social Introversion (Si). Developed later than the other scales, this one assesses the tendency to withdraw from social contacts and responsibilities with two groups—one dealing purely with social participation, the other with general neurotic maladjustment and self-deprecation. Do you know a brand that was once vibrant but has withdrawn from the market, acts complacent, and doesn't project a winning spirit today?

If your brand seems to be under the weather or clearly suffers from any of the symptoms listed above, you should talk to your current customers immediately. More importantly, go talk to and observe potential customers that aren't doing business with you. How do they see you? What's the one thing you could do to improve your relationship with them right now? If you're a nonprofit, go find out where people are volunteering and donating—and what they get out of it.

BRAND SLEEP AND HIBERNATION

Brands aren't always at the top of their game. At best, they're just sluggish and less responsive than they used to be, less capable of delivering the core relevance that customers expect. At worst, brands can behave badly and be deeply offensive.

The longer you've known a brand, the greater the potential disappointment.

Early brand encounters are as familiar as your parents are. Next are siblings. Then extended family. Then friends. Then acquaintances.

Then there are the strangers who treat you badly in the norms of your culture.

Brands behaving badly are deeply offensive, especially when we thought we could trust them. You can name them; I don't have to.

Sometimes what brands need is a good rest. Take Porsche for instance.

Porsche was never deeply offensive, but it was a brand on the way out of existence. A deep financial slumber was beginning to look like a coma in the late '70s and '80s. Then the company discovered its roots, rededicated itself to the core driving enthusiast customer, and emerged in a profitable niche that continues to this day.

The Porsche 911 personifies enduring core relevance and commitment to an idea, yet it has evolved to meet the changing context of technology and customer driving desires, resulting in a mutually beneficial relationship between manufacturer and customer.

The same brand reawakening is taking place at Cadillac.

In the November 24, 2003, *Business Week,* an article by David Welch appeared called "The Second Coming of Cadillac."[5] The article ends on this note: "In a more competitive, global market, Caddy will never see the likes of its glory days of the 1950s, when eight out of ten luxury cars sold in the United States were Cadillacs. Still, it just may become a cool car of choice—and not just for retirees." The crisis that was emerging for General Motors with the Cadillac brand—namely, a customer base that was dying off—has been arrested. "The average age of the Cadillac buyer has dropped to 59 from 64 in 1999."

PRACTICING ADVICE

So what is the advice I give to students seeking crisis management guidance? Look at the culture of the organization. How does it make decisions and on what basis? Here, you will find the predispositions of response in crisis.

You see, brands function as members of your extended family and friends—some you trust and rely on more than others, based on their character. You know them well enough to know on whom you should rely.

The ultimate test for brands, as for family and friends, is when things go wrong. This is when the true nature of brand character is revealed for all to see. When the crisis hits, the brand collective will act instinctively.

If you want a particular response to crisis, you must pursue a cultural change of the organization that manages the brand.

I know many companies, which will remain nameless, that put their faith in process to overcome adversity in crisis. There are procedures, manuals, and audits to ensure compliance with the desired behavior. Process cannot trump culture. The board of directors, a single senior manager, or a remote team that has no knowledge of the process will, acting on its own, ensure randomness in response to crisis.

On the other hand, a strong brand culture known by all members of the organization will ensure a relatively uniform range of response to crisis over time—even without guidance. Cohesive response to all forms of adversity is a highly desirable brand attribute.

Until recently, changing an organization's culture was an off-the-wall or purely theoretical concept. You have the culture you have. Who has time for this culture stuff? We're here to make money or save the world.

Well, I'm here to tell you that more and more success in organizations is now being attributed to cultural factors that can be cultivated and nurtured.

Time and resources are shifting to culture discovery and management programs in the service of creating more enduring organizations and the brands that represent them. Shaping culture will be on the management agenda.

It's early in the 21st century. Do you know what your values are?

Part Two

EXPERIENCING BRANDSCENDENCE

The three elements of Brandscendence, *relevance, context,* and *mutual benefit,* can be developed in specific ways—from very concrete appeals to the senses to more abstract ideas and deeply embedded first impressions.

7

SENSING RELEVANCE

The Power of Perception

"All our knowledge has its origins in our perceptions."
LEONARDO DA VINCI[1]

Executive summary. Techniques to build brand equity include naming, industrial and graphic design, and packaging. Highly successful product industrial design becomes iconic over time, pleasing to the eye and responsive to the touch. Truly effective graphic design marks become recognizable logos where even parts of them ("frags") can represent the whole in the minds of customers. The same can be said of symbolic sounds, such as the AT&T Sparkletone followed by a female voice saying, "Thank you for using AT&T." Entire industries are devoted to refining and manipulating how we perceive taste and smell, and some of these techniques are crossing over into product and service categories that hadn't seen a need for addressing these two senses in the past. When viewed as a whole, a human and organic view of brand management is much more compelling than a structural or mechanistic view, because it is more compatible with the nature of the customer or client.

I KNOW YOU

Great brands understand the five human senses.

Managing a brand around the five senses provides a useful framework for increasing relevance in a variety of contexts. If you have graphic designers, Web masters, industrial designers, or human factors engineers, you have started the journey to organize work around the senses.

Enduring brands are designed to look good and function well.

They sound great—enduring brands know the role that music, audio cues, and spokespeople can play in differentiating and building brand awareness.

Touch is a sensual driver.

Smell is the ultimate attraction and warning system.

Taste is a primal human sense, hence the phrase *You want it so bad you can taste it.*

Truly effective brands strive to mirror human behavior. They explore the senses to evolve over time and provide richer experiences for customers.

The Brand	The Customer
Has form	Sees it
Speaks	Hears it
Has texture	Feels it
Is scented	Smells it
Has flavors	Tastes it

USING THE SENSES TO CREATE ICONS

In the visual world, we recognize Morton salt on the shelf at the grocery store. You can see the dark blue package with a girl moving at a good pace sporting an umbrella over her head and letting salt pour liberally behind her from a container nestled in her arm. This is trade dress designed years ago to convey a "new" benefit—salt that would pour freely, even in high humidity. Yes, clumping salt was a problem, now long forgotten.

Question: Have you ever bought this salt? Lots of people do—and they pay more for it. Not for the benefit of the past but the timeless relevance of the offering and when they first saw and used it. Morton salt imprints on you at an early age in your parent's kitchen. You have it around, not just for salt, but for what the packaging evokes from your past. The girl on the Morton salt package has been updated ever so slightly from one generation to the next, but remains an icon in its category. It's a visual name that is more powerful than the word *Morton* by itself.

There are also signature sounds, tastes, and fragrances that surround us as brand cues. They become names defined by the senses instead of language when we can immediately identify something by them and have preference for them. They become sensory icons when they define a category, whether it be universal fragrance of Johnson's Baby Powder, the unique shape and milk chocolate taste of a Hershey's Kiss on the tongue, or the distinctive rumble of an approaching Harley Davidson motorcycle. We know them, and these brands know us.

THE JUST NOTICEABLE DIFFERENCE

Underinvesting in perception leaves you undifferentiated versus competitors and leaves money on the table. You don't have to be extravagantly different to get noticed, but you do have to invest enough to have a "just noticeable difference."

The just noticeable difference (JND) effect, also known as Weber's Law, is well known to experimental psychologists. It is also a foundational notion in psychophysics, the study and measurement of sensory phenomena. Hold a weight in one hand and an equal weight in the other hand, and you will perceive them as equal. Increase the weight in one hand up to one-fifth more, and you'll still perceive the weights as equal. Weber's Law with repeatable accuracy shows that one-fifth or more weight in either hand will produce the JND effect—and the step function change in perception—so you'll be able to discern a weight difference.[2]

Adapt the JND principle for your brand. Find your brand's JND points and invest in them just enough to differentiate yourself from the background noise of daily life—and from your competition. But realize that investment that's less than the one-fifth JND threshold is just throwing money away.

SEEING IT

My colleague at work who heads the design program for IBM personal computers worldwide likes to talk about "telegraphic innovation."

What David Hill is talking about is creating value in physical space that you can see and immediately conclude that it is valuable.

There is power in staying the course on design. "We have 13 brands that do over one billion dollars a year in sales," says A. G. Lafley, CEO of Proctor and Gamble in *@Issue* magazine.[3] "That's extraordinary when you consider that most of our brands sell for $2 to $5 per unit in the store. We are very attentive to brand creation and innovation. We also, generally, have enough sense not to change a brand identity when we think we've got it right. If you look at a Tide package from 1946, it was orange with a bull's eye graphic and the Tide name in block letters. While we have continuously improved and refreshed the package design, the primary elements are the same."

That sounds like the continuity we've sustained with IBM ThinkPad for over a decade. You can still recognize the IBM ThinkPad introduced ten years ago. It has won numerous design competition awards and tests as iconic in the minds of customers today: black, rectangular, with a red Trackpoint "mouse" embedded in the center of the keyboard.

People still remember the Butterfly keyboard in the IBM ThinkPad 701C notebook computer. When you opened the cover, the keyboard deployed itself to a full size right in front of a 10.4-inch screen. It was industrial design magic.

Rarely do you get to experience inspiration and get paid for it, but I do when working with people like David Hill and John Karidis—the distinguished engineer who invented the magic keyboard—and Dr. Kazuhiko Yamazaki who graciously collaborated on an Appendix in this book. Lee Green, who heads corporate design for IBM, is also someone I count in good company, along with the remarkable Richard Sapper who has been our external industrial design consultant for the past 20 years. Richard is the designer of the iconic IBM ThinkPad notebook computer, now in the market for over a decade and in the 11th year selling over 20 million worldwide, more than any other notebook computer brand. Working with these gentlemen is a privilege.

For more insight on how business strategy, market research, and industrial design come together to serve customer needs, see Appendix B for the case study I wrote with Dr. Yamazaki, "Seeing Relevance: Listening and Leading in User-Centered Design."

Another example of instant visual recognition is the Louis Vuitton line of luggage and accessories. The interlocking LV mark repeats itself amongst several other gold symbols on distinctive brown leather. Get on any global airline flight, and you're likely to see several pieces of Vuitton luggage come on board.

Absolut Vodka has done a superb job of being visually consistent yet playful in advertising executions.

The red and white Coke can and the slightly green, curved Coke bottle are both icons in their own right for the same product.

FRAGS

I was captivated by the spring 2002 issue of *@Issue* magazine, a journal that covers the intersection of business and design. On pages 14 and 15 was a spread called "Brand Frags."[4] Take a look at Figure 7.1.

In 1984, design planner and theorist Jay Doblin of the respected Doblin Group noticed how brands have become paramount to corporate identity in the minds of consumers. To illustrate the power of effective brands, Doblin created a quiz out of fragments of national and global logos, which he flashed on a screen a few seconds at a time. Doblin call the quiz "Frags." Here, we've updated Doblin's 20-year-old quiz with some contemporary logos. See if you can name the brands based on the close-up portions shown. You will probably be surprised by how many you can identify—a compelling argument for why distinctive graphic branding, applied often and consistently, is a key to a strong corporate identity program.

HEARING IT

I remember being told about an experiment in the early days of television that is useful for our discussion about "hearing brands." Researchers wanted to understand the perceived benefits of enhanced sound in television sets, so they set up a control program to watch on the screen and had a variety of audio playback systems to map sound to the picture.

What the respondents reported was unexpected but very enlightening. The better the fidelity of the sound, the more subjects reported a better seeing picture—clearer, brighter, sharper, and so forth. The television "viewing" experience was just that—a package deal of video and audio that is reported in the language of sight, that being the dominant sense organ.

FIGURE 7.1 *Brand Frags*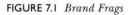

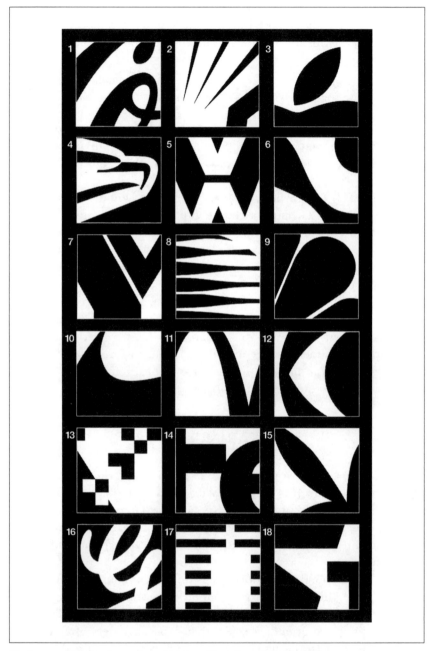

The key to which Frag belongs to which brand is at the end of this chapter.

Reprinted with permission from *@Issue: The Journal of Business and Design*, Vol. 8, No. 1 (Spring 2003), 14-15. Published by Corporate Design Foundation and sponsored by Sappi Fine Paper.

Even with sight being the reported winner, this contest does provide a compelling case for branding that addresses the ear rather than the eye to improve the overall customer experience with a brand.

Branding with sound, or "sonic branding," is a niche market. In developing a suite of sounds for IBM ThinkPad, I spent some time with Scott Elias, one of the founders of Elias Arts. This is a team of 70 people who have come together as a business to brand the world with sound. They've done suites of music to orchestrate the Olympics and beeps and chirps for PDAs.

Elias really believes in starting with the brand intent, so that the sounds they create really "say" what the brand is trying to convey. Listen in to a conversation we had in December 2003 about his company and competencies—and the intersections with Brandscendence after giving him the broad brushstrokes of this project. We started at a high level comparing notes, then got down to the specifics of sonic branding.[5]

> Elias: There is something in the world of sociology called "gift exchange" and the notion that everyone has a gift. If an individual has a gift and they can identify and claim that gift and then share it, they understand what they have to offer of real value. I think organizations and companies would do well to understand, not what their vision is, but what the organization's purpose is. When they do they can attract individuals to the organization who might want to bring their gift within the organization and those for whom the organization and its products can use that gift. In a living systems sense, they serve the evolutionary purpose of that organism and the society at large.

> KC: It's the difference between someone seeking a job versus someone understanding they could have a role to play.

> Elias: Absolutely. That there is a role for the organization also, as there is with a firm such as Patagonia. Although the organization may make clothing or gear, the organization's purpose is that of protecting the environment. The point of linkage is if you give people good gear at a reasonable price, and give them time to spend time in the environment, they'll want to protect it. In some ways, that relates to context. Would the organization be willing to define its role within a certain context?

> KC: I'm interested in your thoughts about the role that sonic branding plays in the overall brand mix. Put it in the context of living systems theory, as we've discussed, versus the relatively rigid metaphors of a Newtonian world.

Elias: These are the things we speak about in what we call "sound commerce." Sound commerce is about relational exchange: ecology of relationship, quality of connection, and reciprocity of exchange. The question we're asking in terms of sound is, "How will this grow emotional currency?" Emotional currency is what we think is key to growing emotional stakeholders. The simplest question here is, "How does it make you feel?" So sound becomes an emotional currency for all the levels of commerce. And for us, what you call mutual benefit, we call "rich commerce" or reciprocity of exchange. We use sound to reveal and augment personal investment in relationships to a company, brand, or product.

We then talked about a hypothetical sports company where *winning*, as a core value being delivered to customers, ladders up to notion of *play* as a larger world than sports.

Elias: How does "play" have a role in an evolutionary context? We can then look at the relationships between extraordinary athletes and ordinary athletes—and the relationship extraordinary athletes have to spectators. We then begin to define the universe of extraordinary athletes and their teams—and look at ordinary athletes and their relationships—and begin to hypothesize about how that might be dimensionalized with music and sound. What happens really quickly is the whole importance of winning or losing. Its not that this goes by the wayside—it's just that you come up with so many other reasons that someone might be involved in a sport. And if you think about it as beyond sport, the role of play and all these other reasons people are invested, then you start to move from there into some of the other dimensions of play. We then group products in what they do in terms of play.

Customers were reporting that one product makes you faster, one makes you freer, one makes you feel more connected.

Music can then take on a life around that, and that might be reflected in everything from advertising to retail environments to the company's role in the Olympics, and they start telling many different sorts of stories. If you take the examples of Nike, Starbucks, or Apple as culture-defining brands—these are value-based brands at the core of their DNA. They've also identified a paradox that exists within society—tears between the mechanical and living systems worlds or, as Nike has identified, the tear between what we're capable of, what our potential is, and what our practice is. They do identify that paradox and create a bridge; in the case of Nike, it's the bridge between potential and practice when they say, "Just Do It."

KC: Let me ask you a question to bridge my readers from your world to something they already know. In our language, we talk about tag lines in advertising, value propositions to drive product portfolios and connect them to customers, and brochures and Web narratives to describe fully what you're about to buy. Every one of these provides the ability to go into more depth with words. What is the scale in the sonic branding world?

Elias: There are several specific elements in what we would call an identity package. The first step for us would be the notion of a mnemonic—the desire to call attention and also aid in memory. These generally aren't used for a long period of time. The next higher state is signature, usually associated with a firm. The next step up is identity. What's difficult for us in the world of logos is that sound has a much higher need to be refreshed—it's what we call the "fatigue factor." You want enough of the same sound so the brand can be safe, secure, and identifiable—and then get other dynamic messaging by using volume, length, coloration—all within what we call a "sound identity system."

KC: What would help amplify your views of the sonic branding world for my readers?

Elias: We work in the area of relational exchange in trying to create a different qualitative connection for the brand than what people are currently working with. The way I see it, sound is, but needs to be more clearly, a metaphor for 21st-century commerce, the notion of "rich commerce." We're looking at how music and sound really are another way to touch, connect, and grow and evolve the brand. We see people having three connections to the brand. One is the material connection—how they connect with it at a physical level. Then, how they connect with it at an informational or intellectual level. Then, how they connect with it at an aspirational level. So I think the power of music is that it is scalable, it is contextual, and most importantly, it speaks to where consumers are. Music is something that needs to be refreshed, and don't think of that as a bad thing, because people change over time. Let's say reliability, performance, and power—the fact is that music and sound can define that differently over time while still delivering that sort of experience. So the brand can continue to be relevant, while the definition changes over time, and that is one of the greatest powers of music, that it continues to be relevant, it continues to express the same values differently to meet people where they are and evolve with them over time.

Thanks, Scott.

AT&T'S SPARKLETONE

If you've ever dialed into the AT&T long distance network, you've likely heard the AT&T chime, followed by a female voice that says, "Thank you for using AT&T." I can personally attest to the value of this audio branding, especially when I'm out of the country. AT&T calls this an "audible signature."[6]

Composer Susanne Ciani developed the chime sound in 1988 and the "chordal flourish" you hear at the front of every AT&T routed call. The voice you hear is that of professional announcer Pat Trumble.

Why create a Sparkletone? Pay phone competition was spreading, and AT&T wanted to signal to customers that they were getting service from them, not a competitor. The Sparkletone was introduced initially for callers making operator-assisted and calling card calls while away from home. Immediately after a "bong" that tells the customer to enter a calling card number, the caller would hear a short version of today's Sparkletone with the "chime" and Pat Trumble saying "AT&T."

In the sonic branding game and as an audio symbol for trust and authenticity, the AT&T Sparkletone is one of the best and most enduring examples around.

FEELING IT

Have you ever had a massage?

If not, I highly recommend it. Especially think about having one after a long, transoceanic flight.

Let this section of the book provide the permission to get a massage, because nothing in the world puts you in touch with feeling it more than a whole body rub down.

The most sensitive part of your body for touch is the hand, especially the tips of your fingers. There are more receptors in these tiny areas than any other place, rendering the finger royalty in the land of touch.

The origin of the IBM Trackpoint mouse in the center of a notebook keyboard was divined from this insight. Introduced in 1992 on the first IBM ThinkPad 700C notebook computer, Trackpoint is a small, red knob found in the middle of the keyboard. Ted Selker, who was with the IBM Almaden Research Center and is now at MIT Media Lab, started work on this short, isometric joystick in September of 1987. Trackpoint leverages both the sensitivity of the forefinger and the placement on the QWERTY keyboard. (Look at the characters on the top-left row of a keyboard and you'll see the letters Q-W-E-R-T-Y, and that's what we call the keyboard in our industry.) Not having to move your hands from the home row position to grasp a mouse creates a great deal of efficiency when typing and manuevering around a computer screen.

There are lots of places you'll find brands that associate themselves with feeling—clothing, soap, fabric softeners. How the fabric feels against the skin, both in its inherent properties and the way it's woven. What the clothing is washed in, how your hands feel when moving them together, how your hair feels when lathering it. What residual properties a fabric softener leaves in clothes to make them feel soft.

There are specifically designed feelings associated with the controls in the cockpit of an airplane or the driver's seat in a car. Remember the story about my wife's Mercedes? The feeling of the interior was no accident. Mercedes works hard to provide a consistent driving encounter for its customers over time.

OXO International has made a name for itself by adding a dimension of touch to its line of household appliances. From potato peelers in the kitchen to tools for the garden, OXO "is dedicated to providing innovative consumer products that make everyday living easier."[7]

The line of products is known as OXO Good Grips. The feel in the hand of these offerings is what sets them apart from the competition. You've probably seen the racks of OXO products in a store, and they not only feel good in your hand, they look like they would feel comfortable in your hand. The visual design signals what you will experience with the sense of touch.

Max Farber founded OXO out of a personal passion for cooking and a love for his wife, who experienced mild arthritic pain when using a conventional vegetable peeler. He collaborated with Davin Stowell and his team at Smart Design to come up with a new, more comfortable peeler. The resulting product, the OXO Good Grips Swivel Peeler, is the foundation of what OXO today calls Universal Design—products designed for everyone to use. Although OXO is a very young company, founded in 1990, the core relevance of what it does is so compelling that it has the DNA to be an extremely enduring brand.

In addition to retail stores, you can also find the OXO Good Grips Swivel Peeler in the permanent collection of the Museum of Modern Art, along with several IBM ThinkPad notebook computers.

SMELLING IT AND TASTING IT

Smell and taste are combined for discussion purposes, because they work together so closely and affect each other. The primary industry players with basic technologies to support taste and smell have offerings that appeal to both senses. One of the largest players in the world is even functionally named this way: International Flavors and Fragrances (IFF), second in sales only to the Swiss company, Givaudan.

"The flavor industry is highly secretive," writes Eric Scholsser in his *Atlantic Monthly* article, "Why McDonald's Fries Taste So Good."[8] "Its leading companies will not divulge the precise formulas of flavor compounds or the identities of their clients. The secrecy is deemed essential for protecting the reputations of beloved brands."

One firm tracking the flavor and fragrance industry is Leffingwell & Associates. Their Web page shows industry revenue is pretty much evenly split between flavors and fragrances—fragrances accounting for 51 percent, flavors 49 percent, of the worldwide market (source: IAL Consultants, June 23, 2000). This worldwide market, according to Leffingwell, was estimated at $15.1 billion in 2002.[9]

In the spirit of Brandscendence, the players in the smell and taste game go back a ways. Revenue leader Givaudan, with $1.9 billion in global sales, traces its origins back to Dodge and Olcott of New York, started in 1796. IFF, with $1.8 billion in sales, started as Stafford Allen & Sons in 1833, primarily as a sandalwood oil and clove oil producer.

When I was growing up, the father of a good friend of mine worked as the head of one of the world's largest packaged foods companies. During one summer, when my buddy was doing a summer job there, he brought home an amazing kit. It was a flavor kit. It contained a lot of small vials that had basic flavors. When combined in the right amounts, they would mimic tastes found in nature—or ones that couldn't.

We familiarized ourselves with the basic elements of taste—sweet, bitter, sour, acrid, etc., by mixing the flavors with tap water. Then we tried combinations suggested by the kit instructions—and some that weren't. I won't go into all the concoctions we made, but it did give me a first glimpse into what you could do with the tool of flavor.

Let's take a category where you could choose taste or smell as the leading sense to enchant a customer: coffee.

Industry leader Maxwell House talks about taste. Smiling people enjoying the satisfying taste of Maxwell House Coffee.

Folger's, on the other hand, is all about aroma. Folger's shows customers smelling coffee as if it were a fine wine. In television ads, Folger's never quite reaches the lips—but is always associated with a warm and friendly home.

Folger's uses the knowledge that our first impression of coffee is when we smell it as children—when our parents are drinking it. This is a strong component of the archetype or first pattern of thought about coffee: smell as a sensory imprint in the context of a warm and loving home with your parents.

A friend from Germany tells me that the same appeal is found in the Jakobs Krönung coffee brand—serve it and experience complete family harmony.

SENSE LAYERING

Intentionally layering the senses is an effective strategy to pursue in all forms of physical goods and services. Add a sense to increase preference and profit.

In the last example, we compared the taste and smell of coffee. Starbucks and similar retailers take this to the next level by offering an end-to-end coffee experience for their customers. They manage the taste and smell of the coffee served but also appeal to the eye, ear, and hand. Starbucks may or may not be for you, but it does manage the details and make good use of adding dimension—and community—to the coffee consumption ritual.

ADD A SENSE WITH PACKAGING

Have you noticed that the world is being turned upside down and on its side?

From toothpaste to catsup, a packaging revolution is underway that signals "easier to use" to customers across a large number of categories. Any dense liquid or paste is moving from tubes and bottles to stand up containers that dispense from the bottom.

I'm not saying that this trend represents a sustainable competitive advantage, but notice which companies moved into this space first. They're the ones that decided to add a sense to their offering.

Not only am I getting cavity protection, but that toothpaste looks easier to handle and takes up less space. And, once you use it, you realize there's less waste, because you can dispense all the paste with none left over in the container.

Catsup promoted to be thick and tasty now comes out easily, too, when the bottle changes from glass to plastic and is turned upside down.

Brands that adopt these new packaging technologies are thinking about a total customer experience with the product. It's not just the scent of the perfume, it's also about the beauty of the bottle it comes in.

Look behind any bar, and you'll see packaging at work to signal distinctive brands. The vodka section has become increasingly interesting with bottles that approach works of art. Catching the eye provides an introduction to the first sip.

Ziplock brand plastic bags today engage three senses when sealing a bag. In addition to letting your fingers feel the bag seal engaging, several years ago they added a color dimension—when the blue and yellow sides of the seal come together, the seal turns green, a second sensory confirmation that the bag is sealed. The third and newest sensation is a "zipper" sound from sealing the bag. One plastic bag—three sensory cues to tell you its closed. By the way, the Ziplock name is pretty nifty, too. Ziplock is a very descriptive name, and it's coined, allowing it to be a registered trademark. More about this in a Chapter 8, "Stating Relevance: What's in a Name?"

Coke has the can and the bottle as distinctive global visual cues. In the case of the bottle, it has a distinctive feeling in the hand. The company also works with its global bottling partners on the right carbonation pressure, bubble size, and fizz to recreate a uniform set of opening sounds and feeling in the mouth. Of course, the taste and smell of Coke is one of the best-kept trade secrets in the world.

ADD THE NEXT SENSE

Even the most valuable brands have branding opportunities ahead of them.

Microsoft started with a boot-up screen look, then added a boot-up sound for their personal computer operating system. But what does Microsoft feel like?

If GE doesn't sound like something today, perhaps it will in the future.

The Web delivery of smell is just around the corner. Digital scent transmission and communication is underway at a company called DigiScents, and they already have second-generation "scent speaker" named iSmell.[10] If Intel pulls this function into its chipsets and could associate its brand with a smell, what would it be?

If Disney's "Imagineers" have labored long and hard to extend the playful, iconic ears of Mickey Mouse from signs to soap, perhaps they will turn next to a portfolio of what Disney tastes like, adding a new dimension to the brand.

Adding a sense makes sense for any brand. Just make sure that you invest enough to get above the JND threshold and get recognition for it.

C h a p t e r   G l o s s a r y

---

mnemonic, *adj.* **1.** assisting or intended to assist the memory. **2.** pertaining to mnemonics or to memory. **3.** something intended to assist the memory, as a verse or formula. **4.** *Computers.* a programming code that is easy to remember, as *STO* for "store."[11]

Author's note: The Brandscendence formula, $Br = (R+C) \times Mb$, is intended as a mnemonic.

Key *to* **I**nstitutional **I**dentity **L**ogo **F**rags:

1. Coca-Cola
2. Shell
3. Apple
4. U.S. Postal Service
5. Volkswagen
6. Cingular
7. YMCA
8. AT&T
9. NBC
10. Nike
11. McDonald's
12. CBS
13. Xerox
14. FedEx
15. Playboy
16. General Electric
17. IBM
18. Texaco

8

STATING RELEVANCE

What's in a Name?

"The Ancient Mariner *would not have taken so
well if it had been called* The Old Sailor."
SAMUEL BUTLER[1]

Executive summary. Creating meaningful and memorable names is one of the most important jobs you can do in branding. Get the name right, and there's a lot of money you won't have to spend telling people what you stand for or why you're relevant. All too often, marketing professionals fall into the trap of seeking a unique name, where the real task should be to give birth to a new company or offering with a name worthy of the character you expect it to achieve over time. *Meaningful* and *memorable* beat the tar out of purely *unique* every time.

BECOMING THE ACQUIRED

I met my wife in Charlotte, North Carolina. Heidi was working as a magnetic tape librarian for North Carolina National Bank (NCNB). If you want to know where the real money is at a bank, don't go to the teller stations or the vault—go to where the computer records are kept and backed up. That's where the money is, in the transaction records.

Banking as an institutional brand holds up only as well as people's trust in banks as a whole. If the trust erodes, get ready for a run on the banks. It still happens in places around the world where instability reigns.

Back to a story closer to home.

Heidi and I watched NCNB grow over the last 20 years. We have members of our extended family who will retire from this enterprise, so we've kept abreast of its changes.

From a branding point of view, NCNB changed its name to Nations Bank while we lived in Connecticut, signaling the acquisition of banks and expansion outside of North Carolina. This trend continued until a pivotal acquisition again changed the name of the combined organization to Bank of America.

I believe this to be one of the most mature acts of strategic brand naming in recent memory. Why? Consider the facts. More importantly, consider who bought whom in this transaction.

This strategy clearly showed Hugh McColl of Nations Bank at his best. He engineered a deal that would enhance equity for both Nations Bank and Bank of America shareholders. The new, combined entity would have a strong U.S. footprint and have the mass to start working in earnest on the global banking stage.

Make no mistake: Nations Bank acquired Bank of America. This was not a merger of equals in terms of business strategy or negotiation skills.

Now you tell me, when was the last time you can remember when one company buys another company and takes on the name of the company being bought? Come on, it just doesn't happen.

But I suspect that Nations Bank did some market research in advance of the deal being made public. What did they find out? Well, Bank of America just had more equity, sounded bigger, and had been around for a lot longer. Bank of America just projected more trust.

Ladies and gentlemen, set aside your egos and look at the great brand asset we're going to get: the name *Bank of America.* We're all here to make money, so let's go to market with the strongest name we can have as a combined organization. Good move.

Better move: Acquiring companies is notoriously hard to do. The employees and suppliers are, rightly, suspicious of the motives of the acquiring company. When will the consolidations begin, and mostly from what side? Top management will probably choose the goods and services of the deal-maker company.

That bomb was defused with haste as the Bank of America heritage employees realized that the Charlotte-based banking juggernaut was going to take on their brand and rename the new enterprise Bank of America. Hey, they really value us and what we've built! This is more than just a financial deal—there's something in it for all of us.

A GOOD NAME CAN TELL AN ENTIRE STORY

Bernard Arnault of LVMH is described as a "brand manager deluxe" by the *Wall Street Journal*.[2] LVMH stands for several great global brands: Louis Vuitton, Moet, and Hennessy. The *WSJ* article has an inset that describes the five qualities that Arnault believes a star brand must have.

1. *Timelessness.* The brand names and products associated with them must last—what we've been calling in Brandscendence "enduring relevance."
2. *Modernity.* The brand creates excitement and makes consumers discover something new, what "context" provides in Brandscendence.
3. *High profitability.* Arnault cites 25 percent margins for at least 10 years.
4. *Growth.* Brands that aren't growing are not attractive to LVMH.
5. *Something more.* It's the intangible something that you cannot explain—the *je ne sais quoi*. "It's like the word *Dior*—a mix of *Dieu* (God) and *Or* (gold). And you know if you have it or not."

As noted above, these concepts by Arnault are a superb fit with the idea of Brandscendence.

Timelessness is a fit for the concept of enduring relevance in the Brandscendence model, as is the intangible "something more." I call this concept mutual benefit, and it can be tracked through the same profitability and growth yardsticks that Arnault uses to account for both timelessness and something more. Modernity is similar to context—relevance that adapts to create excitement at one level and projects at the next to demonstrate something new.

But, most importantly for a discussion about brand names, Arnault also says, "the name must be an institution." Notice the combination of meanings in the brand name Dior that delivers "something more" to customers.

Dior is a simple yet meaningful name in the French language. The powerful combination of *God* and *gold* is subtle or lost in other languages—but the essence and the ethos of Dior transcends languages as it projects its brand being into other cultures.

KEEP IT SIMPLE

If you don't have a *lot* of money or a way to communicate your idea broadly, don't mess around with unique names for products or services. Simple is best.

If you do have a lot of money and want to own a name, you still may not want to make the investment.

In the naming game, you want the perfect balance of immediate understanding and clarity—and the ability to own and protect the name in all the markets you serve.

For instance, take the title of this book. *Brandscendence* is a combination of the words *brand* and *transcendence*.

You might well ask, "Isn't this a coined term on which you need to spend money for people to understand? Do you have a lot of money to burn on this, or what?" No—but I do have a way to communicate the meaning broadly, in depth, about Brandscendence and what it means. I do so through this book, a quarterly newsletter, and occasional speaking engagements.

I would further point out that Brandscendence is to some extent self-explanatory. If you know the words *brand* and *transcendence,* you likely get a glimpse of where I'm going to take you without even cracking the spine.

If either *brand* or *transcendence* are not part of your vocabulary, the meaning is not readily apparent. My guess was that, for the vast majority of English-speaking readers, the term would be known and valuable, so I embarked on registering it as a trademark. That journey continues even as I write and is another part of the naming process we'll visit in this chapter—protecting names as intellectual property.

Here's another example: the full name of the Boeing Corporation's B-52 Stratofortress, which is both descriptive and powerful. Most people know the B-52 is a military aircraft, but Stratofortress did initially convey the idea of its size and mission without a lot of explanation, before being back-formed to just B52.

On the other hand, the dot-com meltdown provided hundreds of examples of less purposeful or contrived names that required a great deal of expense, or time, to achieve meaning. Many of these names are gone now, but some survive, having reached critical market mass.

Yahoo!, eBay, and Google are all common parlance now, but by themselves, these names are meaningless—neither referring to what the brands are or what they do. eBay seems to be a contraction of *e* for *e-commerce* and *Bay* for the San Francisco Bay Area where the enterprise started. Only recently did eBay start to advertise aggressively to expand its presence, but it provides such a unique virtual marketplace that people really want to use it. The name also has the advantage of simplicity—so the simple yet obscure name eBay gains currency by powerful word of mouth.

Yahoo! is an example of both first mover status and demand generation tie-ins with other powerful brands.

ACRONYMS, COMPRESSIONS, AND BACK-FORMATIONS

AOL spent millions on direct response advertising to build a customer base and expand name recognition. AOL also started out life as America On Line, which captures a value proposition and projects an attitude. Customers later turned America On Line into an acronym, AOL. The name stuck, as did the underlying attitude. AOL is more about communications, chat rooms, and community than it is about a connection to the Internet. AOL Instant Messenger is pure communications—the "walkie-talkie" of the Web.

AOL then proceeded, during its pinnacle of Wall Street valuation, to buy Time Warner, which itself is a merger and acquisition legend.

During mid–October 2003, AOL Time Warner became just Time Warner again. The enduring brand outlived the acquirer. At the time of the acquisition, AOL had the cash, but in the long run, Time Warner has the brand.

Compare a dot-com name to a name such as NetJets—a network of private jets held in fractional lease contracts. The beauty of NetJets is the way that aircraft are forward-deployed to regional airports around the United States. A promise to have a plane ready for any client within six hours of calling is the logistics advantage that sets the company apart. It literally is a network of jets, not just a private jet leasing cooperative. Knowing this, the NetJets name immediately makes sense to the target customer without a great deal of explanation.

Speaking of being in the air, remember when we talked about how long Pan Am has been out of the airline business? Twenty-five years or more, yet how many times has the name been revived as a charter carrier? At least three times that I can remember. Pan Am has so much equity and makes so much sense to the ear, it just won't go away.

Pan Am is a back-formation of Pan American World Airways.

Another famous global name is also a back-formation: FedEx, for Federal Express.

Federal Express essentially yielded over time to what its customers had already done—shortening the name. Federal Express had been referred to as "fed-x" for many years in offices around the world. In the early 1990s, the company performed the branding transformation that brought it into congruence with what customers had already done for themselves.

FedEx is a perfect example of a brand that the customers co-own along with the company that provides the service.

PRACTICING ADVICE

Some enduring names for brands are immediately intuitive for their categories, such as Frigidaire refrigerators (cold air) or Bisquick flour (flour with baking powder added for making biscuits).

To go about creating an equally intuitive name for a new company, product, or service, you need some basic tools. In the naming game, you need the tools of language, by which I mean a dictionary, a thesaurus, and as many books of quotations as you can lay your hands on.

If you are at the task of creating names, or what we call at work the art of "naming," you can buy and have all these books at hand, or you can go to your public library. Some libraries have a room for the staff to meet—see if you can make arrangements to borrow it for a couple of hours. Larger libraries have conference rooms for the convenience of their patrons, sometimes for a nominal fee. The reason I'm suggesting that you work at the library is that the books you want to use are likely in the reference section and can't be checked out.

The next thing to do is get a small work group together. You'll probably gravitate toward a collection of "creative people" who will turn out novel names. OK, good idea, have a few creative types at the table. These are your outside-the-box thinkers. But don't be seduced solely by the call of the creative.

You also need people who will react to the name as your customers might—a couple of folks who seem well grounded and tell it like they see it (or hear it, in this case). These are your inside-the-box thinkers.

Also, if you can, bring an attorney. This is your "Can you own the box?" thinker. Specifically, a good intellectual property attorney with experience in trademark law is a great person to have at the table.

If you're interested in protection under trademark law in the United States only, then visit http://www.uspto.gov. This is the United States Patent and Trademark Office Web site. Here, you can search for registered trademarks and those that are pending.

If you want to know if a name is in use anywhere in the world, just use a Web search engine such as Google and see if anything comes up.

BRAINSTORMING FOR NAMES

Once you've got your team in place, you're ready to start brainstorming for a great name for your new company or offering (product/service).

Divide your time into two parts—a penalty-free creative session where there are no bad ideas and another session where names are critically evaluated. These can be done back to back under the crucible of time, but I recommend two sessions. Do the creative work, let the names sit for a few days—then come back with the benefit of unconscious associations and feelings for the second, critical session. Keep the Internet searches out of the first meeting.

With your selected team in place, start with this exercise: write down all the attributes you'd like to have associated with this new entity. This exercise is especially well suited for single-language companies and offerings. Rank the importance of these attributes. Find all of the related definitions and synonyms for the top ten attribute words.

Now you have the basis for doing recombinant word formations that suggest the attributes you want to evoke but are unique enough for trademark protection.

For instance, here are some names that do a lot of heavy lifting in communicating their offerings in their respective categories.

- *The Joy of Cooking.* The best-selling cookbook of all time.
- *Invisalign.* A new way to straighten teeth without visible braces.
- *Flonase.* A nasal decongestant.
- *Business Week.* A weekly business news magazine.

PC Magazine is a good example of a name that communicates a great deal and has stuck to its guns over the years. I remember standing in the lobby of the Arizona Biltmore Resort talking to *PC Magazine* publisher Michael Miller. We talked about the state of the high-tech publishing business just after the dot-com meltdowns. I pointed out that *PC Magazine* was a standout in what had become a lifeless lineup of *e*-prefaced magazine names.

Miller was rightfully proud of standing his ground with parent Ziff-Davis. While all other editors shifted to e-this and e-that, Miller told them there was valuable equity in the name *PC Magazine* and he wasn't going to change it. Furthermore, he claimed there was still interest in the PC category and it wasn't going to diminish anytime soon. He proved to be right on both fronts. Nice going Michael.

One final word about global linguistics (the science of language). If you're naming outside your culture, beware of the meaning of words in other languages, pronunciations in other dialects, and unintended meanings. For instance, the *th* diphthong is not used in the spoken Japanese language; therefore, *ThinkPad* is pronounced *sink pad* where an *s* is substituted for the *th* sound. While this sounds unfortunate, it has come to mean "hold's everything," a good meaning in the second largest market for notebook computers in the world.

DEFENDING SPAM IN THE
AGE OF THE INTERNET

What I'm dishing up for the dessert course of this chapter is a delicious plate of SPAM, a registered trademark name of Hormel Foods. It's a good study in protecting intellectual property that has a twist of irony. The Internet both creates awareness for the SPAM brand of meat products worldwide in the context of the Internet, while Hormel Foods attempts to balance its interests with the less-than-favorable new context for its brand name.

With permission, this is taken verbatim from the Hormel SPAM Web site.

> You've probably seen, heard, or even used the term *spamming* to refer to the act of sending unsolicited commercial e-mail (UCE), or "spam," to refer to the UCE itself. Following is our position on the relationship between UCE and our trademark SPAM.[3]
>
> Use of the term *spam* was adopted as a result of the Monty Python skit in which our SPAM meat product was featured. In this skit, a group of Vikings sang a chorus of "spam, spam, spam . . ." in an increasing crescendo, drowning out other conversation. Hence, the analogy applied, because UCE was drowning out normal discourse on the Internet.
>
> We do not object to use of this slang term to describe UCE, although we do object to the use of the word *spam* as a trademark and to the use of our product image in association with that term. Also, if the term is to be used, it should be used in all lower-case letters to distinguish it from our trademark SPAM, which should be used with all uppercase letters.
>
> This slang term, which generically describes UCE, does not affect the strength of our trademark SPAM. In a federal district court case involving the famous trademark STAR WARS, owned by LucasFilms, the Court ruled that the slang term used to refer to the Strategic Defense Initiative did not weaken the trademark, and the Court refused to stop its use as a slang term. Other examples of famous trademarks having a different slang meaning include MICKEY MOUSE, to describe something as

unsophisticated, and CADILLAC, used to denote something as being high quality. It is only when someone attempts to trademark the word *spam* that we object to such use, in order to protect our rights in our famous trademark SPAM. We coined this term in 1937, and it has become a famous trademark. Thus, we don't appreciate it when someone else tries to make money on the goodwill that we created in our trademark or product image, or takes away from the unique and distinctive nature of our famous trademark SPAM. Let's face it. Today's teens and young adults are more computer savvy than ever, and the next generations will be even more so. Children will be exposed to the slang term *spam* to describe UCE well before being exposed to our famous product SPAM. Ultimately, we are trying to avoid the day when the consuming public asks, "Why would Hormel Foods name its product after junk e-mail?"

Position Statement on "Spamming"

We oppose the act of "spamming" or sending UCE. We have never engaged in this practice, although we have been victimized by it. If you have been one of those who has received UCE with a return address using our Web site address of SPAM.com, it wasn't us. It's easy and commonplace for somebody sending UCE to simply adopt a fake header ID, which disguises the true source of the UCE and makes it appear that it is coming from someone else. If you have or do receive UCE with this header ID, please understand that it didn't come from us.

Other "spam" Web sites

This is the one and only official SPAM Web site, brought to you by the makers of the SPAM Family of products. All of the others have been created by somebody else. We are not associated with those other Web sites and are not responsible for their content. As a Company, we are opposed to content that is obscene, vulgar or otherwise not "family friendly." We support positive family values, and you can count on us for "safe surfing" by your children.

Thank you for visiting the official SPAM Web site!

We've now examined the aspects of brands that engage the primary senses and are summarized by logos and names. With the senses selectively stimulated, the given name or logo treatment can trigger deeper perceived value, which you want to build up and tap into over time. The next step is fully integrating the customer brand experience.

That's our next chapter—branding that creates context and integrates the end-to-end experience for customers, clients, patrons, and citizens.

CREATING CONTEXT
AND INTEGRATING
EXPERIENCE

"There are many truths of which the full meaning cannot
be realized until personal experience has brought it home."
JOHN STUART MILL[1]

Executive summary. Brandscendence is in high gear when all the senses are engaged to signal core brand relevance in a positive context and mutual benefit is perceived. Creating integrated brand experiences for customers' end-to-end experiences is possible with the general understanding of human senses and the specific knowledge gained by discovering the heart and gut of the customer. Imprints are our first experience with something of a particular type, and these imprints can turn new experiences on their head—causing us to experience what we already know.

SPEED BUMP

For those reading this book who aren't part of the North American culture, a "speed bump" is a raised section of pavement that encourages a driver to slow down or lose the suspension of the car. In prepublication reviews of *Brandscendence,* I was told that this chapter was a potential speed bump for readers. Good idea for traffic control; bad idea for the flow of a book.

I thought about the importance of the ideas in this chapter in the overall content of the book. They're rich and needed, but some would have to go for the sake of clarity—and for those left, I would spend more time simplifying and refining them. The short list that's left is:

- Cultural imprinting
- Archetypes and the collective unconscious
- The value of observational research
- Managing the customer experience

Now that I've repaved the verbal road for you, let's start with the first key idea of this chapter: cultural imprinting.

IMPRINTING

Enduring brands imprint at a deeply personal level at pivotal stages in your life.

Imprinting is an important concept that I was introduced to by Dr. G. Clotaire Rapaille.

In the opening of his book, *7 Secrets of Marketing,* he says, "Cultures, like individuals, have an unconscious. This unconscious is active in each of us, making us do things we might not be aware of."[2] Dr. Rapaille says that all members of a culture share a collective unconscious resulting from common imprints. Imprints "are early emotional experiences that have modeled our minds and our lives into what we are today. These imprints vary from one culture to another, and they are powerful constituents of our minds. Together, they make up our cultural unconscious—the part of our being that makes us feel and react as American, Japanese, or French."[3]

Carl Jung, founder of the Jungian school of psychology and a contemporary of Freud, speaks of the *collective unconscious.*

> There are symbolic thoughts and feelings, symbolic acts and situations. It often seems that even inanimate objects cooperate with the unconscious in the arrangement of symbolic patterns.
>
> There are many symbols, however (among them the most important), that are not individual but *collective* in their nature and origin. These are chiefly religious images. The believer assumes that they are of divine origin—that they have been revealed to man. The skeptic says flatly that they have been invented. Both

are wrong. It is true, as the skeptic notes, that religious symbols and concepts have for centuries been the object of careful and quite conscious elaboration. It is equally true, as the believer implies, that their origin is so far buried in the mystery of the past that they seem to have no human source. But they are, in fact, "collective representations," emanating from primeval dreams and creative fantasies. As such, these images are involuntarily spontaneous manifestations and by no means intentional inventions.[4]

We're talking about core relevance here. Not the kind you can consciously volunteer but something that drives you at the gut level to act and react in certain ways. These images are embedded in each of us as members of a particular society, or coded for symbolic retrieval at a cultural level.

Create a brand that connects the conscious world with unconscious deep imprints, and you have one that will stand the test of time.

Even better, if you have the opportunity, start with the imprint and build a brand on the deep foundation it provides.

In the book *How Customers Think,* Gerald Zaltman opens Chapter 10, "Stories as Brands," with, "The idea that brands are a form of storytelling is not new." Zaltman proceeds to link storytelling and archetypes, where, ". . . memories are *archetypes,* defined as images that capture essential, universal commonalties across a variety of experiences."[5]

BRAND ARCHETYPES

As the keynote speaker for the American Marketing Association's 20th Annual Marketing Research Conference, I had the opportunity afterward to attend some of the breakout sessions. A case study on Kraft Barbecue held my attention.[6]

Here's how I remember the story told in the breakout session.

The microwave oven was just beginning to catch on, and the Kraft people had just come up with a new theme for their barbecue sauce that would address the needs of families that needed quick and easy meals. Just take your favorite meat—chicken, ham, ground beef—put Kraft Barbecue sauce on it, microwave it, and in a jiffy you've got a fast, delicious meal for your brood.

Only one problem with this concept: the more they pushed it in television ads, the more sales dropped. Research showed that families were time-deprived, that people needed the quick and easy meal during the week, and that more households were equipping their kitchens with microwave ovens. What was wrong with this positioning? It really fit the facts, but something was way off in the mind of the consumer.

Kraft proceeded to hire Archetype International, headed by Dr. Clotaire Rapaille whom we mentioned just a moment ago, to diagnose the situation.

In the new round of research, the goal was to discover the archetype or cultural imprint of *barbecue*. What is it? What does it mean to Americans? A cultural imprint is something that all members of a culture share—if you will remember, it is something that Dr. Rapaille calls a "cultural unconscious" and Jung calls a "collective unconscious."

It turns out that *barbecue* is about barbecuing. Barbecue is not so much a type of food—it's a family activity and ritual. Barbecuing is not fast; it's slow. Barbecuing is not modern; it's traditional with roots toward the primitive.

Mom is in the kitchen making a portion of the meal—but the twist in the barbecue experience is that Dad is cooking. Remember that this is an archetype, by definition:

> 1. the original pattern or model from which all things of the same kind are copied or on which they are based; a model or first form; prototype; 2. (in Jungian psychology) a collectively inherited unconscious idea, pattern of thought, image, etc., universally present in individual psyches.[7]

We may or may not agree with the roles—but many people will have imprinted on barbecue this way. The imprint is either direct, through an early family gathering, or through media that portrays barbecuing in this way with these gender roles and this unique experience that is more than food preparation. It's a bonding ritual associated with good times.

With this information in hand, the Kraft people repositioned their barbecue sauce in a series of ads that showed an American frontier family barbecuing, everyone in their traditional roles, smiles on faces, with a slow and leisurely pace.

Sales went up, up, up.

Quick and easy was shifted to slow and traditional—in other words, Kraft Barbecue sauce was shifted from an alien idea to one that is deeply imprinted on the American cultural unconscious during early moments and memories of close family bonding.

"Explicit memories established during emotional situations are often especially vivid and enduring, and for this reason are called flashbulb memories. The classic example is that most baby boomers know where they were and what they were doing when they heard the news JFK had been shot,"[8] writes Joseph LeDoux in his book *Synaptic Self.* More recently, a larger part of the global population probably remembers when 9/11 took place. I know exactly where I was—at the beach vacationing with family. I can see the room, the relatives, the images on the television.

LeDoux continues, "But we are all aware from our daily experiences that we remember particularly well those things that are most important to us, those things that arouse our emotions. Emotions, in short, amplify memories."

The first Kraft "fast and easy" positioning rationally fit the facts for an evolving psychographic shift in reduction of time available for meal preparation and advent of the microwave oven.

This was a very rational positioning with little emotional depth, with the exception of showing a happy family eating a meal in no time. What you would normally associate with food cues were not believed in the context of the new microwave cooking technology. Beliefs about the taste and aroma of meat prepared in microwaves were not positive 20 years ago. Barbecue sauce was ill suited to overcome this objection and was incongruous to the barbecuing archetype.

"Slow and traditional," the new positioning, used visual and sound stimuli to evoke imprints that then drove customer to "smell and taste" the barbecue experience right through the glass on the TV set.

Conventional wisdom would tell us that our accumulated repository of experiences forms the basis of what we know about the world. The irony is, these personal and cultural imprints do something more powerful than that—they cause us to experience what we *already* know.

YOU EXPERIENCE WHAT YOU KNOW

Figure 9.1 shows the text of a real e-mail my spouse received from a friend. We normally nuke junk e-mail or jokes of this kind, but this one caught Heidi's eye, and she sent it to me. It's a great example of how we experience what we already know.

The text is gibberish from a pure language point of view, but Gestalt psychology predicts that we will understand the message because most of the whole is there for us to reconstruct meaning. The same is true for

FIGURE 9.1 *Gibberish or Clear Message?*

———- Original Message ———-
From: (deleted)
To: Heidi
Sent: Friday, September 19, 2003 1:03 PM
Subject: FW: This is wreid sutff!

> Aoccdrnig to a rscheearch at an Elingsh uinervtisy, it deosn't
> mttaer in waht oredr the ltteers in a wrod are, the olny iprmoetnt tihng is
> taht frist and lsat ltteer is at the rghit pclae. The rset can be a toatl
> mses
> and you can sitll raed it wouthit porbelm. Tihs is bcuseae we do not raed
> ervey lteter by it slef but the wrod as a wlohe.
>
> hpoe yuo are hvaing a good dya.
>
>

---

a figure that is essentially a big *C*, but we perceive it as an *O* or complete circle. (See Figure 9.2.)

We see this as a circle, even though it really isn't. We perform an act of completion, just as we do for the text—we get completion and meaning out of experience, context, and the mind's desire to find a way of organizing the experiences around us. Without this organizing ability, the world would be something we would constantly have to learn and relearn—rendering us incapable of dealing with even the simplest tasks.

The newest conventional wisdom is to manage the customer experience so people want to do business with you. A more direct approach would be to frame the experience that customers have with you in terms of what they already know and expect and manage to what they already feel and believe.

Experiments show that, when presented with a known object, people will react to it based on what they already know about it. Creating a new experience is orders of magnitude harder and more expensive than tapping into and amplifying a known experience pattern. There's no comparison.

FIGURE 9.2 *Bic C or Complete Circle?*

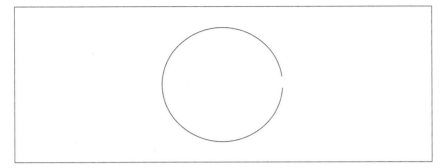

OBSERVING IS BETTER THAN ASKING

I'm a big fan of observational research.

In all honesty, I discount to some extent what test subjects report to me in market research studies. There are techniques to diminish bias, but that's not the issue. People just can't reliably report what they do or—more importantly—why they do it. They can't report what they can't objectively observe and can't report what lies deep inside their unconscious mind that drives behavior.

Figure 9.3 shows a chart I developed with Dr. Stacey Baer, a colleague at work whom I brought on my team to do customer experience strategy, to describe the customer research repertoire.

The chart isn't complete. There are lots of other customer research techniques available, but it did the basic job in telling this story: our internal customers were very familiar with the left-hand side of the chart, not so familiar or comfortable with the right-hand side of the chart.

I would suggest to you that the right-hand side of the chart represents discovering and capturing the insights that will drive game-changing strategies for brands. What the right side won't give you is a lot of numbers. Most of our marketing and management customers want numbers, and with the exception of focus groups, the research techniques on the left-hand side of the chart can generate numbers in quantity.

Think of the market research on the left appealing to the left-side of the brain—the logical side. Think of the research on the right as the more right-brained methods—providing insight that is more creative, less obvious, and generally less likely for competitors to replicate or customers to self-report. I would also say that, although I've listed ethnographic studies in the observational-confirmation quadrant, this body of research techniques can be used equally well for observational-ex-

FIGURE 9.3 *Customer Research Quadrants*

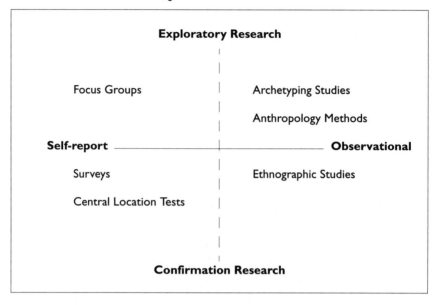

Exploratory Research

Focus Groups   Archetyping Studies

                                Anthropology Methods

Self-report ———————————————— **Observational**

Surveys   Ethnographic Studies

Central Location Tests

Confirmation Research

ploratory research. We did some ethnographic research in airline departure lounges, observing the habits of notebook computer users—and the results were useful for both confirming some things we already knew and inspiring innovation.

A market research program that drives a healthy business and brand strategy will use a blend of all these methods over time to drive differentiation and distinctive insights into customer wants and needs.

This can help overcome what Gerald Zaltman, in his book *How Customers Think,* calls the Titanic Effect.

"*The Titanic Effect, then, is the sinking of a company or brand due to managers' unquestioning confidence in customary, surface-oriented thinking about customers—as if the old paradigm sufficed for both understanding the market and adjusting quickly to market conditions.* This failure to think deeply—particularly to think deeply about business consumers and ultimate consumers—is a failure to question the so-called conventional wisdom."[9]

ADDING THE EXPERIENCE CYCLE

To our experience model that covers the depth of brand meaning, from logical to cultural archetype and distributed among the five senses, we add the dimension of time.

FIGURE 9.4 *Integrating the Experience*

Sense:					
Sight	|	X	X	X	X
Sound	|	X	X	X	X
Touch	|		X	X	X
Smell	|				X
Taste	|				X
		Awareness	Consideration	Purchase	Ownership

In marketing, the purchase cycle is well known:

Awareness → Consideration → Purchase →
Ownership → Service/Support

Depending on the time between purchases, just like the directions on your shampoo bottle: Repeat.

To get to *repeat* more often, businesses talk about lifetime customer value. Brand investments that delight the customer during the ownership experience short-circuit the awareness phase and bring customers back to consideration of your brand or a limited number of brands for the next purchase occasion.

If you plot the five senses against the purchase cycle, you generally get these potentials for sense interaction. (See Figure 9.4.)

Notice in this exercise, there is the growing possibility to delight all the senses through the ownership experience, but there is no sense delighted by service or support. This moves out of the realm of the senses and into pure relationship characteristics that are sensed inside the head and felt by the heart.

Integrating the experience of the customer, both what is being experienced now and the resonance with what has been stored as past experience, is the goal. The experience of now pings one or more of the senses. Current information from the five senses is linked to the accumulated experience of the past connected all the way back to the first imprint.

This turns on its head the notion of "seeing is believing"—because in truth, as we learned earlier, as experiences accumulate we tend to "see what we know." What we already believe forms a robust framework that we use to process and filter information into a cohesive whole.

EXPERIENCING BRANDSCENDENCE

Let's put Brandscendence to work.

Because customers interact with a brand on a cycle, we can take each point in the process . . .

- Awareness (A)
- Consideration (C)
- Purchase (P)
- Ownership (O)
- Service/Support (S)

. . . and map it to the key characteristics of Brandscendence:

- Relevance (R)
- Context (C)
- Mutual Benefit (Mb)

Now, let's put this in a two-by-two grid (see Figure 9.5.) and, in the intersections, assign a value for the stage maturity of the brand.

As a reminder, here are the maturity stages of Brandscendence. For Relevance:

- *Stage 1: Personality development.* Brand as learning child (dependent)
- *Stage 2: Character development.* Brand as learning adolescent (independent)
- *Stage 3: Defined purpose.* Brand as lifelong learning adult (interdependent)

FIGURE 9.5 *Brandscendence Experience Grid*

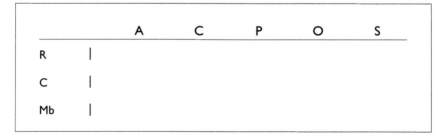

FIGURE 9.6 *Brandscendence Experience Grid*

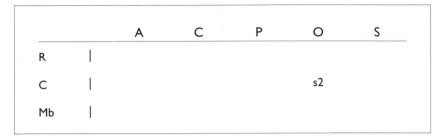

		A	C	P	O	S
R	|					
C	|				s2	
Mb	|					

For Context:

- *Stage 1.* The brand reflects its surroundings and reacts to the environment
- *Stage 2.* The brand proactively adapts itself to the world to increase its success.
- *Stage 3.* The brand projects itself to the world and changes the environment.

For Mutual Benefit:

- *Stage 1: Conditional.* Mere transactions without ongoing relationships
- *Stage 2: Reciprocal.* Formation of customer relationships and memory
- *Stage 3: Integrated.* Sustainable relationships that fuel each other's growth

As an example, in the grid in Figure 9.6, I'm assigning to this hypothetical brand a context stage maturity level of 2, expressed as s2 for the ownership experience.

Now let's populate the rest of the grid.

FIGURE 9.7 *Brandscendence Experience Grid*

		Customer Experience Cycle				
Br Elements		A	C	P	O	S
R	|	s3	s3	s3	s2	s2
C	|	s2	s2	s2	s2	s1
Mb	|	s1	s1	s1	s1	s1

This is a pretty good diagnostic tool. Do you see a pattern in the grid that tells a story about this brand? It says here that is a brand that is a knockout in perceived enduring relevance until someone owns it, and then the stage maturity for relevance goes down a notch. The brand is moderately good at leveraging context, except in service and support. The brand generally functions at a transaction level in terms of mutual benefit, living hand to mouth from one customer purchase decision to the next.

While you were reading the preceding paragraph, did a brand you know pop into your head? If so, you can understand the power of mapping brands in this way. You can then plan to invest in your brand to move it from one stage to the next in the most effective way.

Brands also exist in a web of other brands that push and pull on each other. Understanding brand relationships to other brands is the focus of our next chapter, "Brand Holons."

C *h a p t e r* **G** *l o s s a r y*

---

archetype, *n.* **1.** the original pattern or model from which all things of the same kind are copied or on which they are based; a model or first form; prototype. **2.** (in Jungian psychology) a collectively inherited unconscious idea, pattern of thought, image, etc., universally present in individual psyches.[10]

collective unconscious, (in Jungian psychology) inborn collective psychic material common to humankind, accumulated by the experience of all preceding generations. Cf. **archetype** (def. 2). [1915-20][11]

ethnography, *n.* a branch of anthropology dealing with the scientific description of individual cultures. **Ethnographer,** *n.*—**ethnographic, ethnographical,** *adj.*—**ethnographically,** *adv.*[12]

10

BRAND HOLONS

*"Man shapes himself through decisions
that shape his environment."*
RENE DUBOS[1]

Executive summary. This chapter introduces the concept of brand holons. Brands are both wholes and parts of other brands. Brands exist in the context of other brands, forming brand ecosystems, where stage maturity of specific brands can more or less exert influence on other brands. Understanding the concepts of holons and brand ecosystems can provide deep insight into ways to invest in and extend brands—and the selection of other brands to partner with for mutual benefit.

LEVELS OF ABSTRACTION

If you've been following the thread of thought in the past several chapters, you'll notice that we've been moving from the very concrete to the abstract. Human senses are fundamental. Names conveyed by language are the next level of abstraction. Then we explored putting it all together in an end-to-end customer experience that engages the senses and the mind from conscious thought to emotions and early cultural imprints.

This chapter explores a useful level of abstraction. Normally, abstract and useful can't be used in the same sentence without getting a lot of laughs or sneers from the practical members of our society. But I can assure you that the integrated set of ideas you're about to discover will bring new clarity to the world of branding at work all around you.

FROM STAGE TO WAVE AND BACK

The stages of Brandscendence depicted in Part One might leave you with the impression that you can reach stage three, kick back, and glory in the timeless achievements of your brand.

Not so. Remember: Brandscendence is a journey, not a destination.

Extending from the human development model suggested by Piaget, let's now blend in what we know about the behavior of light. Physics tells us that light behaves both as particles and waves. So do brands.

This dual behavior model from physics also can be applied to brand behavior. Brands behave as particles and as waves, coexisting at each stage of Brandscendence.

Brands are composed of specific instances of behavior in the marketplace—brand particles. They are also a series of patterns that flow out into the marketplace—brand waves. How light behaves can't be explained without both a particle and wave theory and the supporting observations. Neither can brands.

If we take the human development model and fuse it with the language describing the physics of light, we're ready for the next step function change in our conversation about branding.

Please allow me to introduce you to your new best friend in understanding and managing brands: holons.

BRAND HOLONS: WHOLES AND PARTS

Brands exist in the presence of other brands. They are both a whole brand and a part of other brands, and they can be comprised of recognizable brand ingredients.

Adapting and honoring a concept from Ken Wilber, I refer to these wholes and parts as "brand holons." In Wilber's book *A Theory of Everything,* he defines holons as ingredients in hierarchies. It's a very simple and compelling concept.

Wilber says, "A *holon* is a whole that is a part of other wholes. For example, a whole atom is part of a whole molecule; a whole molecule is part of a whole cell; a whole cell is part of a whole organism. Or again, a whole letter is part of a whole word, which is part of a whole sentence, which is part of a whole paragraph, and so on. Reality is composed of neither wholes nor parts, but of whole/parts, or holons. Reality in all domains is basically composed of holons."[2]

I think Wilber might counsel me for corralling the notion of holons into a corner for such a specific use as branding. The concept of holons is expansive and worthy of exploration on its own. However, to make holon theory come alive in the context of branding, I'm going to add my own specific spin to the subject.

For instance, when you buy an IBM ThinkPad notebook computer, you're buying a recognized brand that is by itself a holon. It is composed of many parts that in and of themselves are wholes. Two of these wholes, which are highly visible parts of IBM ThinkPad notebook computers as ingredient brands, are the Intel microprocessor and the Microsoft Windows operating system software.

IBM ThinkPad in turn is a product, a part of what you can buy from a catalog or computer dealer (distribution channels). In the context of these channels as brands themselves, the brand IBM ThinkPad becomes a part of the channel brand holon associated with purchase—whether directly from IBM's Web site, a catalog retailer, or a value added reseller (VAR).

In Figure 10.1 is a map I drew several years ago to describe brand holons for IBM ThinkPad notebook computers. It is an adaptation of an earlier work by Ken Wilber that also included the notion of holons, *A Brief History of Everything*.[3]

This chart provided an integral view of our offering portfolio at a point in time, based on mapping customer research to the holon model. It also pointed to potential adjacent portfolio expansion opportunities.

Try this yourself. Use a brand you know well and try to describe the holon it represents, and then the holons it is composed of, and then the holons it is part of in a larger scheme. When you're done, what you've documented is a brand ecosystem.

BRAND ECOSYSTEMS

Brand holons are by themselves relevant in some specific way that both works upward, as part of larger brand ecosystems, and must be comprised of brand holons that support this relevance. Brand holons manifest themselves in the context of other brands and can be highly adaptive or project themselves to affect the fitness landscape of other brands.

Brand holons, by their very affinity to each other, are mutually beneficial at some level. This mutual benefit can be s1 dependence on other

FIGURE 10.1 *Brand Holons*

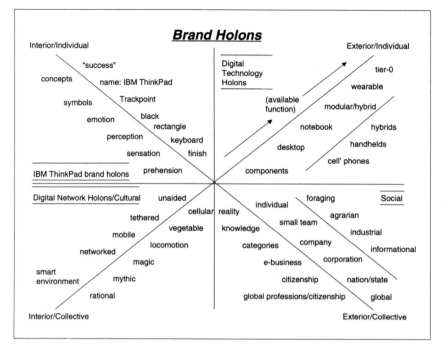

brand holons, s2 independence in delivering the brand's core relevance in the brand ecosystem, or s3 interdependence that creates maximum value for all players in the brand ecosystem.

We're talking about sustainability here. Paul Hawken, the author of *The Ecology of Commerce*,[4] introduces the sustainability issue succinctly when he says in the preface, "Rather than a management problem, we have a design problem, a flaw that runs through all business." He continues, "To create an enduring society, we will need a system of commerce and production where each and every act is inherently sustainable and restorative."[5]

The same could be said of brand holons, where every act is nested in other holons to create a chain of sustainability. Here I need to add some new terms of my own for clarity.

- *Reference holon.* Forms the frame of reference as a single whole/part for looking at the smaller and larger world in which it exists.
- *Subholon chain.* Represents the view of the constant holon down to smaller holon's wholes/parts.
- *Macroholon chain.* Is the view of the constant holon up to larger holon's wholes/parts.

FIGURE 10.2 *Holon Hierarchies*

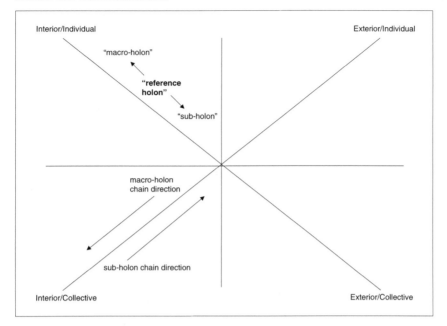

Figure 10.3 shows sustainable and mutually beneficial, from the point of view of the reference holon, must be considered from both sub-holon and macroholon directions.

USING THE THREE ELEMENTS OF BRANDSCENDENCE TO DESCRIBE BRAND HOLONS

Here was our original stage view of the three elements that drive the journey to Brandscendence, where each stage represents a higher level of community, from dependence, to independence, to interdependence.

Now, let's recast this linear view from what we've learned about brand holons. (See Figure 10.4.)

Each brand holon is a whole that has unique relevance unto itself, then exists in the context of other brand holons. There are then the strong or weak bonds of mutual benefit to hold the brand holon chain together. Strong bonds will keep brand holon relationships in place for longer periods of time, weak bonds allow for more promiscuity in the search for stronger brand holon relationships. (See Figure 10.5.)

Adding the Brandscendence maturity stages to the model adds another layer of richness. Each level represents more brand influence

FIGURE 10.3 *The Stages and Attributes of Brandscendence*

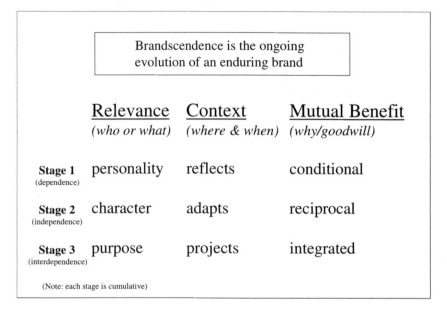

	Relevance *(who or what)*	Context *(where & when)*	Mutual Benefit *(why/goodwill)*
Stage 1 (dependence)	personality	reflects	conditional
Stage 2 (independence)	character	adapts	reciprocal
Stage 3 (interdependence)	purpose	projects	integrated

Brandscendence is the ongoing evolution of an enduring brand

(Note: each stage is cumulative)

that can be exerted on other holons in the brand ecosystem. Note a new theoretical stage being introduced in Figure 10.6—stage 4, a holonic brand level that is integral. We didn't start off with this in the model, because it is a level of brand maturity that doesn't exist today. I have no examples of enterprises operating at an s4 level, but s4 is a desirable place for brands to strive toward. In Figure 10.7 is a representation of the journey to Brandscendence mapped to an integral holarchy that can better explain where an s4 level could take branding practice.

FIGURE 10.4 *The Brand Holon View of Brandscendence*

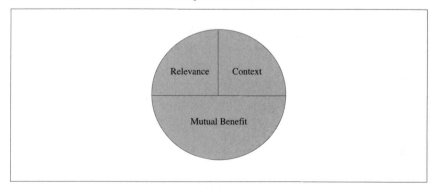

FIGURE 10.5 *The Brand Holon View of Brandscendence*

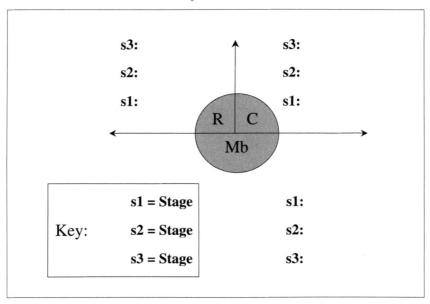

Each stage drives more brand mass, which can exert a gravitational pull on other surrounding brand holons in the brand ecosystem. Let's use an example that many people around the world have personally experienced to more fully explain brand holons.

BRAND HOLONS IN ACTION

Welcome to Walt Disney World's EPCOT Center. EPCOT exists in a web of interrelated brand holons. EPCOT is comprised of world-class brands that are exhibitors from both the commercial world at the front of the park and countries and cultures at the back of the park. EPCOT also exists as part of the Walt Disney World theme park brand, the Walt Disney franchise overall, and as a fundamental ingredient in the Orlando-as-travel-destination brand that has only Las Vegas as a competitor for number of hotel rooms.

EPCOT stands for Experimental Prototype Community Of Tomorrow. It was the last project that Walt Disney launched publicly just before his death a few months later. Mr. Disney was a holonic thinker in the way he interwove his intellectual property. This is more than what they call "synergy" today, where a movie spawns a ton of promotional tie-ins and

FIGURE 10.6 *Brand Step-Function Transformations*

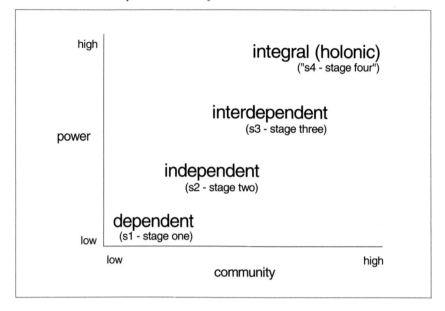

merchandise. Disney nurtured and protected his projects, characters, and properties for long-term stewardship.

EPCOT was originally conceived as a place to work, live, and vacation. The vacation part lives on today in the EPCOT theme park. The work and live part was born years later in Celebration, a community started by Disney on an adjacent property in Florida—from theme park to theme living. Even more faithful to the original idea of EPCOT from a design point of view is Palm City, an resort being built in Dubai, Junari, in the United Arab Emirates. The luxury resort is an island with a layout that resembles a palm tree to maximize exposure to the water. Just as you see in Walt Disney World, where EPCOT is located, Palm City has a monorail, recreation, hotels, entertainment, and, in addition, permanent and rental residences.

As a brand holon, EPCOT is an interesting web of relationships.

Let's move first to the larger brand ecosystem of which EPCOT is a part. EPCOT is part of the larger Walt Disney World theme park located in central Florida. It's a large employer and taxpayer but is also its own government. That's right: when you venture onto Disney property, you've entered a unique place on earth. It's what they call in the travel business a "destination" resort. It's what they call in the commercial world a "foreign trade zone." Unique rules govern a unique destination.

FIGURE 10.7 *The Great Holarchy* Mapped to Brand Theory Metaphors*

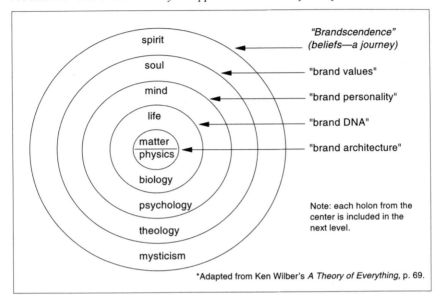

People who work for Disney at EPCOT and all their other theme parks are not employees; they're "cast members," as if the entire park is a giant stage. The technical and design teams working at Disney are called Imagineers to underscore their role in engineering and designer imaginative experience for park patrons. Both the cast member and imagineering monikers are meant to underscore core relevance for the Disney employee and deliver a unique experience for the customer.

Disney pays attention to the details. The meteorologist on site monitors changes in the weather that will then drive menus and merchandise. Hot weather will trigger more refreshment stands to open based on patron density in the park. A potential rainstorm will signal all storefront concessions to roll out carts full of Disney character umbrellas to streets and sidewalks. Rain's over—the carts roll back out of sight. Disney has a strong sense of context for its guests.

EPCOT is also home to both exhibitor companies and countries. At the front of the park are theme attractions from AT&T, General Motors, Kodak, United Technologies, and other companies. Countries include Canada, China, Japan, Norway, United Kingdom, and the United States. These exhibitors are part of a mutually beneficial holon web that reaches down to the core of Disney's ethos and up through the visitors it entertains from around the world.

These brand holons point to a path of integral brand practices that fully show dedication to core relevance, sensitivity to context, and higher paths to sustainable mutual benefit. Try mapping your own brand holon product or organization map soon and see the insights and implications tumble forth.

OK, we've reached a pretty high level of "useful abstraction" in this chapter. In the next part of this book, "Brandscendence in Action," let's examine the world of brands with examples of companies and organizations that are doing it right.

Part Three

BRANDSCENDENCE IN ACTION

The three elements of Brandscendence, *relevance, context, and mutual benefit* work in slightly different ways, depending on the industry, product, or service. Here we see the principles of Brandscendence in action in the air, where we rest, on our plates, and in business-to-business transactions around the world.

11

TAKE ME AWAY

Travel and Transportation

"What this country needs is an ocean in the mountains."
PAUL SWEENEY[1]

Executive summary. The travel and transportation industry represents one of the largest segments of the global economy. Brand categories have unique gifts they can offer their customers, and in the case of travel and transportation, you have the opportunity to invite people into "your home." You can simply offer a hotel room or airline seat, or you can think of the patron as a guest in your world. When they see the inventory of rooms or seats available at any given moment, which brands see a transient level one transaction just to sell one or a level three, ongoing, interdependent relationship at stake? Do you see a body with a credit card or a valued guest you want to keep for a lifetime?

"BE MY GUEST"[2]

You've been blindfolded.
Without sight, your ability to hear and smell is heightened.
You're led out of a car and can hear street traffic noise behind you and smell the internal combustion fumes of a city in motion.

Footsteps forward and through a revolving door reveal a new world on the other side—you hear light classical music in a quiet space, and the smell of flowers replaces the odor of carbon monoxide.

The blindfold is removed and sight is restored. You've been here before.

I've had the privilege of traveling to many places around the world. I've been here before. It's a Ritz Carlton Hotel. These hotels have a luxurious sameness to them. You know you're home—wherever you are in the world.

The other strategy is to have a collection of properties under an umbrella brand that stands for superb hospitality in context—and that is the experience you get with another of my favorite hotel brands—the Four Seasons.

Four Seasons Hotels both are and are not the same worldwide. They are a hotel brand that stands for superb global service, while architecture and locations actively reflect the local culture.

"Be My Guest" is not just this section's title; it's the book with Conrad Hilton's name on it that reflects the philosophy of the Hilton Hotel chain. It has a nice ring to it, reflecting the desire of Hilton to have hotel *guests* staying at their properties, not just people with money paying for temporary accommodations.

Hotels have something going for them that is unique in the branding world—the ability to create a hospitality experience that you live in from time to time.

Disney theme parks take this to the next level when you stay o their property. Disney knows why you're there—to be entertained on vacation—and can optimize the experience end-to-end. To be on site at Disney is to be at the intersection of hospitality and entertainment, and the location creates mutual benefit for both Disney and the patron. Disney captures more share of the wallet from families on site than from families that stay off site, and people vacationing in the park—be it Orlando, Tokyo, Paris, or Anaheim—get an immersive vacation that is a better experience.

RITZ BRAND COMMANDOS

While vacationing one winter several years ago in Aspen, Colorado, the front page of the local newspaper had a compelling story of brand management in action. Evidently, the Ritz-Carlton Hotel in town—one of the finest—had not been keeping up with the maintenance standards set by the parent company. The hotel had been purchased by offshore interests a few years earlier, and Ritz-Carlton was worried that its brand was being tarnished by this property.

Saturday night, in the middle of the winter ski season, a raid was conducted. At midnight, a warrant was presented to the night staff of the hotel to hand over all Ritz-Carlton logo and signature elements.

The executive offices were purged of all Ritz-Carlton letterhead.

The rugs at the entry and in the elevators with the Ritz logo were removed.

Glassware, memo pads, flower vases and arrangements, towels, terrycloth robes, flatware—all were swept away in a few short hours while guests in the hotel slept.

In the morning, a letter was under the door of every guest room informing them that they were no longer staying at a Ritz-Carlton Hotel, a brief and polite description of the reason for the change, and a thank you for previous patronage. Waking up to that letter must have been a shock. Wandering through the hotel without these signature elements would leave you with a definite "something's missing here" feeling.

Ritz-Carlton was serious about its brand equity across its entire franchise system and did something clear and powerful to protect it.

WHERE WE'RE GOING

Where people go when they want to get away is captured in this table from the 2003 *Time Almanac.*[3]

The World's Top Tourism Destinations
(international tourist arrivals)

2000 rank	Country	Arrivals in 1999 (million)	Arrivals in 2000 (million)	Percentage change 1999/2000	2000 market share
1.	France	73.0	75.5	3.4%	10.8%
2.	United States	48.5	50.9	4.9	7.3
3.	Spain	46.8	48.2	3.0	6.9
4.	Italy	36.5	41.2	12.8	5.9
5.	China	27.0	31.2	15.5	4.5
6.	United Kingdom	25.4	25.2	-0.8	3.6
7.	Russian Fed.	18.5	21.2	14.5	3.0
8.	Mexico	19.0	20.6	8.4	3.0
9.	Canada	19.5	20.4	4.9	2.9
10.	Germany	17.1	19.0	10.9	2.7

What does this mean from a brand holon point of view? In addition to being places to vacation, the destination countries also look a lot like strong economic trading partners.

They are places that can be considered generally safe for the visitor.

In over half the cases, the destination is also associated with a popular cuisine, such as French, Spanish, Italian, Chinese, Mexican, or German.

Overall, they represent cultural and economic interdependence, a Brandscendence s3 attribute.

So when people come to see America, where do they visit?

Top States and Cities Visited by Overseas Travelers in 2002

State	Overseas Visitors (thousands)	Market Share
Total overseas travelers	25,975	100.0%
California	6,364	24.5
Florida	6,026	23.2
New York	5,922	22.8
Hawaiian Islands	2,727	10.5
Nevada	2,364	9.1
City		
Total overseas travelers	25,975	100.0%
New York, NY	5,714	22.0
Los Angeles, CA	3,533	13.8
Orlando, FL	3,013	11.6
Miami, FL	2,935	11.3
San Francisco, CA	2,831	10.9
Las Vegas, NV	2,260	8.7
Oahu/Honolulu, HI	2,234	8.6
Washington, DC	1,481	5.7
Chicago, IL	1,351	5.2
Boston, MA	1,325	5.1

These states and cities are powerful brands unto themselves, with tourism campaigns and economic development that keep people coming back.

California, the world's largest net exporter of popular entertainment, is also the biggest tourist draw for visitors from outside the United States. Los Angeles, starring in the role of capital of the film industry, is the second largest city draw, after only New York. San Francisco projects a unique character known around the world, has more restaurants per capita than any other major city in the United States, and is a popular major conference locale.

Florida draws people from around the world to hotels on the water; theme park entertainment in centrally located Orlando; and year-round ocean liner cruises from the ports of Miami, Tampa, and Port Canaveral. Miami is known as the capital of Latin America. The Hawaiian Islands represent a similar warm weather theme, especially attractive to visitors from Asian Pacific countries.

For adult-themed entertainment, Las Vegas is a global destination and second to none in the use of branding techniques to build equity for the town and specific gaming and hotel destinations.

After the demise of the World Trade Center towers, New York City lost one of its most powerful brand symbols. However, the character of New York is now legendary in terms of the will of New Yorkers to survive and rebuild. The loss of the symbol is more than offset by the deposits of goodwill from people around the world who believe in what New York represents. The variety of cultures that meld into what is New York make this one of the most interconnected places in the world and America's number-one tourist destination.

New York is a web of brand holons that reach out to and encompass the cultures that choose to live and work here. The cultures that are less represented are the ones that don't view New York as the same kind of integrating symbol.

WHEN THE LIGHTS GO OUT

I have a buddy at work who recently went to New York when a big chunk of the northeastern United States lost power. He was going across the Triboro Bridge and committed to that route just as the lights winked out and the air conditioning failed. This gave him the opportunity to sleep on the street. The hotel he had booked for several days would not honor his reservation and made no provision for the comfort of its incoming guests. In fact, guests already registered were asked to leave for "insurance reasons." His reaction to this experience was never to stay with this hotel again—not just this property but all hotels carrying its name.

Other hotels in New York behaved better—providing as much comfort as possible to guests in the hotel and, when records existed, accepting the reservations of arriving guests.

Some hotel brands enhanced their relevance to customers in this difficult context, creating tangible mutual benefit under the circumstances—and potentially cementing customer loyalty for life. Others threw the opportunity adversity presented out the window, as opposed to embracing it as a gift.

I was running a meeting in Port Douglas, Australia, and during dinner at a golf club, the lights went out. There were already candles on the tables, so we weren't in the dark. Without missing a beat, staff brought more candles from the kitchen, and dinner proceeded. The night was truly spectacular now, because there were no lights on the ground to compete with the stars.

I started to get quiet reports back from the hotel that, not only was the power out in Port Douglas, but one quarter of Australia was in the dark. There was no firm schedule for when the electricity would return.

The staff of the Sheraton Mirage worked with us all night to consider options for our guests and our meeting plans. All of our presentations were on notebook computers; could we run them off small generators, and would we be able to create enough shade for the screen if the meeting were held outdoors? What food would we serve, and how long could we improvise without the use of the electric ovens in the hotel kitchens? When would we just give up, get everyone on planes, and call it quits?

I can say the staff at this hotel made a lasting impression on me. They made the Sheraton brand sparkle under adverse circumstances.

The power came back on at 3:45 AM, rendering all the contingency planning obsolete but leaving a residue of goodwill that has not been forgotten.

HOLIDAY INN

When I was in second grade, my dad accepted a job in Memphis, Tennessee. It was a transfer from the IBM branch office in Kansas City. He was going to work on a project that would transform the hotel industry into the light-speed and capacity-management entity we know today.

His project was the genesis of the Holidex Reservation System.

We spent many nights in Holiday Inns as we vacationed over the years, because dad is loyal to his roots. The same is true for the Weber outdoor grills that we found in the next move, to Deerfield, Illinois (Weber is in Palatine, a nearby suburb), which we still use today.

Holidex was the first online reservations system for the hotel/motel industry. It changed the rules, just as the airline industry was transformed by the advent of the Sabre airlines reservation system in the 1960s by American Airlines. Today, Sabre Holdings is a separate company and includes the Travelocity Web travel service brand, Sabre Solutions brand, and the Sabre Travel Network brand as the core franchise that still represents the world's largest electronic network linking travel buyers and sellers.

I remember dad asking the guy behind the front desk if we could see the reservation terminal in the back room. We sat down at a terminal, punched in numbers and letters at the teletypewriter console, and reserved a room down the road. To me, it seemed like magic. For the bottom line of Holiday Inn at the time, it was magic.

Today, hotels struggle to reassert their relationship with customers in an era of online reservations. The travel industry strategy used to revolve around cultivating relationships with travel agencies and their agents. However, new brands such as Orbitz, Expedia, and Priceline now offer customers the convenience of reservations at the touch of a button. In a fashion after destination retailers such as Nordstroms and Wal-Mart, these online reservation providers become the trusted brand that helps the customer select other brands in the market.

In both cases—through travel agencies or online reservation systems in the hands of the traveling public—the hotels, airlines, railroads, and car rental agencies have taken up the challenge to reassert their brands as worthy of selection over mere price.

Some have taken a positive route to be a better experience, while others have taken a less desirable path, punishing customers for not doing business with them directly. I recently received a letter from a hotel consortium's loyalty program, informing me that if I don't book with them directly, they won't consider upgrading me when I stay with them in the future.

My reaction to this is twofold: 1) this is not brand building—especially the communication telling me explicitly that if I engage in promiscuous booking behavior, I won't be considered for a better room, even if one is available, and 2) the reservation itself now dictates by policy what used to be at the discretion of the front desk staff, who could immediately delight customers upon arrival.

Knowing this policy actually turns me off and discourages me from considering this group of properties in the future.

INTERCONTINENTAL HOTELS

Today, Holiday Inn is part of the InterContinental Hotels Group (IHG). The origins of the InterContinental Hotels Group can be traced back to 1777, when William Bass established a brewery in Burton-on-Trent, trading under his own name. Bass Ale is with us to this day. In 1876, their red triangle trademark became the first trademark to be registered in the United Kingdom.[4]

In 1989, the government passed Beer Orders legislation, which limited the number of pubs that each of the major brewers could own and spurred a major restructuring of the industry. Bass Groups then dramatically cut the number of pubs that it owned to focus on larger outlets. Cash flow generated by its more mature businesses was funneled into developing an international hotel business.

Bass already owned a small chain of hotels, acquired in 1987. The following year, in 1988, Bass purchased Holiday Inns International, then acquired the North American business of Holiday Inn in 1990. Holiday Inn was already the leading midscale hotel brand in the world, founded by Kemmons Wilson in Memphis, Tennessee, in 1952 to cater to family travel. With continued investment, Holiday Inn grew internationally, and other brands were developed to expand the portfolio and build on its strong infrastructure. In 1991, Holiday Inn Express was launched, adding a complementary brand in the limited service segment, and Crowne Plaza was launched in 1994 to move the group into the upscale market. As the business became more purely brand focused, it sold its U.S. midscale hotel assets in 1997, while retaining the branding through franchise agreements.

A further significant advance for Bass hotels came in March 1998 with the acquisition of InterContinental, originally founded by Pan American World Airlines in 1946. It served not only as a quality hotel brand, meeting the international traveler's needs, but also took care of 40,000 airline crew and staff as they flew the airlines' routes. InterContinental added a top-shelf brand to the hotel portfolio with an important global position that complements Bass's wide range of brands, encompassing the midscale and upscale markets. It also brought considerable synergies and cost savings.

The acquisition of Southern Pacific Hotels Corporation (SPHC) in Australia in January 2000 confirmed Bass Hotels & Resort's position as the leading hotel company in the Asia Pacific region. SPHC operated 59 hotels under the Parkroyal and Centra brands across Australia, New

Zealand, and the South Pacific, as well as hotels in select Southeast Asian countries.

With the pace of consolidation in the global brewing business starting to accelerate, Bass entered into an agreement to sell Bass Brewers to a major Belgian brewer in June 2000, for £2.3 billion. This marked the final step in the refocusing of the group from being a vertically integrated domestic brewer to a leading international hospitality retailer—a process that had taken over ten years to complete. It also involved the sale of the Bass name and the subsequent name change to Six Continents, to reflect better the global spread of the group's businesses.

In April 2001, the U.K. Posthouse hotel chain was acquired for £810 million. Many of these hotels are in good strategic locations, suitable for conversion to Holiday Inns, and this will further consolidate the position of the Holiday Inn brand in the United Kingdom and Europe. In May 2001, the InterContinental Hong Kong was purchased for £241 million, strengthening the hotel business' upscale market position in key Chinese and Asian Pacific markets.

IHG today is the most global hotel group and the second largest in the world by number of rooms. The Group has more than 3,300 owned, leased, managed, and franchised hotels and approximately 515,000 guest rooms across nearly 100 countries and territories.

UP IN THE AIR

I have earned over a million miles on American Airlines's frequent flier program and quite a few on other airlines. I guess you could say that my seat has been in their seat for many hours. The airline travel experience has changed a lot over the last 25 years that I've been traveling professionally.

Bob Lauterborn, Knight Professor of Journalism and Integrated Marketing Communications at the University of North Carolina at Chapel Hill, pointed out to me one day that early airline travel was modeled after the Transatlantic cruise industry. Flying in the era of Pan Am was an elegant experience. By the way, the name Pan Am has exchanged hands several times, and people still recognize it. There was a lot of brand equity in the name Pan Am, and I expect it to be back again some day.

Bob says that the airline industry story has advanced, and more and more, successful brands in the air are based on the Greyhound business model—in other words, bus or commuter train service. The era of elegance is fading for most of the public.

On a recent trip to France, I realized that first class was gone on reconfigured American Airlines planes. Business class was comfortable enough and, as advertised, economy class had also been changed to offer more leg room between seats.

At the same time, a new phenomenon is emerging that's siphoning off customers who used to sit in first class—and that's the fractional jet leasing companies. I'm familiar with NetJets, the company owned by Warren Buffet, because the lead dispatch manager and pilot is a friend of our family and married to one of my wife's best friends. We went to Chuck and Gail's wedding in Connecticut when he was flying for IBM.

The NetJets business model is very much tied to a well thought-out branding strategy. The NetJets brand is not just about owning part of a jet; at its core, it is a sophisticated logistics company that can forward-deploy aircraft and crew in the same way the U.S. Navy forward-deploys ships and carriers. That leads to an unparalleled level of service for customers: you call, and in four hours, a plane will be waiting for you anywhere there's a general aviation airport in the United States.

I can't talk about the customers that NetJet flies: they really value their privacy, and the NetJet philosophy of discreetness in this regard is akin to that shown by legal counsel or personal assistants. However, when it comes to safety, NetJets will draw the line on the customer always being right. There's no roughhousing in the sky and no illicit substances allowed, and the safety of the crew is as important as the safety of the passengers.

NetJets is a very relevant brand for a self-selected group of time-starved and discerning clients. They are migrating from the disappearing first class cabins to their own on-call aircraft.

Where first class continues to exist and is done well is in some of the state-owned airlines, and Singapore Airlines is generally recognized as the platinum standard in the sky for commercial air service. With its great reputation, I'd like to take a Singapore Airlines flight some day.

SOUTHWEST:
AMUSEMENT PARK MEETS AIRLINE

I recently delivered a keynote speech for the combined Washington, D.C., chapters of the Product Development Management Association (PDMA) and Industrial Design Society of America (IDSA). They offered to pay for the trip, and in the process, I had my first chance to fly Southwest Airlines. It was worth the price of admission.

My first impression of Southwest was like boarding a ride at Disney or a Paramount theme park.

When you check in, your boarding pass is marked *A, B,* or *C*. The first 45 people get an *A* boarding pass, the next 45 *B* boarding passes, and the rest *C* boarding passes. When it comes time to get on the plane, it's all open seating. Everyone lines up under three signs labeled *A–B–C*. The sooner you get in line, the better your chances of getting the seat you want. The *A* seating pass holders get on first and so forth.

The first plane I got on even had bulkhead seating that faced the interior cabin, that is to say backwards to what you'd normally see, as it would be in some trains. For groups traveling together, imagine what a different experience it is to be facing each other for the trip.

Southwest didn't even turn off the engines when it emptied the incoming passengers and proceeded to clean up the cabin and board the next group onto the aircraft. Riding Southwest is more like getting on a roller coaster than an airline. Even the boarding pass chime sounds like a whimsical theme park ride entry sound. The ground and cabin personnel were dressed casually and genuinely seemed to like what they are doing. Announcements were friendly, not orders to comply or else.

I'd say Southwest is well along the way to mapping a journey to Brandscendence.

RAIL ENVY

As an American with a fascination with trains since his grandfather worked for the Santa Fe Railroad as a track construction foreman, I admit to having rail envy. Almost any other country on earth has better passenger rail service than the United States. Amtrak is getting better—but compared to the train system in Europe, it is just a nonstarter. Americans have a car and airline culture.

Then there are the Shinkansen bullet trains of Japan, the Train a Grande Vitesse (TGV) of France, and the ever-dependable and immaculate trains of Switzerland. These trains are brand icons for the countries that have them—adding brand luster to the country in terms of service, technical prowess, and the ability to attract those ever important tourists.

But nothing holds the same awe and mystery associated with the *Venice Simplon-Orient-Express*. This train trip is as much a story as an experience. This train is celebrated in books and film, and it's a trip I'd like to take some day.

Whether a national symbol as the Shinkansen or TGV or the train journey of legend with the Orient Express, these are examples of transportation that move beyond utility to being part of the trip—and are brand destinations unto themselves.

12

FINE WINE TO FAST FOODS

"True individual freedom cannot exist
without economic security and independence.
People who are hungry and out of a job
are the stuff of which dictatorships are made."
FRANKLIN DELANO ROOSEVELT[1]

"To eat, perchance to dine."
KEVIN CLARK (AS HE RIPS OFF SHAKESPEARE)[2]

Executive summary. Most brands could learn something from a restaurant. Whether you're in a five-star room or just driving through for a sandwich, restaurants represent unparalleled opportunities to learn about the nature of customer expectations in a variety of contexts for the communities they serve. The s1 context response is to reflect the cuisine and service of other dining establishments. Stage two brands blend the relevance of the brand and help it to adapt to the needs of various community tastes and traditions. In this chapter, the s3 projective behavior of "being consistent over time" is told in the Niebaum-Coppola Winery story, and "being consistent anywhere you are in the world" is explored with an in-depth look at McDonald's.

FRONT OF THE HOUSE, BACK OF THE HOUSE

Every profession has something instructive to offer others. In the case of running a restaurant, there is a key distinction between "front of the house" and "back of the house." This concept is truly useful to borrow in the service of brand strategy.

The front of the house is where the dining experience takes place. The back of the house is where the cooking is done. To be a great restaurant, you have to be outstanding in both the front of the house and the back of the house. The same is true for brands.

Restaurants on the journey to Brandscendence deliver culinary masterpieces in a wonderful setting with pampered service. Fill in the blanks for your brand: your brand delivers _____ masterpieces in _____ with _____ service.

I learned about the front of the house and the back of the house through friends who let me work in their fine dining steak restaurant for a brief period of time. With my brand-seeking eyeglasses on, I found the experience very instructive.

The first thing you notice when you have access to the entire restaurant is the stark transition between the front of the house where the customer dines, and the back of the house where lots of preparation and cleaning work is done. You start to notice this when you stay in hotels. The doors that lead to service elevators and staff staging areas just barely open. The customer-facing carpeted hallway turns immediately into gray concrete floors, wallpaper turns to concrete, and lighting changes from soft incandescent lights and halogen spotlights on artwork to cold, cost-effective fluorescent lights.

Enduring brands do the same thing. They turn up the volume on the front of the house "dining experience." Read that as the overall customer experience, from the minute you walk in the door until you leave in the case of a restaurant—or, for instance, from the day you buy a car until the day you decide to buy a new car. The front of the house is managed for excellence and customer experience: a world-class dining environment and service.

To provide good value for money, the back of the house is managed for excellence and establishment efficiency: exceptional meals prepared with managed operational costs.

Enduring brands understand the distinction between the showroom and the warehouse and act accordingly—whether in physical space or on the Web.

SLOW AND FAST CULTURE BY CUISINE

The United States is a melting pot, yes. But long after we've assimilated into the nation by language and custom, something lingers—that's the food.

No matter what you eat today and what tastes you've developed over time, nothing imprints on you more than what you eat at home and at family gatherings at an early age.

Different cultures have unique approaches to food and dining—and to the role food plays in the culture. The "slow food" movement in the United States is a reaction of a time-starved population that eats out more than in today. The slow food people preach staying at home and preparing nutritious meals at a leisurely pace—or, next best, dining out where getting in and out quickly isn't the main objective.

I grew up with "TV dinners" that were a new thing at the time. All kinds of stuff was being spun off from the military and space programs—and it wasn't all that good. Today, the frozen meals prepared under a variety of names are vastly improved, but I'd single out Stouffer's for doing a particularly good job. Not only is the Stouffer's food well made, but the packaging is distinctive versus other manufacturers and has held the look for many years.

When you're strolling down the grocery store aisle, you can see the Stouffer's section of products coming up through the standing freezer. You know them: the red boxes with black-and-white type and high-quality pictures on the front depicting the meal inside. Stouffer's stands out from the frozen food brands surrounding it. It has a distinctive character, projects itself as a standard bearer for others to match in the frozen foods game, and is reciprocally beneficial for Stouffer's and its customers.

NIEBAUM-COPPOLA WINERY

I look up from a discussion and see what appears to be a fresco painting of scenes from the classic movie *Apocalypse Now* in the dome ceiling of the conference alcove where we're seated. Yup, that's exactly what it is, and this is the headquarters of American Zoetrope. (*Zoetrope:* a device for giving an illusion of motion, consisting of a slitted drum that, when whirled, shows a succession of images placed opposite with the slits within the drum as one moving image.) Francis Ford Coppola is seated comfortably across the table and talks about his family businesses and his pride, the newly acquired Niebaum-Coppola Winery north of San Francisco in Napa Valley, in the town of Rutherford.

Before leaving the meeting, he produces bottles of red and white wine from the family vintage. The white bottle was enjoyably consumed during a Thanksgiving feast with close friends two years ago. The Cabernet Franc, 1993, bottle 21,510 of 22,860, will be featured for a private gathering and toast when this work is published. Thank you, dear sir.

He also invites my wife, Heidi, and me to visit the winery on our visit to Napa that fall. We do it. Wonderful visit. We enter on the back road and get to meet lead winemaker Scott McLeod and his laboratory, away from the main visitor area under construction. We discover that there is a history to this land being preserved, so in the spirit of Brandscendence, I'd like to share it with you.[3]

Facts about the Niebaum-Coppola Estate
- Total estate acreage: 1,654.56
- Total vineyard acreage: 195
- Total bearing acreage: 174
- Acreage by variety:
  - Cabernet Sauvignon: 81 acres
  - Merlot: 39 acres
  - Zinfandel: 30 acres
  - Cabernet Franc: 11 acres
  - All others (Chardonnay, Viognier, Dolcetto): 13 acres

The Niebaum years. Gustave Niebaum was born in 1842 as Gustave Ferdinand Nybom in Helsinki, Finland. He graduated in Helsinki from the Nautical Institute in 1861 and set sail for Alaska as commander of his own ship three years later. After exploring the Pribilof Islands and the Aleutians, he sailed into San Francisco harbor in 1867 with a cargo of furs worth $600,000 and founded the Alaska Commercial Company. Niebaum became a wealthy man and, in 1879, purchased the Inglenook property at Rutherford. He would not only be a wine connoisseur but a world-class producer and expert in the world of wine.

To accomplish his personal goal of knowing as much as he could about wine and wine making, he arranged to receive every wine publication that was available at the time. With the help of Joseph Baer, a bookseller in Frankfurt, Germany, Niebaum assembled the world's greatest library of texts on wine. He learned his craft from the world's most skilled European winemakers, returning with dozens of vines for field trials in California.

Niebaum wanted to produce Californian wines that would compete favorably with the famous French, German, and Spanish wines that were in favor at the time and commanding premium prices.

In 1887, after six years of construction, Niebaum, Architect William Mooser, and winery designer Hamden W. McIntyre, created a state-of-the art winemaking facility in a massive chateau, 220 feet long and 72 feet wide. Completed in 1877 after six years of construction, the chateau is crowned by a tin roof, with six arched vaults, and has massive oak doors. Sandstone quarried on the estate forms the walls that are several feet thick, the vaults were made with skewed arches stressed by cables from the original San Francisco cable car line, and the exterior is trimmed in brown stone taken from Carver's quarry near St. Helena.

Grapes are harvested quickly when ripe, then cleaned, stemmed, and crushed. The juice goes to waiting fermenting tanks—and the leavings go to the compost pile to become fertilizer, an example of the winery's early dedication to sustainability. After fermenting, the wines are transferred to clean storage tanks for clarification.

Wines are racked in oaken or redwood casks for aging—with the only manipulations happening during the blending process where different characteristics are brought together.

The wines are bottled after further aging in wood, and Niebaum required that Inglenook wines be bottled only in glass. This was a farsighted notion at the time—a law requiring glass bottling would not exist for another half century.

Close attention is paid to detail: every tool is nickel plated to prevent metallic contamination; every bottle is first soaked and then scoured; and at night, the crusher, press, apron, tanks, grape bins, and floors are all scrubbed with soda, then steamed.

"To produce the finest wines, to equal and excel the most famous vintages of Europe, it is necessary to have the right kind of vines, grown on suitable soils, well manured, the most perfect cleanliness in handling, constant care and proper age," said Niebaum. "No art or trick or machinery can make up for the absence of these things."

In 1889, Niebaum's California wines won awards at the Paris Exposition where the Eiffel Tower was dedicated. His goal of making world-class wine was realized in only ten years.

The Coppola years. A century after Niebaum bought the Inglenook estate, Francis Ford Coppola and his wife, Eleanor, arrived in Napa in 1975 looking "for a cottage, a place to write, and a couple of acres to make a little wine." They become owners of a bit more than that—1,560 acres of the former Inglenook Estate, the 19th-century Niebaum residence, and 125 acres of vineyards.

"At first, I just wanted to make enough wine to drink and pretend I was my grandfather," says Coppola. "Even at that point, the idea of having your own wine, with your own label and your own family's name and your grandfather's picture on it, was enough."

Inglenook had been broken up in 1964 and sold to United Vintners. As the Coppolas learned more about the unique history of the estate, they were determined to one day reunite the individual parts (read that as an understanding of the brand holons and the brand ecology of Inglenook). Following the success of *Bram Stoker's Dracula* in 1995, the Coppolas bought the remaining parcels of land from Heublein, Inc. The purchase included the chateau, which Coppola started to restore to its early days of grandeur.

"What I wanted most was the heritage that makes the property unique . . . Heritage is everything. If you have the heritage, you can draw on it forever."

The grounds have been beautifully landscaped, the chateau restored, and the winery put into full production.

Two-and-a-half years of intensive work by many craftspeople is complete, with one of the most impressive additions being the sweeping staircase that greets you as you enter the chateau. The staircase design is by Dean Tavoularis, an architect and set designer for many Coppola films. Four master woodworkers labored for more than a year to create this exotic hardwood masterpiece made of black poisonwood, grenedillo, and jobillo imported from Belize where Coppola owns a resort.

Above the grand staircase is a large, stained-glass window that symbolically depicts the holonic reunification of this historic estate and the now intertwined traditions of two remarkable families.

Eunice Wait writes of the winery in 1889, "Among the many vineyards of the world, there are exceptional properties which have a worldwide reputation for perfection of their wines, and the Inglenook Vineyard of Rutherford, Napa County, can justly claim its place among the vineyards of California and will bear the same relation to them as Chateau Lafite, Chateau Y'quem, Clos Vougeot, and the Johannisberg Claus of Europe . . . ."[4]

The Coppola family has taken this world-class winery into the next era, preserving and restoring the relevance of the past and contextually adapting it for a new generation of customers today. The Niebaum-Coppola Estate continues on its journey to Brandscendence.

UBIQUITOUS MCDONALD'S

I admit to imprinting on McDonald's hamburgers and french fries at an early age, because we were living at the time in Deerfield, Illinois. Deerfield is just outside of Chicago where McDonald's was born. Going to McDonald's was an event, a treat—yes, even a ritual.

I don't eat McDonald's much now—unless I'm out of the country. After a week's worth of another culture's calories, I usually seek out something familiar—and nothing's more familiar in another country than a McDonald's restaurant. Just like the Ritz-Carlton, McDonald's works to maintain a strong familiarity to their restaurants. There are more and more exceptions: some are architectural adaptations to local themes, and others are changes in the menu such as serving wine in France or offering the McTeriyaki burger in Japan.

However, McDonald's does have an arsenal of impressive trade dress characteristics it works hard to build and protect.

Start with the *Mc* part of the name. There are a lot of *Mc* offerings on the menu, including the famous Big Mac sandwich. There is the image of the "golden arches" that is in the logo and in the architecture of the restaurants. Then there is the hamburger clown Ronald McDonald, which is also the name of its charity, Ronald McDonald House, which provides free housing for children staying in nearby hospitals. There's a Ronald McDonald house just down the road from where I live.

No detail is too small in outfitting a Ronald McDonald for duty. The *Wall Street Journal* reported that McDonald's ad agency, Leo Burnett, hired a Los Angeles stylist in 1999 to update the hamburger clown's wavy red hair—and then spent a while thinking about increasing the width of the red stripes on his socks.

"Many clowns covet the gig. 'To be a Ronald is a lifelong career,' says Janet Tucker, past president of the World Clown Association."[5]

Ambassador McDonald's

Many years ago, on a vacation to Switzerland, our friends brought their daughter along. We were staying in the central city of Interlaken, south of Zurich and west of Bern. Andrea wanted a McDonald's hamburger. She knew we were outside the United States but that there must be a McDonald's somewhere nearby, because this looked like a civilized country to the 12-year-old.

Unfortunately for us, the only hamburger joint in the immediate area was a place called the Brotli Bar. Andrea informed us that this was not McDonald's. We visited the Brotli Bar several times during our visit, because it was convenient to our hotel and relatively inexpensive. The adults were doing just fine with rosti (the delicious hash browns of the region) and veal sausages at other local establishments, thank you, but it took a trip to Bern, the capital of Switzerland, to slake Andrea's appetite for a McDonald's burger, fries, and milkshake.

As you would expect, the fare was the same as Andrea was used to ordering in the United States. That's the point. The same Quarter Pounders, the same Big Macs, the same trademark french fries. No matter where you are, the relationship with McDonald's is the same. And the restaurant was busy.

Several Swiss francs later, we were back on the train to Interlaken with Andrea smiling, content in the knowledge that she could now last the remaining day of skiing before landing in New York and heading for a McDonald's.

McDonald's is a uniquely American place that has popped up in a lot of places around the world—but not everywhere. When I travel, having access to a McDonald's is not a given. Not so for Andrea. She took it as an act of faith that there would be a McDonald's in any place worth going to. The company that Ray Kroc founded is managing to make Andrea's perception reality.

McDonald's Goes to Moscow

George Cohon orchestrated McDonald's entry into Moscow. The first store on Pushkin Square had a well-publicized opening with lines stretching around blocks and wrapping around on themselves. Cohon is the founder and senior chairman of McDonald's Canada and is rightfully proud of the Russian venture. I spoke to him in the mid-1990s to talk about his amazing journey to bring McDonald's to Russia. It is a story of good corporate citizenship and "overnight" success—after 12 years of negotiations initiated by Cohon.

The journey began during the 1976 Olympics in Montreal. McDonald's had donated a Big Mac bus to the Soviet team. Cohon stopped by for a visit and started a discussion with a Soviet official about food service for the Moscow Olympics in 1980. The 1980 Olympics was boycotted by Canada and the United States, so his early negotiations with the Moscow Olympic Organizing Committee weren't fruitful. But that didn't stop Cohon from thinking about Moscow.

1986 marked the year Cohon connected with the right people—the Moscow City Council—and asked for permission to open a McDonald's in their city. Two years later, he struck a joint venture deal in the spring of 1988. The Gorbachev government had dramatically improved the business climate for Cohon.

To open in Moscow required creating an entire national infrastructure to support just one store in Pushkin Square. Next, two more were opened, one in Gazetny Pereulok and one on Arbat Street. A food-processing plant would have to be created to make the raw foodstuffs that the restaurants would need. It's known as the McComplex.

Since 1990, there have been beef patties to make, bread to be baked, and catsup and mustard to be packaged at the 10,000-square meter Mc-Complex located in the Solntsevo Region of Moscow.

New strains of potatoes would be introduced to Soviet soil. The scrawny spuds to which Muscovites were accustomed would never do for the long, thin, trademark fries McDonald's serves up to its customers worldwide. Relevance and context were in full action. The core relevance of McDonald's was being protected in the back of the house with the con-textually adaptive introduction of and investment in the McComplex.

The Puskin Square restaurant opened on Wednesday, January 31, 1990, with a crew of 630, making it the largest McDonald's crew in the world. On average, the 2,200-square-metre Pushkin Square location serves over 40,000 customers a day, making it the busiest McDonald's in the world.

Diane Rinehart reports in her *Reader's Digest* article "Big Macs in Moscow"[6] that the team trying to get the first store up and running from the eighth floor of the Minsk headquarters began to think it would never happen. McComplex construction was halted for lack of sand and gravel. The lack of materials availability was remedied 10,000 miles away in California where Cohon was having dinner seated next to Yuri Dubrinin, the Soviet Ambassador to the United States. Cohon casually mentioned the sand and gravel to Dubrinin in table conversation that evening.

Three days later, when Cohon was back in Moscow, his Finnish con-struction manager called to tell him that trucks loaded with sand and gravel were lined up for blocks along the road leading to the McDonald's plant.

I interviewed George Cohon on his way to the airport by cell phone in December of 1993.[7] Here's what we talked about.

> KC: What have you learned about opening McDonald's in Russia that is transferable to the larger family of restaurants?
>
> Cohon: The ability of the Russian people to really excel has been proven: one of the Russian stores has been number one in sales worldwide four years after opening. The ability to go into a country and work with local people who have never worked in our system before—and we get phenomenal productivity from these Russian crews. I think that motivates Canadian employees when they hear about it, and I think that's good.
>
> KC: McComplex is introducing new ways of farming to Rus-sia. Can you tell me more about that?

Cohon: No question about it. I spoke to the Minister of Agriculture, and he was shocked with what we've been able to accomplish in growing, packaging, and shipping to the restaurants. We're helping change the entire way Russia thinks about food.

KC: I think the ripple effect you're creating beyond these stores is that you're introducing very basic agriculture and production techniques this country has been struggling with for years.

Cohon: Food generally has not been grown right, stored right, or transported right to get the most food on the table. We went all the way back into the system to get it all to work right. We went to a local farmer to buy the cucumbers that come back into our big McComplex to make pickles. We invited him in to see how it's done and he said, "Boy, if I had the equipment, and you taught me how to do it, I could do it back at my farm." We helped him get the equipment, and he's doing a wonderful job making all the pickles we need right now.

Staff turnover was also thought to be a concern when the venture first opened. It has not turned out to be an issue at all. The Moscow McDonald's venture employed many university graduates who wanted to experience western management techniques.

Bryan Moynahan reported on the staff in the *Sunday-Times Magazine,* published in Canada. "If I could take these crew people back to Toronto, I'd do it," says Geoff Nakamura, the Canadian responsible for training and development in the Moscow restaurants at the time. "They are easy to train. Staff turnover is much less than in Canada. There is little, if any, absenteeism. We started with 60 Western support staff. Now we're down to seven. That says it all."[8]

McDonald's also started working with the community from day one. Because, "Giving back to the community is a primary part of the corporate philosophy at McDonald's," the Moscow operation would not be an exception. Cohon was elected as the first non-Russian citizen to the board of directors of the International Association of Children's Funds, a Russian charity for children with illnesses, orphanages, and schools.

The Honorable Ella Pamfilova, Minister of Social Protection of the Russian Federation, said, "McDonald's personnel policy, community service programs, and participation in rehabilitation programs for disabled people show its deep and sincere concern for the people of Moscow. McDonald's is helping disabled children receive effective medical care that will enable them to take a more active part in the life of society." Read that as mutual benefit.

Stage Three in Action

Another almost unbelievable McDonald's mutual benefit story is closer to home for the American reader.

It took place in south-central Los Angeles at the time of the first Rodney King trial verdict. Four police officers had been declared innocent of beating motorist Rodney King. In the worst rioting in Los Angeles since the 1960s, the streets turned into scenes from the Middle East.

"Many inner city folks just felt the only response they could make was one of violence," said Harold Patrick, a McDonald's owner/operator. "And so there was extreme looting, burning, just total chaos." This quote and several others are from videotaped interviews that McDonald's did with owner/operators, or what you would call franchisees, after these riots.[9]

The community almost burned to the ground. Billions of dollars were lost as looters ransacked stores, then torched the empty buildings.

In a Los Angeles Channel 9 clip, the television camera panned across from a line of police officers to an intersection with a McDonald's on it: "We'll cross the street here on Western Boulevard and take a look at a McDonald's restaurant. The McDonald's at this intersection is about the only establishment yet to be vandalized."

Despite the heat of the moment, not 1 of 30 highly visible McDonald's stores in the area were touched—and that was no miracle.

The owner/operators say that involvement in their community spared their restaurants long before the verdict was delivered. "We are a part of the community," says Leighton Hull, "not as a business only, but as individual operators who actually care about the community."

The people who worked at the south Los Angeles McDonald's were local citizens, people who knew people in the community, not commuters. In many cases, so were the owners. People knew the owners. They weren't faceless.

In a *Time Magazine* article called "America's Hamburger Helper," Edwin Reingold writes:[10]

The $19-billion-a-year company has often been the target of those who disparage everything from its entry-level wage structure to the aesthetic blight of its cookie-cutter proliferation. But the Los Angeles experience was vindication of enlightened social policies begun more than three decades ago. The late Ray Kroc, a crusty but imaginative salesman who forged the chain in 1955, insisted that both franchise buyers and company executives get involved in community affairs. "If you're going to take money out of a community, give something back," said Kroc, "Its only good business."

As a result, McDonald's stands out not only as one of the more socially responsible companies in America but also as one of the nation's few truly effective social engineers. Both its franchise operators, who own 83 percent of all McDonald's restaurants, and company officials, who sit on boards of local and national minority service organizations, allow the company to claim that its total involvement in everything from the Urban League and the NAACP to the U.S. Hispanic Chamber of Commerce may constitute the biggest volunteer program of any business in the nation.

McDonald's has proven over the years that it is on the journey to Brandscendence at an interdependent s3 level. The brand has relevance with purpose—context that projects—and mutual benefit that is clearly s2 reciprocal, at times approaching an integrated s3 level. Wall Street has rediscovered the Northbrook, Illinois, company as the McDonald's brand continues to evolve. You can see an interdependent entity that is now not just a hamburger haven but a place to get a quick breakfast or a salad for lunch, with roots in the communities where it does business.

13

ENTERTAINMENT AND ENDURANCE

"Life can't be all bad when for ten dollars you can buy
all the Beethoven sonatas and listen to them for ten years."
WILLIAM F. BUCKLEY, JR.[1]

Executive summary. The global entertainment industry is a powerful force in shaping brand preferences and cultural expectations. The United States is a net exporter of entertainment offerings and culture worldwide. Film, music, or other amusements may originate anywhere on the planet to shape people's expectations. But, in the process of entertaining ourselves, the vast majority of entertainment customers must suspend disbelief from their own experiences to embrace the feast put in front of them by a global entertainment industry. We really can't have what we see, but we suspend disbelief to immerse ourselves in the dream.

This chapter also explores the powerful role that product placement can have in the quest to achieve Brandscendence.

GLOBAL BARBIE

I read not too long ago that Mattel has been producing Barbie dolls in Japan with special features for that market, such as black hair and fashions that reflected Japanese culture. Then they did some global market research.

The target customer, girls, don't care if Barbie looks like them. The original blonde haired and blue eyed Barbie is a playtime hit world-wide.

"It's all about fantasies and hair," says Peter Broegger, general manager of Mattel's Asian operations. "Blonde Barbie sells just as well in Asia as in the United States."[2]

I suspect that in exporting U.S. film properties, television programs, and videogames all over the world, we have created the "Barbie effect." A single version of Barbie works because she is a reflection of the single global archetype we have exported in entertainment media that over-arches race and culture.

Whether you find this interesting or disturbing, the implications are practical. If you can tap into the archetypes being exported in media, you can leverage an emerging global culture. If you create global archetypes, you can engineer consent for what you're doing, selling, or orchestrating.

Entertainment brands represent a big chunk of change in the global economy. We all need our distractions after doing our part to make a living and gladly turn over a percentage of our wallets to be entertained and inspired. We briefly disconnect from our own reality to immerse ourselves in an artificially constructed experience. We suspend disbelief to become part of the entertainment's construct, whether it be in the movie theater, on television, or on a stage created just for showcasing the brands that you want to pay for in the middle of Florida.

ENDURANCE LITMUS TEST: ENTERTAINMENT BRAND PLACEMENTS

For a great perspective on branding in the entertainment world, I engaged in an e-dialog with Tom Tardio, President of Rogers & Cowan—a product placement company located in the heart of a global entertainment exportplex, Los Angeles.[3] Product placement is a great place to talk about brands with enduring relevance, because as Tom will point out, they're the only ones that are durable enough for the cinema or television.

KC: Tom, what is the role of the entertainment industry in creating brands and helping brands evolve?

Tardio: Brands use entertainment content (films, TV shows, music, sports sponsorships, events) to build or expand the brand's emotional reach and attachment to its consumer. This is often called the E-Factor. A brand can borrow the entertainment equity that exists in a blockbuster film, highly rated TV show, or popular recording artist and reinforce in its target audience the key personality traits that coexist within the brand and within the entertainment content.

Through association, or entertainment tie-ins, a brand can expand its target audience without disengaging from its core, loyal franchise follower. Entertainment content can also amplify the product attributes of a brand. A perfect example of this is the use of a branded product in a film by a celebrity.

This is best illustrated by the car manufacturers, who use a film to showcase not only the beauty but also the high performance of an auto.

There has been a significant increase since 2000 of the number and types of consumer brands that have engaged in entertainment tie-ins. This is primarily the direct result of the drop-off in readership and viewership in certain young target audiences. The Internet and video games occupy their lifestyle.

Most entertainment content skews to younger audiences, and most brands view entertainment properties as the only vehicle that engages this fickle, fragmented, and brand-disloyal group of buyers with rather large purchasing power. Brands effectively use entertainment content as nonevasive and noncommercial exposures to this audience. However, it must be a natural fit, or the damage in reputation will be excessive to this audience. More importantly, a lot of entertainment content is internationally delivered and accepted. A blockbuster film or rising pop star can be the most common connection to a brand, as it's strategy is applied from one language and country to another. Wherever the pop star is popular, the visuals and messages are commonly received among the target audience.

No other vehicle is as widely available for Coca Cola, Nike, or BMW that can consistently deliver their message. Currently, brand managers are digging deeper and deeper into delivering their message through content, to the point where they are seeking to embed their message in the actual TV show.

This is known as immersive or embedded content and has evolved from the *American Idol* craze to a standard formula for many shows and brands to collaborate on. The application of advertising dollars to embedded content dollars guarantees that the audience will see the message. It also threatens the standard 30-second and 60-second advertising commercial.

KC: Can you distinguish between fads and enduring brands in the product placement world? What do you do differently for enduring brands?

Tardio: Due to the production-to-distribution cycle time for a film, sometimes in excess of 14 months, *fads* are not viable candidates for product placement. However, the shorter cycle time for a TV show or a music video does lend itself to the exploitation of a new product introduction, whether it is a fad or not. The most significant challenge to the placement of a fad-product/brand is that the producer of the entertainment property must feel confident that such introduction will be true to the storyline or theme. It has to be a natural fit, or the viewing audience will notice the disconnect. Inexperienced brand managers are unaware of how protective producers are of their creative elements, and they will not allow exploitation of a product that would damage the credibility and ultimately the success of their content.

In the end, the best use of a product placement is for the brand that has shown an enduring quality and presence. If such brand is a natural fit to the visuals or storyline or script that are created by a producer of a film, TV shows, or music video, then the brand plays an organic role or presence to the viewing audience.

KC: Have you ever thought about or actually performed placement of noncommercial goods or services (nonprofit, religious, government, nongovernmental organizations) into entertainment vehicles?

Tardio: When you don't have a real product, bottled or boxed, then there are serious limitations as to the quantity of placements that can be achieved.

It takes a tremendously creative placement professional to look beyond the script and attempt to create and recommend to the producer the inclusion of a brand through posters, props, or verbal references.

A perfect example is the beautiful posters that exist for certain leisure destinations such as the islands of the Bahamas. The art, or sometimes even the ad campaign visuals, can be displayed on buses, billboards, table-top tents, or part of the background setting inside a travel bureau.

Government programs that have well-recognized logos or characters, such as the Red Cross, U.S. Army (recruitment), or Smoky the Bear forest fire prevention posters are the few that can effectively take advantage of product placement.

Verbal references are seldom achieved unless specifically scripted.

KC: What are your general thoughts about the role of brands in driving business strategy today?

Tardio: The general drop off in demand for products as a result of the overall slowdown in our economy has had a tremendous impact on brand strategy and thus on the role that the brand can have in driving business strategy. Although there are fewer new product introductions challenging the position of a brand, the consumer spending patterns; discounting in the marketplace; and reductions in corporate advertising, promotions, and publicity budgets have resulted in the most challenging period in recent times for brand strategists.

It is tougher to stay true to the brand blueprint when the home office is pushing hard to move more product off shelves and reach strong bottom lines. Old formulas to increase brand awareness are not working well. Fresh strategies are a struggle to introduce in fiscally challenging times and by risk-averse brand managers.

Depending on the product and depending on the demographic, the power of the brand can rise above the challenging landscape by creatively adjusting to changing buying patterns. This is a challenge for many companies, because their management's unwillingness to explore alternative strategies seriously impacts their ability to evolve to a new level. It is important during this adjustment to stay true to the core values that the brand stands for over its history.

KC: What about your own brand—in what ways has Rogers & Cowan changed, and in what fundamental ways has it remained consistent?

Tardio: Rogers & Cowan is a brand in the service business that has been around for more than 50 years. In an industry that has seen numerous acquisitions and mergers that have resulted in a consolidation of quality brands, most of the entrepreneurial individuals that built their brands and had their names on the doors have disappeared. Roger & Cowan has survived because of staying true to four values.

The first two are quality and reliability in service. The agency must deliver the best counsel and results and must do it consistently and dependably over time. These values protect the reputation of the firm and, in a competitive environment, are the price of admission.

The third value is innovation, which is a brand differentiator and allows the brand to set the bar higher for competitors attempting to challenge our leadership position. Innovation means constantly evaluating the changing needs of clients and of the staff.

The fourth value is passion. This is where Rogers and Cowan has changed the most. We recruit and keep the people who are the most energetic and passionate about the company's mission. This is what wins business and keeps employees at the firm. This is the brand emotion that can be the glue through difficult and challenging assignments and times.

Thanks, Tom.

BREAKING THE RULES: REMARKABLE BOSE

Do you know about or own a Bose Wave radio?

This entertainment device was introduced in the market in 1993 as a radio only; then a model followed that integrated a top-loading CD player. The radio-only system was priced in 1993 at $349, and the system with the CD player was originally priced at $499. A decade later, they are the same price.

There's a lot of talk in consumer and entertainment electronics about the commoditization of products, driving profit out of the category. So what's going on at Bose that allows them to hold on to the same price point for ten years—for a radio?

The Bose brand is all about innovation. They do a lot of research in acoustics, funded by reinvesting *all of their profits* back into the company.[4] That's strategic commitment you don't find in every commercial enterprise.

But the Bose style of innovation doesn't lead to fads. The Bose Wave radio is essentially unchanged from its introduction, giving it enduring relevance as a product that sends deposits of goodwill back to the parent company. Using what Bose calls "waveguide" technology not found in comparable systems, this radio is innovation done right the first time. The industrial design is stable and recognizable.

However, as Bob Klein points out in a newsletter from Applied Marketing Sciences, Bose has "refused to play the specifications game."[5]

"The company claims that the ability to produce remarkably rich, lifelike sound from such a small enclosure is what separates the Bose Wave radio from other radios. But don't go looking for specifications like power output in watts or frequency response—that information is not available.

"The people at Bose understand that what is really important is how their radio sounds. And so they refuse to release the technical specifications and that forces customers to listen with their own ears, rather than compare watts and decibels and dollars on a chart."

Whether you see the Bose Wave radio on a television ad, an offer in a credit card mailing, a mail order catalog, or walk into a Bose store, the product is the same and the price is the same. That's really unusual pricing discipline coupled with strong distribution management practices, rivaled in the home electronics industry only by the prestigious Bang & Olufsen brand of Denmark. Bose has held the core relevance of the Wave radio stable while branching out to new market contexts with operations in the United States, Europe, Canada, Australia, Asia, and South America.

Bose, founded in 1964 by Dr. Amar Bose, a former professor of electrical engineering at MIT, knows itself and its customers very well—and is very much on the journey to Brandscendence.

14

BECOMING THE CATEGORY

"Success is a journey, not a destination."
BEN SWEETLAND[1]

Executive summary. What do Q-tips, Kleenex, and Aspirin have in common? They are all such successful brands, they have become synonymous with the category. It is a powerful blessing to be this well known—and a nightmare for the intellectual property attorneys. This chapter will show the great advantages of approaching this category ownership boundary and the pitfalls of stepping over it.

Q-TIPS

Leo Gerstenzang invented the cotton swab, which we know today as the Q-tips brand, in 1923. He observed Mrs. Gestenzang cleaning the ears of their baby with a bit of cotton on a toothpick at bedtime and decided something more durable and safe was needed. The Leo Gerstenzang Infant Novelty Company was founded the same year to market baby care accessories, including the new cotton swabs called Baby Gays.

In 1926, the package labels were changed to Q-tips Baby Gays. *Q* for quality and *Baby Gays* for who knows what. During the late 1920s, the

Baby Gays part of the name was dropped, and the product continued on as just Q-tips.

KLEENEX

A year after Leo Gerstenzang invented Q-tips, June 12, 1924, was the date that the facial tissue category was invented and introduced as the Kleenex brand. In the United States, if you want a soft paper tissue, you ask for a Kleenex. In Germany, you'd ask for a Tempo. In both cases, the brand name has become the generic reference for the product category.

Kleenex is a registered trademark of Kimberly-Clark Worldwide, Inc. Since Kleenex created the category, the brand name quickly took over in common usage to describe these new paper tissues.

Kleenex was originally introduced as a superior way to remove cold cream, a "cleansing tissue," but the product gained elasticity on its own as consumers started to use it as a disposable handkerchief during the 1930s.

ASPIRIN

The Bayer AG product, Aspirin, is a registered trademark in over 80 countries around the world, including Bayer's home country of Germany. In the United States, aspirin has become a generic category name.

Dr. Felix Hoffman worked for Bayer and, in 1897, synthesized acetylsalicylic acid as a remedy for his father, who suffered from rheumatoid arthritis. The predecessor was salicylic acid. It was taken for fever, pain, and reduction of inflammation but was poorly tolerated by patients. The new acetylsalicylic acid was both effective and much better tolerated in clinical trials. In 1899, the new acetylsalicylic acid product was launched in Germany under the trademark Aspirin.[2]

Molly Wade McGrath, in her book *Topsellers USA*, offers this story as part of aspirin's journey to becoming generic in the United States.

A month after the 1918 armistice (WWI), the government offered the Bayer stocks for sale at public auction. To the highest American bid would go a large plant, a relatively little known product called *Aspirin,* a substantial number of physician's drugs, and a line of dyestuffs.[3]

Evidently, this plant was making the Bayer acetylsalicylic acid product, and the new owners would continue using the Aspirin name. But, without trademark protection and enforcement, aspirin would become the name for the category in the United States.

STYROFOAM

What we refer to as styrofoam cups in everyday conversations is actually a rezgistered trademark of Dow Chemical Company. The real generic name of the product is foamed polystyrene. But that's not what we say.

Even Webster's Dictionary states: "Styrofoam, *Trademark*. A brand of expanded plastic made from polystyrene."[4]

Dow introduced Styrofoam as a trademarked form of polystyrene foam insulation in 1954. Back in 1839, German druggist Eduard Simon discovered polystyrene as a substance isolated from natural resins, and organic chemist Hermann Staudinger built on this work and published his theories on plastic polymers in 1922. By 1930, BASF developed a way to commercially manufacture polystyrene, and in 1937, Dow Chemical introduced polystyrene to the U.S. market.[5]

Dow seems to turn a blind eye to the everyday use of the word styrofoam, but the company clearly leverages it as an authentic material in building insulation, craft, and floral arrangement applications. In these instances, Dow refers to "STYROFOAM Brand Foam" for the craft and floral uses, and "STYROFOAM extruded polystyrene insulation" for the insulation products.

When you go to Dow's Web site about Styrofoam as a trademark, here is what they say:[6]

STYROFOAM® is a registered trademark of the Dow Chemical Company for its distinctive Blue® insulation product used primarily in the construction industry. It is not used in the manufacture of disposable foam products, such as food packaging, cups, plates, coolers, or egg trays. These disposable products are made of either molded expanded polystyrene beads or a thin extruded polystyrene sheet, neither of which are manufactured by Dow in the United States.

So, the next time you get a cup of java to go, remember, you can't drink coffee from a STYROFOAM cup—because there is no such thing!

The "official" position Dow has taken is with a healthy wink, because the use of the word *styrofoam* in everyday discourse helps Dow in the specific instances where it does bring products to market.

LEVERAGING THE TREND

Tim Triplett, in *Market News,* writes, "Generic fear to Xerox is brand equity to FedEx."[7] There you are, the two basic reactions you can have when society takes your trademark and uses it in new ways. As we discovered with SPAM—defend your turf (Xerox) or go with the flow (FedEx). You choose.

Triplett writes:

> Letters from lawyers rarely contain good news. True to form was the form letter I received several years ago, castigating me for using the word *xerox* in an article.
>
> The word was part of a quote as I recall, but I should have known better. There is no such verb as *xerox.* Documents are not xeroxed; they are copied.
>
> Companies have to protect their brand names, and those letters from attorneys are one way to assure that a brand name doesn't degenerate into a generic term.

Triplett goes on to describe Federal Express embracing the customer-conjured FedEx, as we discussed in Chapter 8, "What's in a Name?." In the case of FedEx, they're leveraging the participatory energy of the customer to boost their brand equity.

TRADEMARK/GENERIC HALL OF FAME

The English language contains lots of examples of a brand name becoming the category. Some even take on a second meaning or a crossover cultural idea. If you can't find a capitalized word in the dictionary, you can be sure the trademark word has crossed over into common use in the language to describe the category.

Here is an incomplete list of trademark names that have crossed over, with some hall of fame candidates that also have a second meaning.

Brand Names	Category	Cross-over cultural idea
Aspirin	acetylsalicylic acid	
Astro-Turf	artificial grass	
Band-Aid	sterile adhesive bandage	stop-gap measure
Crayola	colored wax pencils	
Dumpster	large trash receptacle	getting rid of a bad idea
FedEx	overnight delivery service	
Formica	plastic laminate surface	
Hallmark card	greeting card	
Hoover	vacuum cleaner	rapid eating
Jello	gelatin desert product	state or consistency
Kitty Litter	disposable pet litter	
Kleenex	disposable paper tissue	
Laundromat	self-service washing store	
Levi's	blue jeans	
Life Saver	hard candy	
Mace	non-lethal tear gas	
Nike	sport/tennis shoes	
Plexiglas	thermoplastic polymer	
Popcicle	frozen confection on a stick	
Realtor	real estate agent or firm	
Scotch Tape	clear adhesive tape	
SOS pad	steel wool with embedded soap	
Styrofoam	foamed polystyrene	
Tabasco	hot sauce	
Thermos	vacuum bottle	
TV Guide	television listing periodical	
Walkman	portable music playback	
Vaseline	petroleum jelly	
Velcro	fastening tape	

WHAT TO DO AS YOU APPROACH BEING "KING OF THE CATEGORY"

Is being the category desirable? Yes and no.

Yes, because you're the king of all brands in the category . . .

. . . and no, because you've potentially lost your unique, differentiating brand name in the marketplace, because everyone refers to your brand name as the generic category name.

What to do? There are several tools at your disposal to leverage this situation.

First, use graphic and industrial design. What you've lost in language, you can differentiate and own visually.

Also, leverage the parent company brand.

It's not just a walkman—it's a Sony Walkman with Sony industrial design. It's not just a band-aid—it's the trusted Johnson & Johnson Band-Aid with the J&J trade dress. It's not just scotch tape—it's the authentic Scotch brand tape from 3M with the distinctive Scotch plaid trade dress.

These are brands we know and use every day. But what of the unseen brands that drive the economy just out of sight? Next, our journey takes us into business-to-business commerce and the world of B2B brands.

15

BUSINESS-TO-BUSINESS BRANDS

"A great society is a society in which men of
business think greatly of their functions."
ALFRED NORTH WHITEHEAD[1]

Executive summary. You might think that brand building is only for "consumer brands." This chapter dispels that notion right away with three dynamo brands: Square D, Caterpillar, and Bechtel. They understand the power of branding in a business-to-business (B2B) setting. Square D and Bechtel have demonstrated it for over 100 years each, and Caterpillar is not far behind with 75 years under its belt. This chapter also introduces a business-to-business brand you may have wondered about as you drive around the United States—please let me introduce you to Fuelman.

B2B

There's a lot on the books about what the dot-com people called B2C, or business-to-consumer brands. There's much less documentation about the brands that drive the infrastructure of the planet—the B2B, or business-to-business brands. These brands are the backbone of the global economy.

Names like IBM, General Electric, Cisco, JP Morgan, Accenture, Archer Daniels Midland (ADM), Borg-Warner, Caterpillar, Applied Materials, Solectron, Flextronics International, Honeywell, United Technologies, and Goldman Sachs are all U.S. examples of strong business-to-business brands. Examples of B2B brands outside the United States include names such as Siemens of Germany, Mitsubishi of Japan, Matsushita of Japan, LG of Korea, Samsung of Korea, and Swiss Re of Switzerland (reinsurance).

Here's a 100-year old brand you may never have heard of: Square D.

If you have a circuit breaker box in your home, you have Square D to thank, regardless of the brand you have installed. It is in the business of protecting people's lives in the process of efficiently distributing, managing, and controlling electricity.

"Very few brands that have been around for 100 years can claim that they meet the same essential needs of society as when they began," says Chris Richardson, president and CEO of the North American Division of Schneider Electric. The Square D brand is the leading face of Schneider Electric in the United States, with Schneider world headquarters located in Paris.[2]

Square D started as McBride Manufacturing Company in Detroit. In 1915, the Detroit Fuse and Manufacturing Company began marketing a new sheet metal version of its cast iron enclosed safety switch. The cover of the new sheet metal product had an embossed *D* (for Detroit) in a square border, and customers quickly started asking for the "Square D" switch. Just like the customer-driven Federal Express name change to FedEx that we discussed earlier, the firm changed its name to Square D Company in 1917.

In a press release marking the 100th anniversary of the company, Robert P. Fiorani, vice president of communication for the North American division, says:

> In brand studies conducted over more than four decades, the SQUARE D trademark continues to be among the most recognizable brands of its kind.
>
> The North American brand strength of SQUARE D was an asset that Schneider Electric prized when the two companies merged in 1991, and it continues even stronger today. Whenever end users, contractor, builders, or engineers make a choice

among electrical brands, SQUARE D comes to mind as a preferred brand. We continue working to enhance the perception of the SQUARE D brand and Schneider Electric as the most focused, customer-oriented provider of electrical distribution, control, and automation solutions in North America and wherever our multinational customers may be operating.

My only advice for this overall success story: if the Square D brand is so strong, why not leverage it for the entire $8.7 billion dollar business instead of just the $2.7 billion North American revenues? Remember Bank of America? Square D is so much more memorable than Schneider Electric—I suggest they consider changing the global enterprise name to the flagship brand name to increase sales, trust, and market capitalization. Just a thought.

UNIQUE ASPECTS OF B2B BRANDS

Business-to-business brands appeal to a specific customer set not visible to the general public. They have strong followings and relevance in their respective categories, but they don't necessarily take out newspaper ads, sponsor high-impact sporting or cultural events, or appear on television. They more likely show up in industry trade magazines, in direct mailings to the customers, and through a captive sales force or strong partner distribution network.

Companies such as Borg-Warner aren't on the lips of the men and women at large, but talk to someone in the automobile industry, and they'll surely know this vital supplier. Swiss Re is a reinsurance company that's only known to other insurance companies, because insuring insurance concerns is a world away from daily business transactions but is pivotal in the world of insurers. In each instance, the industry provides context for the brand.

The Fuelman brand is one you've likely seen at a truck stop or large gasoline station. You've seen the brand identity on signs at these fueling stations—an anthropomorphic gas pump that stands at the ready to fuel commercial vehicles and equipment. It's not a brand you'd likely use, unless you're a business or nonprofit organization with trucks, or a state or local government. So what is Fuelman?[3] It's a U.S. network of commercial fueling locations that provides customers with reports of all purchase transactions on a weekly and monthly basis. It saves customers time and expense and works like an ATM card—with a few added features.

When employees purchase fuel or services with a Fuelman card, they enter a PIN code and the vehicle's odometer reading. This provides enough information so all purchases are consolidated onto one statement. The Fuelman network statements show consumption patterns that identify potential fraud, thus protecting the customer from fuel theft and credit card abuse.

Commercial fuel goes into commercial equipment. Let's take a look at one of the next brand macroholons up this B2B value chain.

MOVING THE EARTH

Here's a brand I bet you know without having done business with the company: Caterpillar. You've likely seen the distinctive bright yellow heavy equipment building a road or at a construction site.

Caterpillar is a $20.15 billion business with more than half of the revenue coming from outside the United States. The company is the world's leading manufacturer of construction and mining equipment, diesel and natural gas engines, and industrial gas turbines. The company is over 75 years old and manufactures today in 50 U.S. locations and in 65 other locations around the world.[4]

What sets "Cat" apart from the competition is:

- *Relevance.* A customer support system and logistics network that is unparalleled in the heavy equipment industry. You keep customers up and running in industries that can't afford an idle day.
- *Context.* A network of dealers in more than 200 countries and rental services through more than 1,200 outlets worldwide. This "glocal" set of resources and relationships—global resources, local relationships—is a powerful combination for Caterpillar.
- *Mutual benefit.* From the Caterpillar Web site: "Named to the Dow Jones Sustainability World Index in September 2002, Caterpillar is recognized for successful integration of long-term economic, environmental, and social aspects into business strategies that benefit all stakeholders. Caterpillar's commitment to social responsibility ensures our ability to meet today's needs without sacrificing the ability to meet the needs of future generations."

If Cat makes the tools that help move the earth, then let's again take a look at one of the next brand macroholons up the chain, a global company that builds with big construction tools like the ones Caterpillar makes.

BUILDING THE WORLD

In 1898, Warren Bechtel was grading railroad beds with a mule-drawn scraper in the Oklahoma Territory. My grandfather, S.A. Clark, was not far behind as a track foreman for the Santa Fe railroad. My dad and his sister lived in the track foreman's residential railroad car and got a good portion of their early education in one-room schoolhouses on the Oklahoma prairie. As the track moved forward, so would the school—an interesting way to grow up.

Well, what Warren Bechtel started in Oklahoma has also grown up to become a global, still privately held, enterprise that has completed over 20,000 projects in 140 nations.[5]

Bechtel not only does construction; it manages projects that themselves become brands and national symbols for the organizations that fund them. Bechtel's projects over the years include:

- Helping put together the Six Companies consortium that built the Hoover Dam in the United States (1931)
- Trans-Arabian pipeline project (1950s)
- Jubail industrial complex in Saudi Arabia
- St. James hydroelectric plans in Quebec, Canada
- Northern California's BART rapid transit system

Bechtel currently has 44,000 employees in 60 countries and 50 offices around the world. Here are a few notable statistics that give you an idea of the scale of this business-to-business brand and what it has built since 1898.

- 85,000 kilometers (km) of pipelines
- 27,300 km of highways
- 21,500 km of fiber optic cable and 11,000 cell sites
- 20,000 km of wastewater networks
- 9,500 km of railroads
- 3,000 km of aqueducts
- 365 fossil-fueled power plant units and 150 nuclear generating units
- 250 new wastewater treatment facilities and 106 new water treatment works
- 105 dams, 300 dikes, and 400 service reservoirs
- 80 ports and harbors and 80 airports and airport systems
- 30 metropolitan rapid transit systems
- 25 new towns

"We can build anything, anytime, anywhere," said Stephen Bechtel, who took over the company in 1933 after the death of his father. He pioneered the concept of the turnkey project and vastly expanded the portfolio of projects the company would take on through the 1960s.

Bechtel describes itself as a "can do" company—which seems to sum up what the Bechtel brand has been doing for the last millennium. It is relevant as a large construction project contractor and shows s3 purpose in everything it does. It has proven that it understands context and goes beyond mere adaptation—it demonstrates and ability to project itself as a B2B brand wherever it does business around the world.

Bechtel gets selected as a trusted partner for these immense projects, because it operates in a way that is mutually beneficial at an integrated s3 level. It leaves a residue of goodwill behind in every place the company does business, leaving the borders open for future business across countries, cultures, and time.

Chapter Glossary

anthropomorphic, *adj.* **1.** ascribing human form or attributes to a being or thing not human, esp. to a deity. **2.** resembling or made to resemble a human form: *an anthropomorphic carving.*[6]

THE NEXT STAGE

What, on the technology and social frontiers, will drive relevance, context, and mutual benefit in the future? What can we do to move past stage three Brandscendence to stage four and beyond? Some of the answers for the journey ahead are outlined in BrandNext.™ Branding is also emerging as a useful discipline for the nonprofit and nongovernmental organization (NGO) world and can be applied to a unit of one—you.

16

BRANDNEXT™

"Integrity has no need of rules."
ALBERT CAMUS[1]

Executive summary. Brand strategy holds the power to redefine organizational strategy at large. It can focus resources and select valuable customers by being relevant. It can create a high performance culture that adapts to shifting context or projects and creates the context to which others must respond in the marketplace. Branding must lead in the creation of mutual benefit that drives more value for all the players in the brand ecosystem. This chapter will explore harnessing the energy of change, understanding the technologies that will transform and enhance branding, and looking beyond stage three interdependence to integral brand practice.

THE FUTURE OF RELEVANCE: PRODUCTS ARE SOLIDS, CUSTOMERS ARE LIQUIDS

"Products Are Solids, Customers Are Liquids" is the evolution of a keynote presentation I developed in 1997 for a New Directions for News Conference in Los Angeles, California.[2]

After delivering this presentation several times, I received an evaluation card from one of the people in the audience saying, "It was a life-changing event." She took the time to hand to it me personally and told me she would never look at product development and service planning the same way again. Well, given that kind of feedback, we can't go without sharing this idea with you.

Here's the basic idea behind staying relevant over time.

There are three primary focus areas that can be affected by the energy of change:

1. Customers
2. Products/services (offerings)
3. Organizations that provide them

Each can be in one of three states, depending on the energy of change driving them. They can be:

1. Solid
2. Liquid
3. Gaseous

Here is what this looks like when laid out as a grid.

	Customers	Products/Services	Organizations
Gas			
Liquid		*(States based on the energy of change.)*	
Solid			

At each intersection, there is a potential outcome implied by the energy of change (a dimension of context) when applied to customers, the stuff they buy, and the organizations that produce and deliver products and services.

Too little energy, and the whole system starts to wind down.

		Solid	
	Customers	Products/Services	Organizations
Gas			
Liquid			
Solid	stagnating	unchanging	dissipating

Without harnessing the energy of change, the customers are stagnant, the offerings don't change, and the energy of the organization dissipates. You can think of "buggy whip" stories over the years, where the customers disappear because the need for the offering goes away, along with the company that didn't change enough to remain relevant.

If you think about it, a buggy whip manufacturer was in the business of making the horse go. If the horse was replaced by the engine, the buggy whip company would need to adapt to make the pedals and throttles that would make the new forms of transportation go.

		Liquid	
	Customers	**Products/Services**	**Organizations**
Gas			
Liquid	*grows/learns*	*changes/evolves*	*adapts/survives*
Solid	*stagnating*	*unchanging*	*dissipating*

You'd want customers that grow and learn; your offerings to change and evolve; and your organization to adapt, survive, and succeed. The liquid state is the ideal state for competent responses to change.

The gas state is achieved when the energy of change is just too much for the organization to absorb or direct in useful ways. Rather than evolution, the organization suffers from revolution in the marketplace and disappears, because the fitness landscape has changed so radically, the organization can't survive.

		Gas	
	Customers	**Products/Services**	**Organizations**
Gas	gone	gone	gone
	(fad/burn out)	(ahead of its time)	(revolution)
Liquid	grows/learns	changes/evolves	adapts/survives
Solid	stagnating	unchanging	dissipating

Similarly, the customers invest themselves in fads and burn out on the category, rendering the products and services for these flighty customers, at worst, cinders from a hot fire or, at best, simply ahead of their time.

As a brand steward, I watch our team at work agonize to listen in a variety of ways to get the specifications right in our personal computer offerings. At some point, you have to "freeze the specs" to manufacture something for the physical world. We encourage an adaptive culture that can simultaneously listen to the outside world while also having the discipline to periodically "get solid," to make tangible products without lots of costly midcourse corrections.

An implication of the solid-liquid-gas model is that enduring brands adopt the liquid state to remain relevant across the customer-offering-organization continuum. Be a liquid and move with the fractal flows of tastes and temperaments of the marketplace, while still being true to your brand's core relevance.

CONTEXT ON STEROIDS: RFID

Parts of the future are here today, depending on where you are on the planet. You just have to know where to look.

For instance, your brand is about to go into broadcasting.

Several years before the dot-com meltdown, I was delivering a speech to a marketing crowd at a convention called Internet World. I told them that, for all the money going into porting stores into cyber-space, bringing the Internet into stores was going to be a more transfor-mational shopping experience. For example, there would be end-cap displays with Internet connections to the items on the shelves of that aisle. These shelves can tell you about the products sitting on them.

Thanks to an initiative by Wal-Mart, this idea is about to become real in the United States at a product level by 2005. Using radio frequency identification (RFID), the same technology the Defense Department uses to track 400,000 items, Bentonville (the Arkansas headquarters of Wal-Mart) is about to mandate radio-tagging all of its merchandise com-ing in from suppliers.

"On November 4, Wal-Mart's top 100 suppliers are convening near Bentonville, Arkansas, for what amounts to a United Nations of retail," reported *Fortune* magazine in the November 10, 2003, issue.[3] "Imagine strolling into Wal-Mart to buy the new DVD of *The Matrix*. As you take it off the shelf, a radio signal alerts an employee to restock, telling him where in the backroom to find *The Matrix* and giving a warning ping if he mistakenly slides it onto the *Legally Blonde* shelf. Meanwhile, forget going through the checkout line: an electronic reader scans the items in your cart and automatically charges your debit card."

The leading German retailer *Metro* is already showcasing a store of the future with LCD-panel equipped shopping carts that can sense RFID-tagged items in the store. Your brand has just gone into broad-casting.

RFID-tagged merchandise will be able to self-describe itself to you. If you're standing in front of a Maytag dishwasher in the store and want more information about it, pull out your radio-enabled handheld computer or personal digital assistant (PDA). You'll pick up the manufacturer and model number from the RFID tag on the dishwasher, then connect directly to the Maytag Web site for that product, using either the store's 802.11 wireless network or your wide area network (WAN) subscription account from your cellular telephone company.

The screen on your PDA or the LCD panel on your shopping cart will tell you everything you want to know about the item you're thinking about buying.

The manufacturer can also give you an incentive to buy on the spot just for visiting the Web site. Actmedia, now Newscorp America Marketing, invented The Instant Coupon Machine—you know, the red boxes in the stores that spout coupons in front of the merchandise. When this was deployed, it changed the role of coupons. It went from redemption in days or weeks by clipping newspaper and magazine coupons to redemption in minutes inside the store. It also changed coupons from being a purely below-the-line discounting incentive to being an incentive to try something new or to impulsively switch brands on the spot.

The RFID-tagged product cannot only produce an incentive on the spot, it can customize the offer based on context. How many do we have in inventory in this store? Provide a discount at either end of the supply curve: too many, provide a discount to move the merchandise; none in stock, provide a discount to have the customer wait for delivery to prevent brand switching based on availability. Don't want to play the price game? You can also extend the warranty or change other terms and conditions of the sale.

WIRELESS WANDERLUST AND THE ROLE OF BRANDS

In a few short years, many more wireless marketing and branding practices than just RFID will be an integral part of the customer experience—from awareness, consideration, purchase, ownership, upgrade, service, and support.[4]

Wirelessly connected customers are potentially more impulsive. The volume and variety of opportunities that the customer opts into for a variety of devices, from cell phones to PDAs to notebook computers, may increase the likelihood of impulse purchases. These buying decisions will take place in the stores, on the street, and in your hand.

The role of brand is in the "opt in" part. Only the brands you know and trust will gain your permission to present information and offers to you on your wireless personal devices. The ubiquitous/anonymous nature of the Web gets personal again with brands that will want to connect with you 24/7. Be careful: "Bluejacking" is already beginning to emerge—bluetooth-wireless-enabled personal area network wireless connections that can steal your personal information at the time of transaction. The personal/convenient continuum is a tricky slope.

Wireless marketing techniques also may change the nature of the customer's perceptions of time. Expectations accelerate as customer choices increase and demands are quickly met. Customers will easily become accustomed to faster speeds throughout the processes of access, buying, and delivery.

Choices become more "time-place based," retrieving the notion of shopping in a store. PCs connected to the Internet today do not have a sense of place—place is irrelevant to globally networked devices.

With the addition of cellular and global positioning satellite (GPS) technologies, place becomes relevant again. The specific opportunities in a time and place for a consumer become more like the physical shopping mall than the global, Web-based business-to-consumer (B2C) or just-in-time practices of business-to-business (B2B) transactions.

Wireless technologies not only provide more global communications opportunities, but they also do the reverse: geographically local and immediate opportunities for individuals and businesses.

This means: "What do I need now?" (individual or organization)

This means: "Where is it closest?" (physical space)

This means: "When is it available?" (timing of transaction)

The networked nature of wireless connections trades these considerations of immediacy with the overall cost of the transaction. Perhaps the lowest-cost offering is close and available, or not. The choice is in the hands of the user.

Wireless marketing then potentially introduces the paradox of being convenient while also providing so many choices that buying becomes complicated for the consumer. Again at this point, brands assert themselves as the trusted intermediaries for people and larger organizational entities. Brands have the ability to cut through complexity for customers with value propositions that can create trust over time.

Wireless WAN networks will also be the infrastructure of choice for the developing world. It's expensive to string wires or lay fiber optic cable—so voice and data in emerging economies and the third world will be decidedly wireless. This means that every marketing practice used in wired economies will be adapted to wireless in these emerging markets.

The key change in billing practices that will make a big difference in WAN networks is placing the burden of inbound calls on the caller, not the wireless subscriber. When you answer your cell phone today in North America and in most other parts of the world, you pay to connect with the caller. If this burden shifted to the caller (voice) or sender (data), then wireless telemarketing becomes possible. It's impossible without this change.

The network or the handset will have a filter that immediately lets in numbers the customer has programmed to receive and store the rest for response later. An incentive such as microcredits against subscriber bills will be provided to encourage customers to return stored calls.

Local area networks (LANs) make connections at home, work, and public places such as airports more likely. Wireless LAN standards, such as 802.11, provide device users with the opportunity to connect with networks such as the Internet without going into a public cellular network. These wireless connections are more secure and make possible virtual private network connections (VPN). It's like having your own high-speed network connection wherever you are in range of an 802.11 transceiver.

LAN marketing methodologies are just being conceived today. In a world with lots of wireless LAN connections, the ability to segment customers will be a pivotal consideration at the beginning. Only the affluent, early adopters, and global businesses will go for wireless LAN connections. The self-selecting nature of this segmentation is very compelling for marketing professionals in search of high-income demographics.

Work is already underway to provide wireless LAN connections in aircraft. When the second war in Iraq broke out, I was in France skiing. There was no television that week, only the BBC shortwave broadcasts. Coming back on a Lufthansa flight from Frankfurt, I was enrolled in a high-speed LAN pilot program. With an Ethernet connection from the aircraft's satellite antenna to my seat, my IBM ThinkPad became my temporary television—I could watch the live CNN feed from their Web site and get visual impressions of what was going on in the Middle East.

When tied into an airplane's LAN, the ability to provide fee services and in-flight shopping experiences reaches a new level. In some respects, you can envision airfares being subsidized by marketers who want to rent eyeballs glued into a seat for an extended period of time. "This segment of your trip is brought to you by . . ."

Personal area networks represent the real change in immediacy that people don't see or understand yet. Transactions scale so that peer-to-peer exchanges of information take place. Peer-to-peer means one device talking directly to another device. This means that your notebook computer will wirelessly exchange data with your cell phone or PDA. Your refrigerator and pantry could do a self-inventory and load a grocery list onto your handheld device. The frozen dinner will tell your microwave oven how to set itself using a wireless instruction label on the package.

The benefits from the exchange are expanded and enhanced for both companies and the customers they serve. In the past, customers got products and services, and companies got the customers' money and attention. Now customers and companies get access to each other—customers get real-time relevant information and offers, and companies get to know customers in more depth to tailor offers they'll really want. A company will have the opportunity to present flexible offers to customers when the firm may have a critical need to move merchandise. "Proximity bartering" also becomes possible, to exchange value for value without the need for money changing hands—little eBay exchanges on the street.

The fractal emergence of wireless markets is well underway. The patterns are taking shape. The customers are learning. The methods to reach these markets are being invented now. We can already perceive the small fractal pattern of the revolution wireless technology will cause and how marketing professionals may use it. Wireless will be disruptive for some but lucrative for those who deliver on the immediacy, relevance, and mutual benefits that wireless marketing techniques can bring to customers and companies worldwide.

HYPERBANDWIDTH AND VIRTUAL REALITY

The tetradic reversal on wireless is fiber optic enabled hyperbandwidth and the possibilities of virtual reality and telepresence it makes possible.[5] Certain aggressive forms of online gaming and cybersex will initially taint these new immersive technologies and give them a bad name.

Branding will again need to assert itself to give this new world relevance beyond immediate gratification and to show that it serves customers in a transcendent way that delivers mutual benefit. The context and content will have to change. But this kind of immersive technology will change what it means "to go shopping." The experience will echo what happened when sending stores into cyberspace rendered them two-dimensional, which then inspired the brick-and-mortar stores to fight back with "smart stores" that will deliver a better customer experience. Same technology parts—reconfigured to different ends. Cyberspace counterattacks by bringing a three-dimensional shopping experience to you wherever you have access to high bandwidth and a terminal equipped for telepresence.

Expect these isolated patterns to replicate themselves and spread. This is what I call the "fractal emergence of markets"—a metaphor, based on fractal geometry theory, that was pioneered by IBM research scientist and mathematician Benoit Mandelbrot. You've likely seen pictures based on fractals where the base pattern is very small at the center, repeats itself, and grows exponentially at the edges. Good ideas do the same thing. Wireless is a great idea already spreading rapidly with fractal precision, with virtual reality and telepresence right behind it.

THROWING OUT THE BOOKS

I learned a valuable lesson in high school from educator Ed Rsczyck, who taught my earth science class. The year I had his class, something very interesting was happening: a new theory was spreading like wildfire across the scientific literature. It was called "plate tectonics."[6] What at the time was a new theory caused a step-function change in thinking in the earth science community, and Mr. Rsczyck had the presence of mind and the authority to set aside our textbooks, which were steeped in the older geosyncline theory.[7] For the rest of the year, we worked from *Scientific American, National Geographic,* and other articles he found to create a living textbook for the class. I'd find this situation quite often in college later on, but for a ninth grader, it was quite a lesson in complex adaptive behavior.

In the course of writing this book, I've had to reconsider a few things myself, setting aside some old ideas to make room for new ones. As I said in the preface, this book represents a frozen moment in time, my accumulated thinking deposited on paper during the year 2003. Even in this year, my thinking has moved forward about this last chapter and where branding is going.

THE FUTURE OF MUTUAL BENEFIT: REVISITING RETURN ON RELATIONSHIPS

A book that never hit the shelves ten years ago was titled *Return on Relationships*™ (*ROR*). Its ambitious goal was to make intangible equity an important topic in managing an enterprise. I intentionally created a phrase with the same cadence and structure used throughout the financial community: return on investment (ROI), return on assets (ROA), return on capital (ROC), and so forth. Its assertion was that you could direct resources to influence measurably the revenue and profit of commercial entities. While I didn't make much progress on this turf as I would have liked, Kay Lemon, Valarie Zeithaml, and Roland Rust surely have, as you can see in Appendix C, "Putting the Brand and Branding in Context: Customer Equity Marketing Metrics."

Another insight has occurred to me that has more to do with language and worldview than quantification of brand equity. The standard terms used in the world of branding draw more from the world of myth and spirituality than the standard terms of scientific management that are widely embraced in the practicing workplace today.

Standard Management Concepts
Facts (foundation of reality)
Numbers (to inform)
Plans (to guide)

Standard Brand Concepts
Beliefs (foundation of reality)
Stories (to inform)
Values (to guide)

Want to know why it's hard to have a great branding conversation in some workplaces? You're not speaking the same language. Most of the management language and concepts come from a mechanical, left-brained worldview, while brand language is more right-brained, integrative, and conceptual. Are they mutually exclusive views? Absolutely not.

My mistake with *Return on Relationships* was to assume that I could just rename some right-brained concepts using left-brained language. The framework was too weak. Trying to convert beliefs into facts, or stories into numbers, isn't going to work very well. The mistake was in pure conversion. Wrong idea. We need to bridge the left-brained, logical, fact-driven worldview with the right-brained, conceptual, belief-driven world. We started on that journey in Chapter 10 about brand holons. Now, as New Orleans-trained chef Emeril Lagasse would say, "Let's kick it up a notch!" with memes and spiral dynamics.

THE POTENTIAL OF INTEGRAL BRAND PRACTICE: MEMES

John Petersen, president of the Arlington Institute (a Washington, D.C., beltline future studies think tank), invited me to attend a leadership seminar held during the summer of 2003. There, I heard Don Beck talking for the first time about spiral dynamics—based on the work of Clare Graves, professor emeritus of psychology at Union College in New York—and the concept of memes—based on the work of British biologist Richard Dawkins and, later, Mihaly Csikszentmihalyi.

Dawkin used the word *meme* to "describe a unit of cultural information comparable in its effects on society to those of the chemically coded instructions contained in the gene on the human organism."[8] This quote is from Csikzenminhayli's book, *The Evolving Self,* and as he points out, Dawkin's term *meme* was 20 years old at the time of his book in 1993. It is now 30 years old and is coming into its own.

I purchased the book that Beck wrote with Christopher Cowan, *Spiral Dynamics: Mastering Values, Leadership, and Change,* and read it, even though writing was more the order of the day in 2003 than reading. This I made time for—it was rapidly changing my thinking about the future of brand strategy.

Beck and Cowan elaborate in *Spiral Dynamics,* saying:[9]

Mihaly Csikzenminhayli uses the expression *meme* to contrast with *genes* in identifying the origins of human behavior as opposed to physical characteristics.

A meme contains behavioral instructions that are passed from one generation to the next, social artifacts, and value-laden symbols that glue together social systems. Like an intellectual virus, a meme reproduces itself through concepts like dress styles, language trends, popular cultural norms, architectural designs, art forms, religious expressions, social movements, economic models, and moral statements of how living should be done.

Memes act much like particles. Spiral Dynamics proposes the existence of another wavelike metameme, a systems or values meme (vMEME). These vMEMEs are organizing principles that act like attractors for the content-rich memes that Dawkins and Csikzenminhayli describe. Big vMEMEs are the amino acids of our psychosocial "DNA" and act as the magnetic force that binds memes and other kinds of ideas in cohesive packages of thought. While they are initially shaped in each human mind, vMEMEs are so vital, they reach across whole groups of people and begin to structure mindsets on their own. vMEMEs establish the pace and process for gathering beliefs. They structure the thinking, value systems, political forms, and worldviews of entire civilizations. vMEMEs are linchpins of corporate cultures and determine how and why decisions are made. Our individual MEME stacks are central to our personalities and set the tone for relationships and whether we are happy campers or restless souls.

In an early presentation of his findings to the National Institutes of Mental Health in Washington, D.C., in 1973, Clare Graves warned that he was about to "crawl forth on a fragile limb."[10] Human systems, he would argue, reflect different activation levels of our dynamic neurological equipment; i.e., our brains' chemical wetware, complex cell assemblages, and billions of potential neuron connections. "As man solves the problems of existence at a level," Graves contended, "new brain systems may be activated and, when activated, change his perceptions so as to cause him to see new problems of existence." Instead of beginning only as passive hardware without content (Locke's *tabula rasa* or blank slate view), it turns out the normal human brain comes with potential "software-like systems" just waiting to be turned on—latent upgrades!

What we're talking about here is new ground and is somewhat controversial. The facts supplied by physical inspection of genes versus the speculative nature and behavior of memes gets the social sciences in trouble all the time. Edward O. Wilson, in his enlightening book *Consilience: The Unity of Knowledge,* captures the spirit of this debate quite well in the chapter, "Genes to Culture:"

Gene-culture coevolution is a special extension of the more general process of evolution by natural selection.

The nature of the genetic leash and the role of culture can now be better understood, as follows. Certain cultural norms also survive and reproduce better than competing norms, causing culture to evolve in a track parallel to and usually much faster than genetic evolution. The quicker the pace of cultural evolution, the looser the connection between genes and culture, although the connection is never quite broken. Culture allows a rapid adjustment to changes in the environment through finely tuned adaptations invented and transmitted without correspondingly precise genetic prescription. In this respect, human beings differ fundamentally from all other animal species.[11]

Below is a table showing the vMEMEs color-coded, with their popular names and basic motives highlighted.[12]

vMEME	Popular Name	Basic Motives
Beige	SurvivalSense	staying alive through innate sensory equipment
Purple	KinSpirits	blood relationships and mysticism in a magical and scary world
Red	PowerGods	enforce power over self, others, and nature through exploitative independence
Blue	TruthForce	absolute belief in one right way and obedience to authority
Orange	StriveDrive	possibility thinking focused on making things better for self
Green	HumanBond	well-being of people and building consensus get the highest priority
Yellow	FlexFlow	flexible adaptation to change through connected, big-picture views
Turquoise	GlobalView	attention to whole-Earth dynamics and macro-level actions

The implication in spiral dynamics theory is that memes awaken latent capacities depending on what life conditions we're facing at any given time. Just as outlined in the Brandscendence stage model, and as discussed with brand holons, each stage represents a step-function change in perspective and thought-processing, and each stage includes and incorporates the previous levels. Beck and Cowan provide, for discussion purposes, their thumbnail of human development. Notice the time compressions of each interval.[13]

100,000 years ago	Beige	Survival	To be human, not just animals
50,000 years ago	Purple	Mystical	Forming tribes, magic, art, spirits
10,000 years ago	Red	Exploitative	Warlords, conquest, discovery
5,000 years ago	Blue	Absolutist	Literature, monotheism, purpose
1,000 years ago	Orange	Materialist	Mobility, individualism, economics
150 years ago	Green	Humanitarian	Human rights, liberty, collectivism
50 years ago	Yellow	Integrated	Complexity, chaos, interconnections
30 years ago	Turquoise	Holistic	Globalism, ecoconsciousness, patterns
Today?	Coral		To emerge and be observed . . .

I submit that if the vMEME that Beck and Cowan postulate is the meme package for individual and societal level information, there can be a mirror brand meme, or bMEME that is an attractor package representing the values of these societies and the members of them. Further, I believe that, if orchestrated properly, bMEMES can be used as a catalyst to move more members of a society from one level to the next. In this case, branding as a profession and the brands it nurtures become less s1 and s2 mirrors and more of an s3 posture—projecting the values of the next meme stage and offering an invitation to emerge in the next level.

BMEMES AND INTEGRAL BRAND PRACTICE

Spiral dynamics explains a lot about the world we're living in right now. Can you look at the last table and see some current global conflicts presented in the context of different worldviews? Can you see companies, organizations, and countries trying to reorient or rediscover their relevance in the context of discontinuous changes taking place all around us? That kind of thinking would be a move toward s4 integral brand practice.

FIGURE 16.1 *Brand Step-Function Transformations*

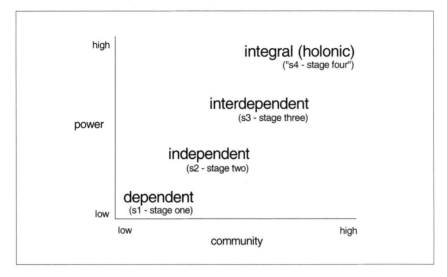

What characteristics would s4 integral brand practices have? I suggest that s4 would embody *timeless* relevance, have an *ubiquitous* context, and possess *transcendent* mutual benefit. I admit, these are lofty goals. S4 is a purely theoretical and aspirational level—but one worthy striving for over time.

Chaos theory suggests turbulence along the way to s4 integral brand practice. In some cases, brand relationships are moving up the spiral with increasing global interdependence and cooperation. In other cases, brand relationships are moving down the spiral to defend themselves, as the lower survival memes reassert themselves as part of our consciousness. When you add s4 to the Brandscendence stage model, here's what it looks like.

	Relevance	**Context**	**Mutual Benefit**
Stage 1 (dependent)	personality	reflects	conditional
Stage 2 (independent)	character	adapts	reciprocal
Stage 3 (interdependent)	purpose	projects	integrated
and a proposed . . .			
Stage 4 (integral)	timeless	ubiquitous	transcendent

The bMEME mirrors the vMEME as a values attractor system. The bMEME is simultaneously a brand holon, composed of relevance, context, and mutual benefit stages. S1 dependent brands behave, in general, like the beige and purple memes described by Beck and Cowan as survival and mystical spiral dynamics levels. S2 independent brands seem to have a lot in common with the red, blue, and orange memes: exploitative, absolutist, and materialist. S3 interdependent brands share values with the green and yellow memes: humanitarian and integrated. The proposed s4 integral brand level would share turquoise and coral meme characteristics: holistic—and the emerging coral level yet to be understood and documented.

The implication is that, by understanding the vMEME suggested by spiral dynamics, we have the opportunity to craft powerful and meaningful bMEMES that increase the possibility of creating and managing enduring brands. Appendix D offers a "vMEME Communications Strategy" created by Don Beck that presents another view of how vMEMEs can be used and applied.

Because this chapter is supposed to provide a glimpse of where branding will take us, let's leave this discussion for another time so my thinking can gestate and mature on the implications of spiral dynamics and the bMEME for the practice of branding.

If you have examples to offer of a bMEME or brand holons in action, just send a note to me at bmeme@contentevolution.net. I can't promise to respond to every note, but thanks to anyone who takes the time to look around for emerging Brandscendence and share it.

17

BRANDSCENDENCE IN THE NONCOMMERCIAL WORLD

"We are healthy only to the extent that our ideas are humane."
KURT VONNEGUT, JR.[1]

Executive summary. The concepts of Brandscendence work just as well in the noncommercial world. Governments, nongovernment organizations, and nonprofits can all thrive by paying attention to the three essential elements of enduring brands: relevance, context, and mutual benefit. These noncommercial entities fit into brand ecosystems as distinct brand holons, and as we discovered in the last chapter, the notion of memes takes us to another level of understanding about brand interactions between cultures.

NEW DIRECTION

This chapter started out in a different direction. It was meant to show that some nongovernmental organizations had risen above others in the delivery of humanitarian services across borders. In the fall of 2003, I had to alter my views.

A poster child for this idea was the Red Cross. We're still going to look at this phenomenon that is more of a movement than an organization. However, it is clear that the Red Cross is a brand holon that ties its backing primarily to the first world for the benefit of all humankind, and this ancestry is enough to make it hateful for some people, no matter what it does.

The Red Cross generally doesn't get attacked in the course of doing its work, but it did in Iraq in October 2003. Within days, the word came from Geneva that Red Cross workers would pull back to surrounding countries, leaving the local Red Crescent workers (also part of the Red Cross movement) alone to continue the work at hand. We'll come back to the Red Cross shortly.

For now, let's talk about an unexpected event that lifted the brand of a formerly little-known United Nations agency to prominent status. The circumstances and subsequent performance of this agency may have lifted it to international prominence, but you could tell through its actions that it had already been on the journey to Brandscendence.

OUTBREAK

The first I heard of SARS was when turning on a television in an airline departure lounge at the Stuttgart International Airport after arriving from the United States. The picture hadn't even come in yet, but the CNN news announcer was telling the world not to travel to international hub airports because of an outbreak of this new killer bug called SARS. You don't get much more international than Stuttgart. Oh well, hold my breath, wash my hands, and get on with the trip—too late to do much else.

In a world that still generally demands respect of national borders, came a brooding bureaucracy turned upstart inside the United Nations. The World Health Organization, or WHO (pronounced by the initials: *W-H-O*), flexed its muscle and made its voice heard during the SARS outbreak.

Unheard of by the general public, all of a sudden, WHO was on the lips of people on the street and public officials. Entire countries and cities were put on the "do not travel list" of the WHO—previously the province of government state departments around the world. Latent brand authority and authenticity trumped traditional forms of communication. The WHO was effective both in containing SARS and in retreating to a safe distance for another day when the crisis was over.

The WHO had built up a great deal of relevance capital over the years, and in this context, it became a global leader for a brief but important period of time. What the WHO did was also mutually beneficial, because it is cited for containing the spread of SARS and saving lives. In return, huge deposits of goodwill were being made, increasing the WHO's ability to exert authority when the next global health crisis hits.

COMPARING COMMERCIALISM AND COMPASSION: BMW AND THE RED CROSS

In the world of automobile brands, BMW has an enduring phrase that captures the essence of the brand: *the ultimate driving machine*. It is more than a tag line for advertising: it represents a succinct statement about the BMW ethos of "beautiful design, great performance, and excellent service."[2] BMW is an expression about innovative personal mobility and technological leadership.

BMW maps to the three elements of Brandscendence, and notice how the phrase *ultimate driving machine* really does capture a promise to customers and drives BMW's behavior.

1. *A relevant primary idea.* Innovative and unique personal mobility driven by creative ideas (captured in the word *ultimate*)
2. *Contextual brand evolution.* Technology leadership and engineering excellence that evolved from airplanes in 1919, motorcycles in 1923, and BMW cars in 1956 (captured in the word *machine*)
3. *Mutual benefit.* Creating personal mobility for drivers and riders who crave personal freedom (*driving*—both in terms of customers' driving experiences and the company being driven to be a leader in mobility)

Compare and contrast BMW to the Red Cross.

The Red Cross might be thought of as *the ultimate humanitarian experience* (my adapted phrase).

The American Red Cross provides, ". . . relief to victims of disasters and helps people prevent, prepare for, and respond to emergencies."[3]

The purpose of the International Red Cross, ". . . is to protect life and health and to ensure respect for the human being. It promotes understanding, friendship, cooperation, and lasting peace amongst all peoples." The seven principles of the International Red Cross are:

1. Humanity
2. Impartiality
3. Neutrality
4. Independence

5. Voluntary service
6. Unity
7. Universality (equity amongst all Red Cross organizations world-wide)

The Red Cross around the world has achieved Brandscendence.

- *Relevance.* Crosscultural relief and prevention of human suffering around the world
- *Context.* Extending help in crisis wherever it exists
- *Mutual benefit.* Helping others in their greatest time of need (self-esteem for volunteers and people who donate) and being there when you need it (universal goodwill)

MUTUALLY BENEFICIAL: THE AMERICAN RED CROSS

Long before Walt Disney and McDonald's founder Ray Kroc were driving ambulances for the Red Cross, which they both did, the first examples of volunteers in any kind of organized activity began to appear during the mid-1600s. They included the Knights of Hospitaliers of medieval orders, the Sisters of St. Vincent de Paul, and the clergy of the Camilian Catholic order in the late 17th century, who wore black robes with a red cross as they nursed the sick.

Today, the secular American Red Cross is an example of an organization that generates goodwill on a number of levels and fits the Brandscendence model very well indeed. It is relevant in a variety of contexts and mutually beneficial in its behavior of an organization.

The Red Cross operates in the arenas of health and human services: disaster services, blood collection and distribution, AIDS education, health and safety training, and local programs that meet the needs of specific communities. The Red Cross movement provides an international link to world crises and the relief of human suffering.

It is also a nonprofit organization that has weathered an era of erosion in the U.S. volunteer movement. With scandals hitting the front pages of newspapers nationwide over the last decade, all nonprofit organizations have suffered erosion in confidence in the nonprofit sector.

Confidence in the Red Cross was especially stressed as it struggled with a new burden, AIDS, and other infectious diseases in the blood supply. As the leading organization to collect and distribute blood in the United States, the American Red Cross received more than its share of public scrutiny as fear of AIDS spread across the globe.

This, in turn, caused the Red Cross to react not only to the natural disasters for which it is well prepared but also focus time and attention on a lingering disaster building up in the general population. In a sense, the organization just wasn't prepared for this shift in time perspective. The context of time was more like the proverbial frog being slowly boiled, rather than the sharp pang of pain normally associated with Red Cross disasters.

Red Cross teams react swiftly to fires, floods, hurricanes, and other natural disasters. The organization also efficiently collects, tests, and dispatches blood to medical facilities nationwide. In the early '90s, protests mounted against blood bank operations. The organization just wasn't ready to take the longer view these protesters brought to the table. The Red Cross still had a mandate to deliver blood *today;* there was no alternative.

But these voices started to have an effect. They forced the American Red Cross to reexamine itself and take a longer view about why it exists and what its prospects were for survival. It had begun to lose its focus during the turbulent '80s. Essentially, it was a victim of the same trends that caused some businesses to lose their way during the same period.

Businesses went on a diversification and acquisition binge. The American Red Cross also diversified. It created new programs and strayed from the original mission that made the Red Cross successful.

Today, it is refocused and has divested itself of noncore pursuits, as many companies have. Neither the Red Cross nor businesses can afford to be somewhat good at many things—they need to be excellent in a few focused areas and be known for them. Elizabeth Dole, who is now a U.S. senator, lead the American Red Cross in the early '90s and is credited for getting the organization back in focus.

Susan Chira, writing in the *New York Times* in the article, "Power Player, Playing Cautiously,"[4] says that Dole, ". . . has won praise for her stewardship of the Red Cross: fund raising, cost cutting, instituting more stringent blood screening, and responding to a string of natural disasters, including Hurricane Andrew and the Midwest floods."

Because the Red Cross is so dependent on volunteers, it looked in depth at volunteerism in a 1988 report called "Volunteer 2000"[5] and translated what it learned into ten principles.

1. We can broaden our nation's volunteer work force by removing barriers to volunteering.
2. Volunteers are not "free."
3. Volunteers contribute more than meets the eye.

4. *Volunteer* does not mean *amateur*.
5. Volunteers and the organizations they serve must meet each other's expectations.
6. Volunteers must never be exploited.
7. Volunteers make excellent middle and senior managers.
8. When recruiting volunteers, it is more important to place the right person in the right job than to attract volunteers at random.
9. We can help shape government policies on volunteerism.
10. Everyone benefits when nonprofit organizations collaborate.

The Red Cross experience with volunteers is unique, because it considers volunteers to be the backbone of the organization. The report says, "It is safe to say that there are no jobs in the Red Cross that, somewhere in the organization, are not being performed by volunteers. Reliance on volunteers to perform management roles makes the Red Cross volunteer experience unique among nonprofit organizations."

The "Strategy for the International Red Cross and Red Crescent Movement" is a 40-page document that is also known as "Strategy 2010." In the foreword, Princess Margriet, Chairman of the Standing Commission of the Red Cross and Red Crescent in 1999, says, "The aim of the Strategy, through more effective cooperation, is to more fully realize the Movement's ultimate goal: a Red Cross and Red Crescent Movement which is helping victims, improving the lives of vulnerable people and meeting the great humanitarian challenges of our time."[6]

A study conducted by Young & Rubicam for the movement indicates the Red Cross brand evokes feminine and nurturing associations, and somewhat passive, especially in Asian regions. Doctors Without Borders (Medecins San Frontiers, or MSF) by comparison, was seen as more male, and more of an change agent. We'll look more closely at MSF before we're done.

Strategy 2010 is designed to use volunteers in a more effective way in the movement, "to be stronger together in reaching vulnerable people with effective humanitarian action throughout the world"[7] The strategic objectives of Strategy 2010 are:

1. Strengthening the components of the movement
2. Improving the movements effectiveness and efficiency through increase cooperation and coherence
3. Improving the movement's image and its relations with governments and external partners

These objectives should bolster the primary mission statement of the Red Cross and Red Crescent Movement adopted in 1986:

> To prevent and alleviate human suffering wherever it may be found, to protect life and health and ensure respect for the human being, in particular in times of armed conflict and other emergencies, to work for the prevention of disease and for the promotion of health and social welfare, to encourage voluntary service and a constant readiness to give help by the members of the Movement and a universal sense of solidarity in need of its protection and assistance."[8]

DOCTORS WITHOUT BORDERS

A brief note here about the relatively new Doctors Without Borders, or Médecins Sans Frontières (MSF). Founded in 1971 by French doctors who believed that all people have the right to medical care regardless of where they live or the circumstances in which they find themselves, MSF not only delivers medical care as a private, nonprofit organization but is also committed to bearing witness and speaking out against the causes of human suffering.[9]

MSF has sections in 18 countries that bring together 2,500 volunteer doctors, nurses, related medical professionals, and other administrative and engineering talent to deliver aid in more than 80 countries, including Chechnya, Angola, Kosovo, and Sri Lanka.

As the Red Cross study indicated, Doctors Without Borders is seen as more male and a change agent entity. By comparison, the Red Cross evoked feminine and nurturing associations, which are viewed as passive traits. Rather than setting up a competitive landscape, I'd say that Doctors Without Borders is the ying to the Red Cross's yang. MSF filled a void in a space and is now redefining the Red Cross, just as a new media form redefines all the previous media before it.

A toast to both the Red Cross and Doctors Without Borders for the work being done around the world—and to all the other nongovernmental entities out there trying to make a difference in the relief of human suffering.

18

BRAND YOU

*"First of all, it is necessary to distinguish two broad categories
of mental images: reproductive images, which are limited
to evoking sights that have been perceived previously, and
anticipatory images, which envisage movements or transformations
as well as their results, although the subject has not
previously observed them (as one can envisage how a
geometric figure would look if it were transformed)."*
JEAN PIAGET[1]

This is the shortest chapter of *Brandscendence*.
This is about you.
What is the state of your brand?

Relevance. When I interview people for positions at work, whether
they are already employees or potential external hires, I have a standard
question: "What role have you had that is the same at work, at home, and
over time with your family and friends? Why do they call on you? When
do they seek you out?"

Can you answer this question quickly and in-depth simultaneously?
Take the time to work it out, put it on paper, and memorize it. Knowing
your core relevance and being able to state it fast and clearly will take
you places.

Context. Are you able to adapt to changing circumstances? Without changing your core relevance?

Oops! Are you on the journey to Brandscendence, or are you a fad?

Brandscendence: Core relevance changes glacially but contextually adapts to be effective in any circumstance.

Fad: You become whatever the circumstance requires. For more clarity on this thought, rent Woody Allen's *Zelig* from the video store—it's about a person who becomes whomever he is around.

Mutual benefit. Do you practice reciprocal behavior? Do you have a network of people with which you're interdependent over time? Or are you living life in stage one, transaction by transaction?

Look again at the stages of Brandscendence.

	Relevance	**Context**	**Mutual Benefit**
Stage 1 (dependent)	personality	reflects	conditional
Stage 2 (independent)	character	adapts	reciprocal
Stage 3 (interdependent)	purpose	projects	integrated
and a proposed. . .			
Stage 4 (integral)	timeless	ubiquitous	transcendent

Where are you on the journey to Brandscendence?

$$\text{Brandscendence} = (\text{Relevance} + \text{Context}) \times \text{Mutual benefit}$$

Observe the world of brands around you, and spend some time thinking about where you fit in. Come back and reread *Brandscendence* from time to time to refresh your grounding in the basic ideas of the journey and your familiarity with the three elements of enduring brands.

Just for some perspective before we leave each other, let's compare you with the rest of the world. If there were only 100 people on Earth, where would you fall in the context of these facts aggregated by Medard Gabel, who heads Big Picture Small World Consulting, from reliable sources.[2]

If there were only 100 people in the world:

- 30 are under 15 years of age.
- There are more children under 15 in Africa than there are people in North America.
- 7 are over 65.
- 2 have a life expectancy of 80 years or more.
- 6 have a life expectancy of 50 years or less.
- 1 is near death.
- 77 are people of color; 23 are white.

- 49 are female.
- 51 are male.
- 67 are non-Christian.
- 33 are Christian.
- 22 are Moslem.
- 46 live in cities.
- 3 live in countries other than where they were born.
- 20 live on less than $1 a day.
- The 20 richest receive 84 percent of the world's income.
- The 5 North Americans consume 31 percent of the world's energy.
- 14 people are without health care services of any kind.
- 14 adults are unable to read.
- If you own a computer, you are 1 of 8 people who do.
- If you have Internet access, you are 1 of 5 people who do.
- 51 people have not made a telephone call.

What social meme are you part of? How do you relate to the other memes around you?

Focus. The path to Brandscendence patiently waits for the brands you manage—and for you.

A

THE IBM THINK STRATEGY
Melding Business Strategy and Branding

BY KEVIN CLARK AND MARK MCNEILLY

Originally published in *Strategy and Leadership Magazine*
Volume 32, Number 2
Copyright Emerald Group Publishing Limited 2004
http://www.emeraldinsight.com/sl.htm

Kevin Clark and Mark McNeilly are managers in the IBM Personal Computing Division (PCD). They are responsible for marketing strategy, branding, and market intelligence. In the following case study, they review the lessons learned from the launching of the PC Division's Think strategy, a project whose success resulted from the talents and efforts of IBM PCD's executives and employees. Kevin is the author of the upcoming book Brandscendence: Three Elements of Enduring Brands, to be published by Dearborn Press. Mark is the author of *Sun Tzu and the Art of Business: Six Strategic Principles for Managers,* to be published by Oxford University Press.

> *"This time, like all times, is a very good one,*
> *if we but know what to do with it."*
> **RALPH WALDO EMERSON**

In April of 2001, we were pondering the implications of a reorganization of IBM's PC business. Three organizations were now one: the IBM ThinkPad notebook computer group, the IBM NetVista desktop computer team, and the monitors and options area. The IBM Aptiva desktop brand for consumers had already been out of the market for over a year, and all IBM PC products were now out of retail stores. The consolidation of talent and resources posed both opportunities and challenges.

As the managers responsible for branding and marketing strategy, we saw the potential for a new branding approach that would strengthen the positioning of the IBM PC portfolio in the marketplace and signal strategic differentiation. Yet the current brands had varying levels of strength and stood for different things in buyers' minds.

The ThinkPad brand was by far the strongest brand. Announced in 1992, the IBM ThinkPad stood for quality and innovation. Its classic black design was well recognized throughout the industry and had won hundreds of design awards. For end users, research showed that carrying a ThinkPad meant that its owner was a serious business leader who had achieved success. These factors translated into high awareness of, consideration for, and purchases of the ThinkPad line of notebook computers.

The IBM NetVista desktop PC line was less well known. Announced only the prior year, it had not yet had the ability to build brand equity and become known in the marketplace. Furthermore, the prior strategy of the desktop team had focused more on being low cost than on differentiation, a very different position than that of ThinkPad. The monitors and options offerings were known by the IBM brand; they essentially had no subbranding like ThinkPad and NetVista.

Beyond the branding issues, other factors needed to be considered. The PC industry had grown up placing high importance on having the latest technology, yet as hardware capabilities outpaced the demands of software applications, PCs became "good enough." Lower prices and stable offerings had become more important than new technology to business buyers, IBM's major target.

Two questions intertwined: "How should IBM differentiate itself given the new industry dynamics?" and, "How might a new branding approach help communicate this new strategy?"

SHIFTING THE FOCUS OF INNOVATION

"There is nothing more difficult to take in hand,
more perilous to conduct, or more uncertain in its success,
than to take the lead in the introduction of a new order of things."
NICCOLO MACHIAVELLI

The ThinkPad team had long been known for its innovative approach to hardware design and had led the industry with many new products and features. These included several firsts in the area of new product categories, color displays, and media integration. Yet customers were saying that this type of hardware innovation, while still important, was becoming less so.

In response, the new, combined PC team looked for ways to provide innovation "beyond the box," that is, giving business customers benefits beyond the usual end-user productivity enhancements provided by personal computers. This focus was based on customer insight and research that showed that the cost to a business to support a personal computer was four times that of the original purchase. These support costs included such things as rolling out the PCs to end users, helping desk personnel to support end users, and managing the fleet of PCs.

Thus, the IBM PC team's innovation focus shifted beyond the benefits provided to end users to include the information technology department and the business overall. These innovations were in areas such as enabling wireless mobile computing, enhancing laptop security, and making the backing up and restoration of data easier and more fail-safe. This shift in strategy was profound, enabling IBM to position itself more effectively against competitors, whose value proposition was lower purchase prices for vanilla technology. Yet this new value proposition, innovation for business advantage, needed to be communicated to customers.

THINK BRANDS

"The past is but the beginning of a beginning."
H.G. WELLS

We pondered if there was a way to address the branding issues facing the PC division while simultaneously communicating the new value proposition for customers. The most appealing plan was to build off the strength of the ThinkPad brand, extending its name and equity to the other product lines.

Beyond ThinkPad's positive associations and high awareness, the word *Think* itself had a long history and association with IBM, going back to its original founder, Thomas J. Watson, Sr. Back in the early 1900s, T. J. Watson made *Think* the motto of IBM, saying, "We don't get paid for working with our feet—we get paid for working with our heads. Feet can never compare with brains. Thought has been the father of every advance since time began. Knowledge is the result of thought, and thought is the keynote of success in this business." Watson was also responsible for creating *Think Magazine,* an external IBM publication, as well as for the proliferation of "Think" signs on the desks of IBM employees. This tie to *Think* was linked to IBM's heritage for innovation and was such a prominent part of IBM's culture, that it became linked to IBM in customers' minds as well.

Yet a ThinkPad brand extension was also a risky strategy, as it might lead to draining the very equity that had taken several years to build. What was needed was marketplace feedback.

So, in the fall of 2001, a number of Think names were tested for the different products in the IBM PC portfolio: the desktop, the monitors, and the accessories. The worldwide study revealed that using the Think label was perceived to be a "natural extension" of the ThinkPad brand and that customers would be willing to accept the Think label as a brand, if the Think products were compatible and had the same high levels of quality expected of the IBM ThinkPad. In fact, *Think* brought to mind the "good name and good performance of the existing product." Further, using the Think label for the accessories portion of the portfolio was perceived by respondents to "tie all the products together" and create a "stronger bond" between the accessories and computer lines. The respondents recognized the heritage of *Think* and its linkage to IBM, as well as sharing the perception that "IBM is synonymous with quality." Based upon this research study, we foresaw no negative impact on the ThinkPad brand.

With the naming research complete, we went the next step, enlisting the help of our Marketing Advisory Council. Composed of leading marketing consultants, academics, and practicing professionals from around the world, this is a group we had relied on for several years to provide input on IBM PC divisions marketing strategy. The overall view of the Council was very positive. They felt that extending the ThinkPad brand was something IBM needed to do, that it was not a risk but an obligation and that we had a tremendous asset in the word *Think*. They especially believed that tying the introduction of Think brands to a new strategy and value proposition was an opportunity to provide a vision of where IBM would take personal computing, moving the value beyond simply purchasing the hardware to helping companies achieve business advantage through better management of the personal computing assets. The Council's main concerns were twofold: that we ensure that the brand architecture and strategy were thought through end to end and, more importantly, that we didn't give up before we saw results.

To get a PC industry perspective, we also enlisted the help of our Analyst Council. This group is made up of analysts and press from top IT consulting and media companies. Given their interest in industry and technology trends versus marketing, this group provided advice focused more on the business and technology strategy. This Council was supportive of our shifting the emphasis from offering products to solving customers' business problems and improving the return from owning PCs, not just lowering the cost of buying them.

The IBM Corporate Marketing team was also supportive of extending the ThinkPad brand to the rest of the PC product line. However, we were asked to put specific guidelines in place to ensure that IBM's equity in Think and ThinkPad were maintained.

THE SYNERGY OF BRANDING AND STRATEGY

"A plan which succeeds is bold; one which fails is reckless."
KARL VON CLAUSEWITZ

Given favorable market input and corporate support, the next step was to solidify the brand architecture and link it to the business strategy. Extending from the ThinkPad brand name, the NetVista desktop line was renamed ThinkCentre, and the monitor line was given the ThinkVision moniker. The Think Accessories and Think Services names served to link those offering categories to the rest of the family. One of the most important synergies between the branding and business strategies was created by the ThinkVantage Technologies software line. This set of products was at the heart of the beyond-the-box strategy to reduce the information technology costs of companies and boost their productivity. Putting these formerly disparate products under an umbrella brand enabled us to communicate in shorthand the "sizzle" on top of our personal computer "steaks."

The Think strategy was announced on November 4, 2002, in events in 12 major countries with 145 industry journalists and analysts in attendance, resulting in 170 pieces in major publications. Then, in the first quarter of 2003, we released the Thinkers ad campaign, featuring real-life successful people who had used our offerings to gain business advantage. As 2003 continued, the new offerings from the Think family were released: ThinkVision monitors, ThinkCentre desktops, and ThinkVantage technologies.

RESULTS

"Luck is the residue of design."
BRANCH RICKEY

The impact of synergizing our branding and business strategies has resulted in significant business results. The press and analyst coverage of the announcement was universally positive, with the Gartner Group stating, "The Think marketing strategy represents a step forward for IBM to effectively communicate the value proposition behind its "four-pillars" vision. IBM should be able to better market its proposition. While IBM is leveraging the success of the ThinkPad brand, it is also developing a more consistent message." The *Computer Business Quarterly Report* wrote, "TBR believes IBM will be able to better communicate its advantage over competitors with this branding strategy, which will likely boost sales of PCs in the short term."

Organizationally, the PC Division's innovation for business advantage strategy also links well to corporate IBM's new On Demand strategy, which was announced shortly before the Think announcement. The On Demand strategy is focused on making businesses more productive and responsive through IBM's business consulting and technology offerings. Just as importantly, the Think strategy has reenergized the IBM PC team, renewing our purpose and intent.

The advertising campaign was well received, testing extremely well among readers and increasing the awareness of selected Think family products significantly in 2003. More importantly, the Think message and promise of value has resonated with customers, leading them to reconsider the way they purchase personal computers and their expectations of them. Sales, of course, are the ultimate test. In October of 2003, IBM sold its 20 millionth ThinkPad, more than any other laptop brand. While the first ten million unit sales took eight years (1992 to 2000), the second ten million took only three years (2000 to 2003).

LESSONS LEARNED

*"There are so many Thinks that a Thinker can think! . . .
Think left and think right and think low and think high.
Oh, the Thinks you can think up if only you try."*
DR. SEUSS

We have learned much by working through the Think strategy and project. Some lessons dealt with strategy, some dealt with organizational behavior, and some were simply about ourselves.

- *In the new, more competitive business-to-business environment, value is moving beyond just providing products to providing value that improves the customer's business.* Obviously, the more value one can provide to customers, the better. A critical area to consider in doing so is going beyond simply offering an inexpensive product to understanding how your company can help the customer reduce the costs of operating the product. This is especially true when, as in the PC industry, the purchase price is a small fraction of the cost to operate and maintain the product after purchase.
- *Branding and business strategy are inextricably linked.* Too often, companies see branding as "just marketing baloney" to support or (even worse) disguise the true business strategy and promise to the customers. However, as good brand stewards know, a brand's meaning is the sum of the entire experience a customer has with it. Synergizing branding and business strategy leverages the power of both for greater marketplace impact.
- *Look for opportunity in adversity.* It would have been easy to look at our multiple brands, shrug our shoulders, and continue on the same path. However, with any problem, there also lies an opportunity; in our case, it was the chance to meld several disparate brands into a family. Strategically, this reenergized IBM in the PC space and enabled us to send a new message to the marketplace. Tactically, this improved our marketing communications efficiency, because all our investment was behind a single message and family of offerings.
- *Leverage what you have.* Beyond the obvious strength of the Think-Pad brand was an incredibly powerful yet underutilized and dormant resource: the linkage between IBM and *Think*. By reaching back into IBM's history with *Think* and binding it to a strong

modern incarnation of it (ThinkPad), we were able to build a more meaningful and long-lasting branding approach for our PC family.

- *Get feedback to improve your plans.* Crucial to our success was getting input and feedback from multiple sources: market research, our marketing council, our industry council, corporate headquarters, and others. Significant changes were made as a result of these inputs, leading to a better overall strategy and tactics that would ensure positive outcomes.

- *Persistence linked with executive support is essential.* Over all the months of planning, it often seemed as though the Think strategy would be derailed. Any one of these snags could have spelled the end of what has turned out to be an excellent idea. The efforts and persistence of a small group of executives and thought leaders ensured its survival and ultimate success.

Recrossing the Chasm and Demand Innovation

Geoffrey Moore penned the book *Crossing the Chasm* to describe his view of technology adoption by customers. Mapped to the shape of a bell curve are the key stages in Moore's Technology Adoption Life Cycle.

- Innovators: technology enthusiasts (1 percent)
- Early adopters: visionaries (9 percent)
- Early majority: pragmatists (40 percent)
- Late majority: conservatives (40 percent)
- Laggards: skeptics (10 percent)

The Think strategy suggests that, if you have equity in an existing offering category that has already won over even the laggards, you may be able to extend it profitably to new offerings and get it in the hands of the early adopters and early majority sooner. It also points to breathing new life into existing offerings by putting some of the late lifecycle offerings under the umbrella of a more vibrant or innovative category.

Adrian Slywotsky and Richard Wise of Mercer Consulting in their new book, *How to Grow When Markets Don't,* talk about innovation on another dimension: demand innovation. The Think strategy is very much aligned to the Slywotsky and Wise assertion that, "companies skilled in demand innovation understand and exploit a little-known truth: while the product sale may be the culmination of the manufacturer's efforts, it usually marks the beginning of the customer's."

The Think strategy, simply stated, is "Innovation for Business Advantage," with an emphasis on delivering this advantage during first deployment and the complete ownership experience for personal computers. This strategy views customer wants and needs through an end-to-end economic lens.

"This is something most customers can't articulate directly; next-generation needs are often so profound and ambiguous, that customers haven't yet pinpointed them or put them into words," say Slywotsky and Wise. "If you succeed in viewing and understanding your customers through an economic lens, you'll find in time that you've made an important shift—from responding to customer needs to anticipating them."

For IBM in the personal computer marketplace, the intent of the IBM Think strategy is to accomplish just that.

B

SEEING RELEVANCE
Listening and Leading
in User-Centered Design

"Less is more."
MIES VAN DER ROHE

The following is based on a paper that Kazuhiko Yamazaki, Ph.D., and I submitted for the International Council of Societies of Industrial Design conference held in Seoul, Korea, in 2001. It has been updated and adapted for use in this book.

I believe that our collaboration over the years shows through in this work. This particular case study illustrates how we leveraged the brand equity in IBM ThinkPad to address a particular set of customer needs in Japan. Although we decided to move our portfolio to a global base later, the offering described in this paper was very well received by Japanese customers, and a tenth anniversary edition of the IBM ThinkPad based on some of the same design ideas sold out immediately.

Kaz has updated and expanded the original thinking in the paper to make it an appendix for this book, showing how we extended knowledge about a specific customer segment in Japan to global, ultraportable notebook computer offerings around the world. IBM and ThinkPad are trademarks of IBM Corporation.

Executive summary. The purpose of this case study is to demonstrate how to make design stability over long periods of time on notebook personal computer (PC) products. To approach the notebook PC, which has design stability over long periods of time and had become very well known to very special customers as a result, we proposed a leadership design approach. Leadership design comes from listening to end users and leading with innovation to meet their needs.

The case study for the IBM ThinkPad X series will show how business strategy drives investment by listening to users, which informs the design and engineering process to deliver what users truly want. Leadership design comes from listening and leading with innovation to meet user wants and needs.

In this case, a global market research study reached out to many users of mobile computing devices.

One of the user groups was located in Japan, and they provided data that was fundamental for designing a new notebook PC. These new models have a number of user-inspired elements, including a distinctive finish, touch, and feel available only in Japan.

- IBM ThinkPad X30
- IBM ThinkPad s30
- IBM ThinkPad X40, the latest version of the product

The results of this case study showed that listening to users for market research leads to an informed business strategy. A well-informed business strategy leads to designing truly useful and innovative offerings for end users. We listen to the desires of people in their minds and hearts around the world and consider their desires along with our original designs and development inspirations to lead in the marketplace.

INTRODUCTION

Business strategy and brand management must work in unison to create value for stakeholders and end users. Strategy is based on the business design of how value is created for stakeholders. Brand value is the sum of all attributes presented and known in the marketplace and the way in which value is delivered to end users.

Together, strategic business plans and specific offering designs represent a powerful intention to serve the needs of large numbers of people in harmony. Listening to what people want and leading them toward new and useful offerings is crucial for long-term success. This approach is central to IBM user-centered design.[1]

FIGURE A.I *Structure for Listening and Leading*

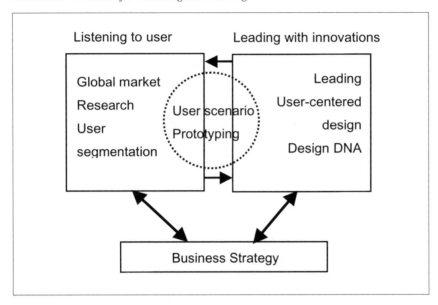

From the user-centered design approach, the collaboration of various types of professionals is important to design information devices. One of the difficulties of collaborations among various types of professionals is that it is not easy for them to communicate with each other, because their backgrounds and the technical vocabularies are different. Creating stories called "user scenarios" and modeling prototype devices is one useful method to share user information. It helps bind what we've heard from end users to useful design innovations.

APPROACH: LEADERSHIP DESIGN

As outlined, leadership design comes from listening to end-users and leading with innovation to meet their needs. In this section, as shown in Figure A.1, the authors describe an approach for leadership design based on their experience of branding and designing the ThinkPad[2] IBM notebook computers.

Listening to Users

Listening and leading has been a key part of the business design for IBM ThinkPad notebook computer offerings. Making ThinkPad a brand people trust is something IBM has worked toward for almost ten years, with the result that people believe the IBM ThinkPad is the notebook computer that helps them succeed.

Extensive market research is used to understand what end users want to do next. The IBM portfolio of technologies and development capabilities is then applied to these wants and needs. Resources are focused on what IBM can do to best meet these needs.

A key part of the business strategy agenda is market research, especially for market segmentation. Today, the IBM mobile computing user segmentation is based on end-user behavior. This includes global travelers, numeric intensive users, commuters, users who want a simpler computing experience, and a unique segment recognized only in Japan–the "status seeker."

User Scenario

Modeling user scenarios is one of the useful methodologies to understand users and share the information among designers and related people.[3] A user scenario has many roles such as system vision, design rationale, usability specifications, functional specifications, user interface metaphors, prototypes, object models, formative evaluation, documentation/training/help, and overall evaluation.[4]

For an innovative design, user scenarios need to be developed for each end-user segment to share the goals and aspirations of these users with a variety of professionals. They use these user scenarios to create and evaluate new ideas. User scenarios are very important tools to collaborate with many professionals around the world and create a common language for this collaboration.

For ThinkPad design, experts in fields such as strategy, marketing, brand management, engineering, industrial design, graphic design, user interface design, and usability are brought together by these end-user stories as user scenarios. For ThinkPad, this story line, or user scenario as we call it here, has been prepared for all IBM ThinkPad users.

A better experience: IBM ThinkPad stands for innovative and easy-to-use mobile computing that is tailored to my needs and delivers a surprising and cool experience.

Also, based on this user scenario, a poster for the image of the ThinkPad experience has been prepared to share the goal across the team, as shown in Figure A.2.

FIGURE A.2 *The ThinkPad Experience*

Leading with Innovation

Leading with innovation is the approach from design to meet customer needs. It consists of leading user-centered design, design DNA, and collaboration with a multidisciplinary team.

Our leading user-centered design approach is the way to design from the user's viewpoint with innovation. Design teams start from user needs and propose several ideas. Also, this approach includes a user-experience design approach in integrating all of the forms and materials for users. To cover all user scenarios, this approach starts with initial awareness of the brand or product, then continues through customer evaluation, purchase, setup, upgrade, and replacement with a later product.

The design team needs to cover product design, graphic design, and user interface design to cover the entire life cycle of users interacting with the device and brand.

Design DNA is an important approach to keep a unified brand image and enhance brand equity in the future. For ThinkPads, the design DNA was selected after studying a global brand research project and af-

FIGURE A.3 *IBM ThinkPad*

ter discussion by the worldwide design team, brand team, marketing team, and an external design consultant.

One innovative way to maintain consistent design DNA while creating innovative design ideas is to collaborate with an external consultant. For ThinkPad, ten years of fruitful collaboration with Richard Sapper of Milan helps keep the ThinkPad design DNA stable and youthful, evolving purposefully to extend the idea that is IBM ThinkPad's basic design DNA.

The form of the IBM ThinkPad notebook computers started as a rectangular black box, but it has been extended several times over the past ten years to incorporate useful features and details that are in keeping with the original design concept. Several different characteristics and details have been added to the IBM ThinkPad, but it still keeps the original concept and design DNA.

CASE STUDY: IBM THINKPAD X SERIES

This case study will document how business strategy drives the investment in listening to users, which informs the design and engineering processes to deliver what users truly want. For this purpose, the ThinkPad s Series was selected as a case study.

Listening to Users for IBM ThinkPad X Series

In this case, a global market research study listened to many users of mobile computing devices. One of the user sets, found exclusively in Japan, formed the foundation for designing and developing the IBM ThinkPad s Series.

User Scenario for ThinkPad X Series

The Japanese Status Seeker category helped focus IBM on serving the needs of an end-user type that was discovered in earlier research—people who believe that IBM ThinkPad is an experience in success. IBM ThinkPad notebook computers help people succeed; people who use IBM ThinkPad notebook computers are seen as successful. This focus on success was very strong in the Japan Status Seeker segment. Following is the simple user scenario for this user segment.

"I want to project a sophisticated high-tech image and use the smallest, hottest technology to reflect who I am."

Leading with Innovation for ThinkPad X Series

In this case, leading user-centered design is based on global user research and real contacts with users in Japan. Also, to cover all user experiences, the design and development teams worked closely with product design and the marketing teams. The design approach is based on ThinkPad design DNA, but the innovations were developed to meet user needs.

These user-inspired elements include an exclusive finish, touch, and fit available only in Japan. The design emphasizes communications, with a built-in antenna in the screen for wireless communications, accompanied by an innovative keyboard for input. The keyboard input and wireless output remain synchronized when the notebook computer is closed, but are held in visual dynamic tension when it is open.

ThinkPad X30 and ThinkPad s30. Following are some of the details of the design that were added to the design DNA as user-inspired innovations.

- *Extended ThinkPad design DNA.* A simple black form is basic ThinkPad design DNA. For this product, the DNA was enhanced with a shiny finish with accent colors for the latch icon and connector and a colored keyboard for improved usability.
- *Compact with usable design.* There are many usability features in this compact notebook, such as the full-size colored keyboard that can be tilted by the battery, ThinkPad buttons, and separate audio controls.
- *Exclusive finishes and touches.* Visually distinctive features are important for status seekers. A new, shiny finishing material was developed. After studying several surfaces, this finish was selected as the best of the black finishes. Also, several other finishes were prepared such as for the palm rest area, which has a soft touch finish; the ThinkPad button area, with a black hair-line finish; and the hinges, which have a metallic finish.
- *Built-in advanced technology.* Advanced technology was built into the system along with the visual design. A wireless antenna was built into the display as butterfly wings, a keyboard light was built into the top of the display, and a long-life battery option makes it easy to attach a large battery.
- *Out-of-box experience (OOB).* The out-of-box experience is important for products. This includes packaging, setup instructions, manuals, CD-ROMs, preloaded software, initial wallpaper and screensaver, etc. For this project, ThinkPad design DNA and ease of use were key concepts. All shipping components were redesigned to help customers have a positive OOB experience.
- *Life cycle.* For promoting the new product, the user-experience design approach was used to cover the entire product life cycle and establish a unified brand image. The approach was to enhance the ThinkPad design DNA, using a Web-based design approach, and make it easy to recognize the design concept quickly.
- *Web design.* The Web is the one of best tools to communicate with many people about interesting products or about problem solutions using our products and services. Previous Web design was a product-oriented approach, but for this project, we tried a human-oriented approach based on human-experience design. Based on user scenarios used for the design itself, user scenarios for users

have been developed with several key images, animations, and text.[5]

- *Brochure design.* Printed materials such as flyers and brochures were designed based on the Web design and content. One of the key concepts was to select ten key points and images to make it easy to recognize the product quickly.

ThinkPad X40.   During the tenth anniversary celebration of IBM ThinkPad, a commemorative edition was produced for the Japan market in 2002. Numbered and rendered with the high-gloss top cover finish, this edition of the IBM ThinkPad X40 (the smallest and lightest member of the IBM ThinkPad family at the time), sold out on the Web within days. Some of these ThinkPads were spotted within weeks on eBay and other exchange sites for twice the street price.

CONCLUSION

The results of this case study show that linking business strategy to what users truly want will lead to the design of truly useful and innovative offerings. We must balance listening to the wants of people in their minds and hearts around the world with leading the art of the possible using original designs and development inspirations.

ACKNOWLEDGEMENTS

For help with this paper, we would like to say special thanks to David Hill, David Sawin, Stacey Baer of IBM Corporation, and Tomoyuki Takahashi of IBM Japan. Also, we would like to thank the marketing, design, and development teams for ThinkPad in Research Triangle Park, North Carolina, and in Japan.

C

PUTTING THE BRAND AND BRANDING IN CONTEXT

Customer Equity Marketing Metrics[1]

BY KATHERINE N. LEMON, ROLAND T. RUST, VALARIE A. ZEITHAML, LOREN J. LEMON[2]

The quartet who penned this appendix are, to my way of thinking, *the* thought leaders in customer equity measurement.

Executive summary. Customer equity is defined as the combination of value equity, brand equity, and relationship equity. Value equity is made up of quality, price, and convenience attributes. Brand equity is composed of awareness, ethics, and perception components. Relationship equity includes loyalty programs, affinity, community, and knowledge-building. Understanding these attributes and measuring them regularly can help target investments that can build an enduring customer constituency.

CUSTOMER EQUITY

While gaining insights into brands and branding is valuable, the reality for every company is that tradeoffs must be made. Competition between various business components is inherent in modern enterprises—

R&D versus production, versus sales and marketing, versus employee compensation, versus you name it. Even within marketing, such tradeoffs are prevalent, involving brand and branding, pricing, service, convenience, relationship marketing, and a myriad of other marketing efforts. Given that no company has unlimited resources to invest and fully fund all the company initiatives that appear to have some incremental benefit, tradeoff decisions must be made.

While determining how such tradeoffs are made among the various components of a business is beyond the scope of this book, metrics are now available to evaluate the relative impact of various competing marketing efforts. So now a hypothetical company marketing chief with $500,000 to spend on marketing efforts has a tool to assist in making such tradeoffs, including decisions regarding brand and branding efforts. The tool also enables the marketing chief to be able to make the case to superiors regarding the value of investing in marketing efforts.

The key metric in this regard is Customer Equity, which is defined as the total lifetime value of a firm's current and potential customer base. Customer Equity views the company's customers as an essential asset of the firm. This metric is customercentric in approach. For, while a firm's products or other offerings will vary from time to time, customers remain the key to long-term success.

Utilizing Customer Equity as the core component, academic researchers have created a framework (the CE Framework) within which tradeoffs among various marketing initiatives (including brand and branding) can be evaluated. The first level of the CE Framework identifies and defines the three primary drivers of Customer Equity. Those key drivers are: value, brand, and relationship. Using such drivers, the CE framework allows a company to determine what matters most to its customers. The company can determine in a more disciplined way, based on such customer insights, where it can best invest its marketing resources to enhance Customer Equity—that is, to grow the value of the customer asset.

Customer Equity Drivers in Detail

Value driver. The value driver is defined in the CE Framework as the customer's assessment of the utility of the firm's offering (product or service) based on the customer's relatively objective perception of what is given up for what is received. In other words, value looks at the customer's basic willingness to part with something (e.g., money) to obtain the company's offering (e.g., product) based on an assessment of the objective aspects of the offering.

FIGURE A.4 *The Customer Equity Model*

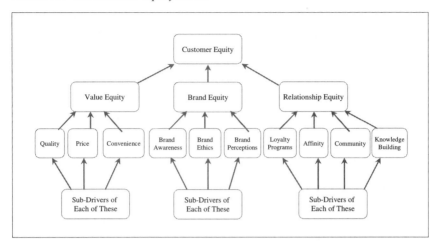

While it is easy to see that, for any given company, there could be a myriad of subcomponents to the value driver, the traditional, and generally quite comprehensive, subcomponents to the value driver are quality, price, and convenience. Under the CE Framework, quality encompasses the customer's perception of the physical and nonphysical aspects of the offering. Price represents "what is given up by the customer," usually money, but other costs may be involved (e.g., having to purchase a device to operate the product). Convenience relates to the time costs relative to obtaining the product and other costs incurred by the customer to be able to do business with the company.

Brand driver.   In the CE Framework, the brand driver is defined as the customer's subjective and intangible assessment of the company's offering beyond the offering's objectively perceived values. This definition is probably narrower than what most people think of when approaching brand and branding. But the power of the definition is that it separates some of the amorphous aspects of a brand or branding efforts and, as a result, makes the branding issue more actionable. The focus here is not management's view of the benefit or value of a brand; rather, the focus is on the actual impact of the brand on the customer's purchase behavior. This permits insights into the tradeoffs that can become actionable to the company.

Like the value driver, there could be a myriad of subcomponents to the brand driver, but the CE Framework conceptually identifies the key subcomponents as: customer brand awareness, customer attitude toward the brand, and company ethics. Brand awareness deals with those company actions that influence and enhance the customer's awareness of the brand. For many offerings (especially consumer package goods), this takes the form of some type of advertising. Customer attitude toward the brand deals with the closeness of the customer's connection to the brand and the customer's emotional ties to the brand. In other words, how much does the customer identify with, or subjectively value, the brand? The final subcomponent is company ethics. While this may not first appear to deal with brand, remembering the definition of the brand driver (i.e., the customer's subjective assessment of the company's brand), it is clear that the company's ethics (or the lack thereof) clearly have a role in such customer subjective assessments. For the purposes of the CE Framework, company ethics deal with company efforts (or lack of efforts) to influence the customer's subjective perceptions of the firm not necessarily related to a specific company offering. Ethics involve charitable or community activities as well as company policies (e.g., privacy and employee relations) and actions (e.g., corporate misconduct).

Relationship driver. The relationship driver is defined in the CE Framework as the customer's tendency to stick with a company above and beyond the customer's objective and subjective assessments of the company's offerings or brands. As with the other drivers of Customer Equity (value and brand), there could be a myriad of subcomponents to the relationship driver, but the CE Framework traditionally looks at the subcomponents of: loyalty programs, special recognition and treatment of the customer, affinity programs, customer community-building programs, and customer knowledge-building programs.

Loyalty programs are ubiquitous. They reward the customer for specific behaviors (e.g., flying on the airline) with tangible benefits (e.g., free tickets). Special recognition and treatment refers to company actions that recognize specific customers with specific benefits not generally available to others (e.g., preferred seating at the theater). Affinity programs seek to create strong emotional ties with the customer by connecting the company's offering with other aspects of the customer's life (e.g., college alumni Visa cards). Community-building programs seek to link a given customer with a group (community) of other like customers of the firm (e.g., Corvette car clubs). Finally, knowledge-building programs seek to create a learning relationship between the customer and the company, such that the customer is less willing to create a relationship with an alternative provider. For example, travel companies learn customer preferences so that subsequent interactions are specifically tailored to that customer based on the customer's stated prior preferences (e.g., seating and food preferences on flights).

Identifying the Key Customer Equity Driver

Knowing the various drivers and their subcomponents of Customer Equity, the firm needs to determine which of the drivers and subcomponents are key to the target customers doing business with that company. This is the critical first step in a company's implementation of the CE Framework. While this step will vary from company to company, the point is for the company to determine which drivers may have an influence on the target customers doing business with the company. This can be determined by a variety of means such as customer one-on-one ethnographic interviews, broad customer surveys or focused surveys, and industry data. After the set of potential drivers and driver subcomponents has been identified, target customers are surveyed to determine their perceptions of the company's and its competitors' performance with regard to the specific CE drivers and subcomponents, and to gain additional data necessary to calculate customer lifetime value (CLV) and Customer Equity.

Once the data is compiled, the company would first determine what drivers and driver subcomponents are most important for the customer to do business with the company. The company would then assess the company's performance on such drivers and subcomponents and compare that with the relative importance to the customer. Finally, the company can evaluate its performance relative to its competitors and the customer's level of importance. For example, a company could determine on a one-to-five scale (five being the most important) that its customer ranks value as a four, brand as a two, and relationship as a three. The company could also determine that its performance levels are: value, two; brand, four; relationship, three. Finally, the company could determine that its primary competitor has the following performance levels in the eyes of the customers: value, five; brand, one; relationship, five. This results in the following bar graph:

The results provide many insights to the marketing chief. One is that, because the customer doesn't weigh brand highly (2) and the company already has a high performance level on brand (4), that the company need not expend additional branding efforts on this target customer group. Further, the customer's competitor is not providing sufficient

FIGURE A.5 *Customer Equity Analysis*

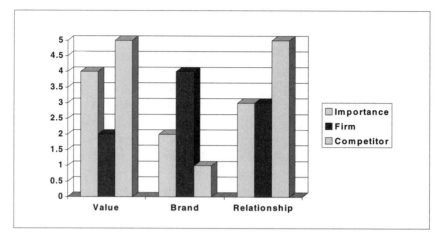

branding efforts relative to the customer's expectations (performance 1, importance 2). With respect to value, the company is not providing value to the target customer relative to the customer importance (importance 4, performance 2). Moreover, the company's competitor is meeting the customer's value criteria (performance 4). So clearly in this case, the company is not meeting the customer's expectations and is at a competitive disadvantage. With such insights, the company marketing chief now will be able to tailor marketing efforts to meet customer expectations and identify and address situations in which the company has a competitive advantage or disadvantage vis-à-vis its competitors.

Scenarios Related to the Customer Equity Framework

Armed with an understanding of the CE Framework, one can now see how certain situations may result in one of the drivers having more importance that the other drivers. While this may vary from company to company, offering to offering, and even target customer group to target customer group, some broad generalizations are possible that help illuminate situations that generally favor one driver more than another.

Value driver. The value driver will be critical when there are discernable differences between competing offerings. If a company's offering is essentially fungible (e.g., gasoline), an objective assessment of the offering's utility is the same regardless of who is making the offering, resulting in little value differentiation other than price. In such a case, other drivers may be more important (brand awareness of *Exxon* or loyalty programs). But, where the offerings differ, a company has a much greater opportunity to make the case that their offering provides more objective utility than the competitor's (e.g., vehicle performance or convenience). This allows for use of value strategies other than just price.

Value is also critical where the customer transaction requires a complex decision process. In such a situation, the customer will be examining tradeoffs, costs, and benefits related to each offering. While some of this will be subjective (e.g., brand name), much of the process will involve the customer's evaluation of objective components of the offering. One example would be the process one needs to go through in selecting a mobile phone calling plan.

Value is also an important feature in B2B transactions. Because the buyer may need to be able to justify the purchase to superiors, the need to articulate objective advantages of the purchased offering from the other competing offerings is critical. Additionally, such transactions have long-term consequences or involve large sums of money that make value critical.

Companies offering new or innovative products or services must address the value driver to overcome customer reticence or lack of understanding regarding such a "really new" offering. Such a company can address either the utility component (e.g., faster download speeds), the "what the customer has to give up" component (e.g., only $19.95 a month), or often both to create the possibility that the customers will purchase the offering.

Brand driver. As noted throughout this book, brands and branding often play a role in company marketing efforts. But, as we have pointed out, brands and branding will not always be the critical driver of Customer Equity. Nevertheless, in many situations, brand and branding will be key. For example, brand is very important in low-involvement, repetitious, or routine transactions. This is often the case with consumer packaged goods such as groceries and beverages. Once a company has successfully made the customer brand aware and brand loyal, it is difficult for competitors to move that customer to other products.

Additionally, brand is critical in situations where the offering is highly visible to others or in some ways "identifies" the customer. This involves high-end offerings such as luxury automobiles and other visibly "labeled" goods (e.g., Abercrombie & Fitch clothing). Because the brand is what the customer is, at least in part, purchasing is the ability to be connected to the brand, and the brand is critical.

Brand is also important to offerings that are particularly sensitive to customer word of mouth. Positive word of mouth can be enhanced by strong branding, making the customer susceptible to greater subjective approval of an offering simply because it carries a brand that they have heard good things about. Branding can also be especially important in situations where there is negative word of mouth. In such situations, focusing on branding efforts to defeat the negative word of mouth could be critical.

Finally, brand can be important to "credence" offerings; i.e., where it is difficult to evaluate the offering prior to acquisition. In other words, the brand attempts to establish a positive effect on the customer so that the customer will still acquire the offering, even in light of such uncertainty. A great deal of business school marketing education is based on such an approach. An executive education program offered by a "top ten" business school may be perceived as more desirable, even though the customer (attending executive) has no way of objectively making that determination in advance.

Relationship driver. The emergence of the Customer Relationship Management (CRM) bandwagon may make it appear that relationship is the key driver of customer equity in almost every case. However, blindly jumping on that bandwagon has resulted in a great deal of wasted time and money for things like loyalty programs in cases where the customer really doesn't care about such matters. By using the CE Framework, managers can intelligently determine whether such efforts are worthwhile.

While much maligned, loyalty programs can be critical to drive customer equity. This is particularly the case where carefully crafted programs create in the customer's mind the idea that the aspirational value of the reward is greater than the actual cash benefits. At least early on, this was the case for airline frequent flyer programs, where the aspirational value (e.g., "I'm going to Hawaii for free.") was seen as greater than the actual cash benefit (three cents a mile).

Also, certain products lend themselves strongly to customer community building, yielding additional customer interactions. For example, membership in the HOGs (Harley Owners Group) keeps Harley-Davidson customers connected to the company and yields additional customer equity (e.g., their successful clothing line).

Offerings requiring the customer to opt out also depend a great deal on the relationship driver (e.g., newspaper subscriptions). The objective in such situations is to maintain the relationship with the existing customer so they are not inclined to opt out, either because of disaffection or actions of competitors.

Customer Equity Framework Strategic Decision Making

Once you have determined the key drivers and subcomponents to driving Customer Equity for your company, the power of the CE Framework becomes apparent. Armed with that information, you can determine how you are doing on things that matter most to your customers—both in isolation and in comparison to your competitors. This knowledge will give a company the ability to be responsive to the wants and needs of its customers and the marketplace in general. Intelligent tradeoffs may now become clear. You may not want to spend the $100,000 needed to improve your loyalty program, when the customers are much more receptive to brand advertising. In other situations, you may find that brand advertising has less of an impact on your existing or targeted customers than improving the quality of the offering.

Clearly, nothing occurs in isolation, and just because one driver may be more important than another does not mean that you should ignore the other drivers of Customer Equity in your marketing efforts. But with the Customer Equity Framework, management has the ability to prioritize among the various marketing components in a disciplined manner.

BRAND AND BRANDING IN CONTEXT

Returning to the theme of this book, using the Customer Equity metric and the CE Framework, management can make decisions regarding branding efforts in a customercentric approach. Because a key purpose of brand efforts is to get the customer to do business with you and to keep doing business with you, such an approach is essential. This metric and framework should also help management avoid investments in branding efforts that might have little payoff or might come at the expense of other marketing efforts that could be more effective. Finally, in those situations where brand and branding efforts are crucial, the metric and framework will help make the case for the company making the investment in critical branding efforts.

Author's Note

I would like to thank Katherine Lemon, Roland Rust, Valarie Zeith-aml, and Loren Lemon for contributing this updated view of their work in customer equity marketing metrics to *Brandscendence*. This appendix adds a dimension to the work that wouldn't have been possible without the expertise and pioneering work these marketing thought leaders have done in the study of customer equity and lifetime customer value.

D

THE COMMUNICATIONS
MODEL FOR MEMES

vMEMES	Best Source	Best-Fit Approach
BEIGE	Caretaker Provider	Biologic senses—touch, taste, smell, sight, hearing Physical contact rather than symbols
PURPLE	Caring chieftain or shaman Counsel from the revered elders From within the tribe/clan group Signals and omens from spirit realm Word of ancestors and their ways Collective sense of supportive peers	Traditional rites, rituals, ceremonies Includes mystical elements and superstitions Appeals to extended family, harmony, safety Recognizes blood bonds, the folk, group Familiar metaphors, drawings, and emblems Minimal reliance on written language
RED	Person with recognized power Straight-talking Big Boss One with something to offer Respected, revered, feared other Celebrated "idol" with reputation Someone of proven trustworthiness	Demonstrate "What's in it for me, now?" Offer "Immediate gratification if. . ." Challenges and appeals to machismo/strength Heroic status and legendary potential Flashy, unambiguous, reality-based, strong Simple language and fiery images/graphics
BLUE	Rightful, proper kind of authority Higher position in the One True Way Down the chain of command According to the book's rules and regulations Person with position power and rank In compliance with tradition and precedent As directed by divinely ordained Power	Duty, honor, country, images of discipline Self-sacrifice for higher cause and purpose Appeal to traditions, laws, established norms Use class-consciousness, knowing one's place Propriety, righteousness, responsibilities Ensure future rewards and delayed gratification Assuage guilt with correct consequences
ORANGE	One's own right-thinking mind Successful mentors and models Credible professionals and "gurus" Prosperous, successful, elite contacts Advantageous to the self image Resulting from own observations Tried-and-true experience, experiment	Appeal to competitive advantage and leverage Success motivations and achieving abundance Bigger, better, newer, faster, more popular Citations of experts and selected authorities Experimental data and tried-and-true experience Profit, productivity, quality, results, win Demonstrate as best of several options
GREEN	Consensual communitarian norms Enlightened friend/colleague Outcome of participation and sharing Result of enlightenment, becoming Observation of events here and now Responsive to affect/feelings/emotions Relative to situation and people at hand	Enhance belonging, sharing, group harmony Sensitive to human issues and care for others Expand awareness and understanding of inner self Symbols of equity, humanity, bonding Gentle language along with nature imagery Build trust, openness, exploration, passages Real people and authentic emotional displays
YELLOW	Any useful information source May adopt BEIGE through GREEN Competent, more knowing person/entity Relevant, more functional data Merge formal sources and hunches Individualized explorations/discoveries Media congruent with message	Interactive, relevant media, self-accessible Functional "lean" information without fluff The facts, the feelings, the instincts Big picture, total systems, integrations Connect data across fields for holistic view Adapt, mesh, blend, access, sense, gather Self-connecting to systems and others usefully
TURQUOISE	Experience of discovery Learning in communal network Holistic conception of multiple realities Any being in the TURQUOISE sphere Knowing systems across the planet Reawakened deep brain capacities Reliance on holistic consciousness	Multidimensional chunks of insight Use multitiered consciousness to access Renewed spirituality and sacrifice to whole Ecological interdependency and interconnections Macro (global) solutions to macro problems Community beyond nationalities or partisanship High-tech and high-touch for experiential
CORAL, ETC.		

This Meme Communications Strategy chart is supplied by Don Beck and is reprinted with his permission.

Preface

1. *Webster's New Universal Unabridged Dictionary* (New York, NY: Barnes and Noble Books, 1996).

2. Ibid.

3. Ibid.

Chapter One

1. My favorite book of quotations: Dr. Lawrence J. Peter, *Peter's Quotations: Ideas for Our Time* (New York, NY: William Morrow and Co., 1977).

2. "Brands in an Age of Anti-Americanism," *Business Week*, Asian Edition, August 4, 2003, 47–49.

3. Anjan Chatterjee, Matthew E. Jauchius, Hans-Werner Kaas, and Aurobind Satpathy, "Revving Up Auto Branding," *The McKinsey Quarterly* 1 (2002): 134-143.

4. Ibid.

Chapter Two

1. Dr. Lawrence J. Peter, *Peter's Quotations: Ideas for Our Time*, 494.

2. This endnote is inclusive of these books and authors.

- David A. Aaker, *Managing Brand Equity: Capitalizing on the Value of a Brand Name* (New York, NY: The Free Press, 1991).
- David A. Aaker, *Building Strong Brands* (New York, NY: The Free Press, 1995).

- Roland T. Rust, Valarie A. Zeithaml, and Katherine N. Lemon, *Driving Customer Equity: How Customer Lifetime Value Is Reshaping Corporate Strategy* (New York, NY: The Free Press, 2000).
- David A. Aaker and Erich Joachimsthaller, *Brand Leadership* (New York, NY: The Free Press, 2000).
- Kevin Lane Keller, *Strategic Brand Management: Building, Measuring, and Managing Brand Equity* (Upper Saddle River, NJ: Prentice Hall, 1998).
- Marc Gobé, *Emotional Branding: The New Paradigm for Connecting Brands to People* (New York, NY: Alworth Press, 2001).
- Marc Gobé, *Citizen Brand: 10 Commandments for Transforming Brands into a Consumer Democracy* (New York, NY: Alworth Press, 2002).
- Laurence Vincent, *Legendary Brands: Unleashing the Power of Storytelling to Create a Winning Market Strategy* (Chicago, IL: Dearborn Trade Publishing, 2002).
- Sam Hill and Chris Lederer, *The Infinite Asset: Managing Brands to Build New Value* (Boston, MA: Harvard Business School Press, 2001).
- G. Clotaire Rapaille, *7 Secrets of Marketing in a Multicultural World* (Provo, UT: Executive Excellence Publishing, 2001).
- Gerald Zaltman, *How Customers Think: Essential Insights into the Mind of the Market* (Boston, MA: Harvard Business School Press, 2003).

3. Jean Piaget and Barbel Inhelder, *The Psychology of the Child,* New York: Basic Books, 1969, 2000; originally published in French as *La Psychologie de l'enfant* by Presses Universitaires de France, Paris, 1966.

4. Ralph Stacey, *Complexity and Creativity in Organizations,* San Francisco: Berrett-Koehler Publishers, Inc., 1996.

5. From the eBay Web site home page, *Company Overview, Our Mission,* http://pages.ebay.com/community/aboutebay/overview/index.html, November 2003.

6. Marshal McLuhan & Bruce R. Powers, *The Global Village: Transformations in World Life and Media in the 21st Century,* New York: Oxford University Press, 1989, 9, chapter "The Resonating Interval." The McLuhan Tetrad is a metaphor that when drawn looks like a double Mobius loop, with these features at each corner of the four-sided loop figure, here asked as questions: "1. What does any artifact enlarge or enhance? 2. What does it erode or obsolesce? 3. What does it retrieve that had

been earlier obsolesced? 4. What does it reverse or flip into when pushed to the limits of its potential (chiasmus)?"

7. Transcribed from a dialog with Scott Elias, president of Elias Arts, New York, December 13, 2003.

8. From the eBay Web site home page, *Company Overview, Our Mission,* http://pages.ebay.com/community/aboutebay/overview/index.html, November 2003.

Chapter Three

1. Dr. Lawrence J. Peter, *Peter's Quotations, Ideas for Our Time,* 474.

2. "The Top 100 Global Brands," Interbrand/Business Week 2003.

3. "BMW: Will Panke's High-Speed Approach Hurt the Brand?" *Business Week,* 9 June 2003, 57-60.

4. Scott Davis and Michael Dunn, *Building the Brand-Driven Business* (New York, NY: The Free Press, 2003).

5. Molly Wade McGrath, *Topsellers USA* (New York, NY: William Morrow and Company, Inc., 1983), 16.

6. Ibid.

7. *Webster's New Universal Unabridged Dictionary,* 1996, xv–xvi.

Chapter Four

1. Dr. Laurence J. Peter, *Peter's Quotations: Ideas for Our Time,* 1977.

2. Ralph Stacey, *Complexity and Creativity in Organizations* (San Francisco, CA: Berrett-Koehler Publishers, Inc., 1996), 204-205.

3. Noel M. Tichy and Stratford Sherman, *Control Your Destiny or Someone Else Will* (New York, NY: Doubleday, 1993).

4. Martha Lagace summary of Douglas Holt, "Building Brandtopias: How Top Brands Tap into Society," *HBS Working Knowledge,* 24 June 2002.

5. Adrian J. Slywotzky and David J. Morrison, *The Profit Zone: How Strategic Business Design Will Lead You to Tomorrow's Profits* (New York, NY: Times Business, Random House, 1997), 6-8.

6. *Webster's New Universal Unabridged Dictionary,* 1996.

7. Ibid.

8. Ralph Stacey, *Complexity and Creativity in Organizations*, 287-288.

Chapter Five

1. Dr. Laurence J. Peter, *Peter's Quotations: Ideas for Our Time*, 1977.

2. Sarah Lyall, "Regular Guy on a Laugh Track," *New York Times*, 1 July 1993, sect. C, 5.

3. Frank S. Moore, LL.B of the New York Bar, *Legal Protection of Goodwill* (New York, NY: The Ronald Press Company, 1936), 42.

4. George R. Catlett and Norman O. Olson, *Accounting for Goodwill* (American Institute of Certified Public Accountants, Inc., 1968), 37.

5. Carl Bass, Practice Fellow, Financial Accounting Standards Board (FASB), interview by the author, transcribed from audiocassette, December 1994.

6. Ibid.

7. *Webster's New Universal Unabridged Dictionary*, 1996.

8. Ibid.

9. Ibid.

10. Ibid.

11. Ibid.

Chapter Six

1. Dr. Laurence J. Peter, *Peter's Quotations: Ideas for Our Time*, 1977.

2. Statistics from: Stephen A. Greyser, "Johnson & Johnson: The Tylenol Tragedy," *Harvard Business School Case Study* HBS 9-583-043 (1982).

3. John Cobb and Herman Daly, *For the Common Good* (Boston, MA: Beacon Press, 1989), 138.

4. Cheryl L. Karp, Ph.D, and Leonard Karp, J.D., *MMPI* (American Academy of Matrimonial Lawyers, http://www.aaml.org/MMPI.htm, November 2003).

5. David Welch, "The Second Coming of Cadillac," *Business Week*, 24 November 2003, 80.

Chapter Seven

1. Dr. Lawrence J. Peter, *Peter's Quotations: Ideas for Our Time*, 1977.

2. Daniel N. Robinson, *The Great Ideas of Psychology* (Oxford University and Columbia University, The Great Courses 660, no. 6); related, from the course guide, "Weber's Law Concerns Sensitivity to Differences between Stimuli; Fechner's Law Concerns the Magnitude of Sensations," 19.

3. *@Issue: The Journal of Business & Design* 9, no. 1 (Fall 2003), 2. Published by Corporate Design Foundation.

4. *@Issue: The Journal of Business & Design* 8, no. 1 (Spring 2002), 14-15. Published by Corporate Design Foundation.

5. Scott Elias, president of Elias Arts, interview by the author, 13 December 2003.

6. Background information on the AT&T "Sparkletone" provided by Heidi Mantz, creative director, AT&T brand identity, in the brief, "AT&T Sparkletone: Did You Know?" October 2003.

7. Information about OXO adapted from the company's Web site, http://www.oxo.com, November 2003.

8. Eric Schlosser, "Why McDonald's Fries Taste So Good," *Atlantic Monthly*, January 2001, 50.

9. Information adapted from the Leffingwell & Associates Web site, http://www.leffingwell.com, November 2003.

10. Ethan Smith, "Smells and Whistles," *The Industry Standard*, 2 October 2000.

11. *Webster's New Universal Unabridged Dictionary*, 1996.

Chapter Eight

1. Dr. Lawrence J. Peter, *Peter's Quotations: Ideas for Our Time*, 1977, 345.

2. Marketplace, "Brand Manager Deluxe, How LVMH's Arnault Matches Wild Designers, Iconic Label to Commercialize Creativity," *Wall Street Journal*, 10 October 2003, sect. B, 1.

3. Official SPAM Web site, Hormel Corporation, http://www.spam .com.

Chapter Nine

1. Dr. Lawrence J. Peter, *Peter's Quotations: Ideas for Our Time,* 1977.

2. G. Clotaire Rapaille, *7 Secrets of Marketing,* 9.

3. Ibid., 13–14.

4. Carl G. Jung, *Man and His Symbols,* (New York, NY: Doubleday & Company, 1964,) 55.

5. Gerald Zaltman, *How Customers Think,* 211 and 213.

6. Raj Rajaratnam and Jill Orum, Kraft Foods Corporation, "The Caveman Is Alive and Well," presentation at the American Marketing Association, 20th Annual Marketing Research Conference, Sheraton Harbor Island Hotel, September 1999.

7. *Webster's New Universal Unabridged Dictionary,* 1996.

8. Joseph LeDoux, *Synaptic Self: How Our Brains Become Who We Are* (Harmondsworth, Middlesex, England: Viking/Penguin Group, 2002), 221. Author also cites for "flashbulb memories" these references: Brown and Kulik, *Cognition,* 1977, 5:57-99; Christianson, *Mem. Cogn.,* 1989, 17:435-43; Neisser and Harsch in *Affect and Accuracy in Recall, Studies of "Flashbulb" Memories,* edited by E. Winograd and U. Neisser (New York, NY: Cambridge University Press, 1992).

9. Gerald Zaltman, *How Customers Think,* 288.

10. *Webster's New Universal Unabridged Dictionary,* 1996.

11. Ibid.

12. Ibid.

Chapter Ten

1. Dr. Lawrence J. Peter, *Peter's Quotations: Ideas for Our Time,* 1977, 172.

2. Ken Wilber, *A Theory of Everything: An Integral Vision for Business, Politics, Science, and Spirituality,* (Boston, MA: Shambala Press, 2001) 40.

3. Diagram adapted from Ken Wilbur's *A Brief History of Everything,* 74.

4. Paul Hawken, *The Ecology of Commerce: A Declaration of Sustainability,* (Harper Business, 1993), xiii.

5. Ibid., xiv.

Chapter Eleven

1. Dr. Lawrence J. Peter, *Peter's Book of Quotations: Ideas for Our Time,* 1977, 472.

2. Conrad Hilton, *Be My Guest,* published by Hilton Hotels and found in hotel rooms right next to the religious texts in nightstands around the world.

3. From *Information Please* © *2003,* reprinted from source: "The World's Top Tourism Destinations (international tourist arrivals)," source: World Tourism Organization (WTO); "Top States and Cities Visited by Overseas Travelers in 2002," source: U.S. Department of Commerce, International Trade Administration, from Statistical Abstract of the United States, 2001.

4. Adapted from the Intercontinental Hotels Group Web site, http://www.ichotelsgroup.com.

Chapter Twelve

1. Dr. Lawrence J. Peter, *Peter's Quotations: Ideas for Our Time,* 1977.

2. Ibid.

3. Adapted from the Neibaum-Coppola Winery Web site, http://www.neibaum-coppola.com, December 2003.

4. Eunice Wait, *Wines and Vines of California,* (San Francisco, CA: 1889).

5. "Ronald McDonald Is Such a Busy Clown, How Does He Do It?" *Wall Street Journal,* 29 May 2003, sect. A, 1.

6. Diane Rinehart, "Big Macs in Moscow," *Reader's Digest,* June 1991, 4.

7. Transcribed interview with George Cohon by the author, December 1993.

8. Bryan Moynahan, "Feeding the 50,000," *The Sunday Times Magazine* (Canada), 29 November 1992, 3.

9. "McDonald's amid the '92 L.A. Riots," McDonald's Corporation videotape #MC-1237, 7 May 1993.

10. Edwin Reingold, "America's Hamburger Helper: McDonald's Gives New Meaning to 'We Do It All for You' by Investing in People and Their Neighborhoods," *Time,* 29 June 1992, 66.

Chapter Thirteen

1. Dr. Lawrence J. Peter, *Peter's Quotations: Ideas for Our Time,* 1977, 342.

2. "One-Toy-Fits-All: How Industry Learned to Love the Global Kid," *Wall Street Journal,* 29 April 2003, sect. A, 1.

3. Tom Tardio, interview by the author, e-mail, July 2003.

4. Bose Corporation Web site, http://www.bose.com, November 2003.

5. Bob Klein, "Secret Specifications," *AMS Voices: An Idea Sheet from Applied Marketing Science* 14 (November 2003).

Chapter Fourteen

1. Dr. Lawrence J. Peter, *Peter's Quotations: Ideas for Our Time,* 1977, 454.

2. The World of Aspirin, Bayer Web site, http://www.aspirin.com/faq_en.html, November 2003.

3. Molly Wade McGrath, *Topsellers USA,* 136.

4. *Webster's New Universal Unabridged Dictionary,* 1996.

5. Mary Bellis, "Polystyrene and Styrofoam," http://inventors.about .com/library/inventors/b1polystyrene.htm.

6. Dow Chemical Web site, http://www.dow.com/styrofoam/na/about/regtm.htm, November 2003.

7. Tim Triplett, "Generic Fear to Xerox Is Brand Equity to FedEx," *Marketing News,* 15 August 1994, 12.

Chapter Fifteen

1. Dr. Lawrence J. Peter, *Peter's Quotations: Ideas for Our Time,* 1977.

2. From the Schneider Electric, North America division, Square D Web site, http://www.squared.com, November 2003.

3. Adapted from the Fuelman of Michigan Web site, http://www.fu elmanmi.com, December 2003.

4. Adapted from the Caterpillar corporate Web site, http://www.cat .com, November 2003.

5. Adapted from the Bechtel corporate Web site, http://www.bech tel.com, November 2003.

6. *Webster's New Universal Unabridged Dictionary*, 1996.

Chapter Sixteen

1. Dr. Lawrence J. Peter, *Peter's Quotations: Ideas for Our Time*, 1977.

2. Kevin A. Clark, "Products Are Solids, Customers Are Liquids" (keynote presentation first delivered at the New Directions for News Conference, Los Angeles, CA, December 1997).

3. Matthew Boyle, "Wal-Mart Keeps the Change," *Fortune*, 10 November 2003, 46.

4. This section on wireless branding adapted from the chapter, "The Future of Marketing in a Wireless World," that I contributed to: Frederick Newell and Katherine Newell Lemon, Ph.D., *Wireless Rules: New Marketing Strategies for Customer Relationship Management Anytime, Anywhere* (New York, NY: McGraw-Hill, 2001) 176-185.

5. The concept of "tetrad structure" is found in Marshal McLuhan and Bruce R. Powers, *The Global Village: Transformations in World Life and Media in the 21st Century* (New York, NY: Oxford University Press, 1989). Page 11 is where the authors say, "The tetrad helps us to see 'and-both,' the positive and the negative results of the artifact." An artifact in this case is any technology. Page 8 asks these questions about the structure of any technology tetrad (artifact): "1. What does any artifact enlarge or enhance? 2. What does it erode or obsolesce? 3. What does it retrieve that had been earlier obsolesced? 4. What does it reverse or flip into when pushed to the limits of its potential (chiasmus)?" Example as found on page 176: "Committee: (A) Enhances group image of authority; (B) Obsolesces individual responsibility; (C) Brings back dialog; (D) Reverses from specialized job to corporate role."

6. Plate tectonics is "a theory of global tectonics in which the lithosphere is divided into a number of plates, each of which moves on the plastic asthenosphere more or less independently to collide with, slide under, or move past adjacent planes. (1965-70)" Also: the *lithosphere* is "1. the solid portion of the earth (distinguished from the atmosphere). 2. the crust and upper mantle of the earth." and the *asthenosphere* is "the region below the lithosphere, variously estimated as being from fifty to several hundred miles (eighty-five to several hundred kilometers) thick in which the rock is less rigid than that above and below but rigid enough

to transmit transverse seismic waves." From *Webster's New Universal Unabridged Dictionary,* 1996.

7. Geosyncline is "a portion of the earth's crust subjected to downward warping during a large span of geological time; a geosynclinal fold. (1890-95)" From *Webster's New Universal Unabridged Dictionary,* 1996.

8. Mihaly Csikszentmihalyi, *The Evolving Self* (New York, NY: Harper Collins, 1993), 120.

9. Don Edward Beck and Christopher C. Cowan, *Spiral Dynamics: Mastering Values, Leadership, and Change* (Malden, MA: Blackwell Publishing, 1996), 30-31.

10. Ibid.

11. Ibid., 51.

12. Edward O. Wilson, *Consilience: The Unity of Knowledge* (New York, NY: Alfred A. Knopf, 1998), 128.

13. Beck and Cowan, *Spiral Dynamics,* 41.

14. Adapted from Beck and Cowan, *Spiral Dynamics,* 50-51.

Chapter Seventeen

1. Lawrence J. Peter, *Peter's Quotations: Ideas for Our Time,* 1977.

2. From the BMW international Web site, http://www.bmw.com, March 2003.

3. Adapted from the American Red Cross Web site, http://www.red cross.org, March 2003.

4. Susan Chira, "Power Player, Playing Cautiously," *New York Times,* 20 October 1993, sect. C, 1 and 12.

5. *Volunteer 2000 Study: Findings and Recommendations* (American Red Cross, December 1988).

6. *Strategy for the International Red Cross and Red Crescent Movement,* Resolution 3—Approved by the Council of Delegates in November 2001, report from the International Committee of the Red Cross Web site.

7. Ibid.

8. Ibid.

9. Adapted from the Doctors Without Borders Web site, http://www.doctorswithoutboarders.org, July 2003.

Chapter Eighteen

1. Jean Piaget and Barbel Inhelder, *The Psychology of the Child,* (New York, NY: Basic Books, 1969, 2000); originally published in French as *La Psychologie de l'Enfant* (Paris, France: Presses Universitaires de France, 1966), 71.

2. Data sources from the teachers guide for the *BigPictureSmallWorld* movie, http://www.bigpicturesmallworld.com.

Appendix B

1. http://www.ibm.com/easy, *IBM User-Centered Design,* 2000.

2. K. Yamazaki, T. Takahashi, H. Shima, S. Kimura, and E. Shibata, "ThinkPad760 series" (in Japanese), *Annual Design Review of JSSD* 2, no. 2 (1977): 44-47; K. Yamazaki, "Design for Wearable Computer" (in Japanese), *JIDPO Design News,* no. 244 (1998): 36-43; K. Yamazaki, "User Interface Design for Notebook Style Computer" (in Japanese), *7th Human Interface Symposium,* 143-146, Kyoto, Japan, 1991; K. Yamazaki, "Universal Design Approach to Portable Computers" (in Japanese), *Technical Report* (Information Processing Society of Japan), no. 81 (August 2000): 33-38; J. Nielsen, *Usability Engineering* (Academic Press, 1993).

3. J.M. Carroll, *Scenario-Based Design–Envisioning Work and Technology in System Development,* (New York, NY: Wiley, 1996); J.M. Carroll, *Making Use of Scenario-Based Design of Human-Computer Interactions* (Boston, MA: The MIT Press, 2000); K. Yamazaki, "Study on Design Method by Using Video User Scenario," *CHI2001,* New Orleans, 2001; "IBM PC experience" (in Japanese), http://www.ibm.com/jp/pc/experience, 2001.

4. J.M. Carroll, *Making Use of Scenario-Based Design of Human-Computer Interactions* (Boston, MA: The MIT Press, 2000).

5. "ThinkPad i-Series s30" (in Japanese), http://www.ibm.com/jp/pc/thinkpad/tpis3015/tpis3015a.html, 2001; "Digital Gadgets" (in Japanese), http://www.ibm.com/jp/dg, 2001.

Appendix C

1. This chapter is based on: Rust, Zeithaml, and Lemon, *Driving Customer Equity;* Rust, Lemon, and Zeithaml, "Return on Marketing:

Using Customer Equity to Focus Marketing Strategy," *Journal of Marketing* (2004, forthcoming).

2. Katherine N. Lemon is Associate Professor at the Carroll School of Management, Boston College. Roland T. Rust is the David Bruce Smith Chair in Marketing and Director of the Center for e-Service, Robert H. Smith School of Business, University of Maryland. Valarie A. Zeithaml is Roy and Alice H. Richards Bicentennial Professor and Area Chair of Marketing, Kenan-Flagler School of Business, University of North Carolina at Chapel Hill. Loren J. Lemon, JD, is an attorney based in Lexington, Massachusetts, who specializes in marketing and business transaction law.